# Professional
# Public
# Executives

# Professional Public Executives

Edited by Chester A. Newland, Director, Federal Executive Institute

Published by The American Society for Public Administration

## PUBLIC ADMINISTRATION LIBRARY

Published by the American Society for Public Administration

*PAR Classics* Series

1. **Professional Public Executives**
   Edited by Chester A. Newland

2. **Perspectives on Budgeting**
   Edited by Allen Schick

*Copyright © 1980 by the American Society for Public Administration*

All rights reserved. No part of this book may be reproduced or transmitted in any form or by any means, electronic or mechanical, including photocopying, recording, or by any information storage and retrieval system, without permission in writing from the publisher.

> The American Society for Public Administration
> 1225 Connecticut Avenue, N.W.
> Washington, D.C. 20036

Library of Congress Catalog Card Number: 80-81209

International Standard Book Number: 0-936678-00-3

# Preface

WITH THIS volume by Chester A. Newland and a companion volume by Allen Schick the American Society for Public Administration launches a new publications series entitled *PAR Classics*. From time-to-time the Society will commission volumes containing the best articles from the pages of *Public Administration Review* on a given topic over the history of the *Review*. The selection of articles will be by a volume editor with expertise in the subject area. The editor will contribute an introductory article for purposes of stage setting, tying themes together, presenting overviews, or summarizing the state of the art.

We hope the *PAR Classics* series will prove most useful to scholars and students of public administration alike and that these volumes will make a special contribution to the field.

Ray Remy, *President*
American Society for Public Administration

March 1980

# Contents

Preface .................................................... v

Professional Public Executives and Public Administration Agendas
    *Chester A. Newland* ....................................... 1

Notes on the Governmental Executive: His Role and His Methods
    *Donald C. Stone* ......................................... 31

The Senior Civil Service
    *Leonard D. White* ........................................ 49

Executive Development After Ten Years
    *Marshall E. Dimock* ...................................... 60

The Senior Civil Service and the Career System
    *Paul P. Van Riper* ....................................... 71

The Need for Elected Leadership
    *Dorothee Strauss Pealy* .................................. 85

The Manager *Is* a Politician
    *Karl A. Bosworth* ........................................ 90

Who Are the Career Executives?
    *Earl H. DeLong* .......................................... 99

Executive Leaders—Career and Political
    *John B. Blandford* ...................................... 102

A New Look at the Career Civil Service Executive
    *W. Lloyd Warner, Paul P. Van Riper, Norman H. Martin,* and
    *Orvis F. Collins* ....................................... 108

Equipping Men for Career Growth in the Public Service
*John J. Corson* .......................................... 120

Politicians for Hire—The Dilemma of Education and the Task of Research
*Norton E. Long* .......................................... 134

Developments in Government Manpower: A Federal Perspective
*Roger W. Jones* .......................................... 143

Executive Preparation for Continuing Change
*John W. Macy, Jr.* ........................................ 151

Can City Managers Deal Effectively with Major Social Problems?
*Keith F. Mulrooney* ...................................... 156

Separate Career Executive Systems: Egalitarianism and Neutrality
*Lloyd D. Musolf* ......................................... 168

The Future Executive
*Harlan Cleveland* ........................................ 178

The American Public Executive in the Third Century
*Frank P. Sherwood* ...................................... 185

The City Manager: Professional Helping Hand, or Political Hired Hand?
*Richard J. Stillman, II* .................................. 194

Professional
Public
Executives

CHESTER A. NEWLAND*

# Professional Public Executives
# And Public Administration Agendas

MANY PROFESSIONAL public executives function today at the junctures of public affairs where politics and administration merge or are one. They are at those pivot points where crucial problems are dealt with and major decisions of governance are made. These top professionals, their roles, their administrative/ political environments, and how they do their jobs constitute a foremost agenda of public administration. It is in these public executives and their interface functions that the field may most nearly discover a distinctive identity. If pursued, it may be there that the greatest promise lies of some identifiable public administration theory.

The *Public Administration Review* has reflected main currents of thinking and practice about professional public executives since the 1940s. The principal focus of related *PAR* articles and symposia has been on executive workforce needs and developments in the United States national government. Beginning with an article by Leonard White on the Second Hoover Commission's proposal for a Senior Civil Service, federal executive service issues have been discussed in *PAR* by such prominant figures as Marshall Dimock, Paul Van Riper, John Corson, Roger Jones, John Macy, Harlan Cleveland, and Frank Sherwood. From its beginnings in the 1940s, however, *PAR* concerns with executives have been broader than the national government. The first extended article on the governmental executive, by Donald Stone, reflected his knowledge and interests in city and other local public managers, state executives, and senior federal civil servants. City management has been a continuing topic in *PAR*, with symposia edited by Charles R. Adrian in 1958 and by Keith Mulrooney in 1971, as well as other major articles, including the final one in this collection by Richard Stillman, II.

Here, the focus is on changing public executive roles and performance, on legal/institutional executive work force provisions, and on related public administration agendas. Building on the rich collection from *PAR*, current and developing roles of professional public executives are first discussed in this article. It is clear that leading city managers in the 1980s perceive their roles differently than most did three or four decades earlier. Leaders among these professional local government executives may, in fact, stand distinctly apart from American organizational executives generally, including many career federal government executives, in their role perceptions and performance. But U.S. federal executives are also in crucial times of change. The adoption in 1978 of the Senior Executive Service was, in some respects, a culmination of efforts started in 1935 and given focus by the Second Hoover Commission in the 1950s. The SES also reflects special concerns of the late 1970s. Because of their importance, these SES provisions and the initial developments associated with them are specifically discussed in the third part of this article, following a review of past prescriptions for career public executives. Finally, the focus here is on more generic and basic concerns of public administration as related to professional public executives. On the other hand, they are the old issues of how political and administrative systems clash and destabilize one another, mesh as one, or are differentiated but merged to get things done. And perhaps more basic, they are concerns with what gets done. What values are reflected in the roles—the expectations—of professional public executives and in such important institutions as the new Senior Executive Service and the International City Management Association (ICMA)?

## Changing Roles of Professional Public Executives

At the end of the 1970s, an ICMA Committee on Future Horizons issued a report, *New Worlds of Service*,[1] looking toward the year 2000 and the changing responsibilities of professional local government managers. The committee's work reflected experiences of executives who had already led their profession through major changes in the 1960s and '70s. Kansas City, Missouri's manager, Robert A. Kipp, who as president of ICMA appointed the Future Horizons Committee, had reflected as follows in 1977 on changes in city councils and in the city management profession: "The relatively homogenous 'board of directors' city councils that often existed prior to World War II are largely creatures of the past. Today, for city councils and city managers alike, it's a new ball game."[2] Long before the seventies that game was in an arena where politics and administration are joined. As early as 1958, the *Public Administration Review* had published the article in this collection by Karl Bosworth, "The Manager *Is* a Politician." Those dimensions of local government managers' roles are first discussed in this part of this paper.

Second, current roles of U.S. federal executives are briefly examined in this section, though much that is relevant to that topic is deferred to the later discussions of the Senior Executive Service.

State level executives are not separately dealt with there, although the *PAR* article by Lloyd Musolf does discuss the California Career Executive Assignment system.

### Local Public Executive Roles

By 1980, 2,792 appointed city managers or chief administrative officers served local governments in the United States, and about half of the people living in all jurisdictions of 10,000 population or larger lived in those communities.[3]

Local councils of governments and a variety of special district governments were also served by appointed chief executives.[4] Most of those managers considered themselves professionals and belonged to the ICMA. Some 4,000 other ICMA members (many non-corporate) included assistant mangers, interns, and others with professional interests in the field.

Generalizations about so diverse a group are hazardous, but their important roles and qualities have been easy to discern for a long time. They perceive themselves foremost as professional public managers; they are mobile in practice; they engage one another in conferences and other developmental activities; they write, talk, and read about their work; and they optimistically share public service values of constitutional democracy. Significantly, many see themselves as the nexus of policy formulation and implementation processes and as interorganizational specialists, as reported in several articles in this *PAR* collection.

In his 1965 article, Norton Long described city managers as "politicians for hire"—essential managerial mercenaries who need to have capacities to govern wisely. Social changes of the late 1960s and '70s brought special challenges for local public executives, as described in the article by Keith Mulrooney in this collection. Tom Fletcher, then city manager of San Jose, in a 1971 *PAR* article not included here described the changing roles as follows:

> What is the manager of today? Is he an administrator? professional? technician? manipulator? or a politician? In all probability, the modern city manager has elements of all of these. Certainly the old image of the manager as the professional administrator, dealing with the techniques of engineering and finance, is gone.[5]

That description of roles corresponds to Robert Kipp's conclusions about the nature of "the new ball game": "Many citizens—and a few city managers—hold the mistaken belief that the manager's role is to 'run' the city government. That may have been true once in some cities, but not today. ... Today, the manager's role in the local governing process is that of a facilitator and a source of support to the council as it takes new directions and steps into new areas."[6]

A development of the late 1970s which illustrates some further reaches of city managers' facilitative roles was a National League of Cities Council Policy Leadership Program.[7] That activity went in a direction suggested in a 1958 *PAR* article by Dorothee Strauss Pealy in this collection. It was an effort to improve city council's performance through team training processes facilitated by an outside party. The program was tested in 1979 in four council-manager cities: Wichita, Kansas; San Jose, California; Long Beach, California; and Fort Worth, Texas. The program related to roles as identified in a 1979 ICMA report from an Amsterdam conference of city managers:

> The city manager is not in a position to decide unilaterally what the objectives of the organization (the city) are. This is the role of legislative

authorities in the city. However, our interviews reveal an unfortunate tendency for elected bodies to neglect this role in favor of more immediate political payoffs. Consequently, the manager must assume the additional responsibility of being a subtle developer of processes which will help elected officials establish clear city objectives.

Instilling a commitment to process among elected representatives often places the manager in a very vulnerable and sensitive position. The nature of councils–collections of individuals–often makes them resistant to even a basic level of process skills such as working in a group setting. But this is a responsibility that several of our participants have assumed.[8]

**Commitment to What?**

Acceptance by local government managers of this responsibility reflects a strong commitment to effective democratic processes. The principal aim is to help elected officials to provide some sense of (or consensus on) general political directions while being sensitive to diverse interests. This delicate responsibility involves managers professionally in helping to find agreement, if not consensus, on policies.

Dallas city manager, George Schrader, who chaired ICMA's 1978-79 Future Horizons Committee, summarized relevant perspectives of that group, stressing "Greater day-to-day involvement [of managers] in concerns of elected officials" and "More emphasis on brokering among interests in the community, negotiating among conflicting interests."[9]

The future challenge was seen by the ICMA group as more than simply the old and difficult one of balancing responsiveness to short-term general and particular interests. They concluded that other professionally articulated values must be brought to the process. Professional public executives' roles were perceived by them as importantly distinct from those of politicians, whose different roles, in turn, were stressed as basic to democracy.

This orientation was fundamental to the committee's 20-year projection for the profession: "To shape and to adapt to the changes between now and the year 2000, the profession must be even more idealistic."[10] Four public service ideals were highlighted, as follows, in that report:

> The prime ideal of the profession must be that of excellence in management. . . .
> We must be the strongest believers in democracy. . . .
> The concept of equity is also one of our ideals for the future. . . .
> Our commitment to ethical conduct should remain high.[11]

Although that idealism dominated the ICMA Committee's conclusions, that viewpoint resulted from an extended effort to look realistically at prospects and responsibilities of the profession. From the perspectives of 1978-79, hard challenges were projected for the 1980s. Large problems of American society generally were confronted: inflation, unemployment, and economic dislocations; resource scarcities; and cultural malaise. Major challenges of urban governance were probed: centralization and federal government determinism; growing interdependency, from local through international levels; and governmental incapacities—expanding responsibilities outstripping authority and resources. But optimism, nontheless, dominated.

Hopeful signs found by the group for future urban governance included these: (1) demonstrated, growing capacities for networking in complex interrelationships; (2) growing recognition of limits of scale in public organizations; (3) escape by public administration from intellectual traps of all-purpose organizations; (4) expanding scientific and technological capacities; and (5) valuing by people of disciplined professional expertise balanced by democratic authority in urban governance.

Those sorts of *professional* perspectives led these local government executives to conclude their Future Horizons effort with a commitment to development of a code of ideals to complement ICMA's long-standing and influential code of ethics. In the words of the Committee: "This would be an affirmative statement of ideals of the profession that goes beyond the ideal of ethical conduct. These ideals should include strong expressions of a belief in democratic values and processes. The strength of constitutionally representative democracies, needs for social justice, dedication to equity in regulation and service delivery, a conservation ethic, and the importance of continually striving for excellence in local management."[12] In large respects, the Committee dealt with the issue raised in the 1965 *PAR* article by Norton Long: How can practitioners be equipped professionally to govern wisely?

### Expectations of Federal Executives

It is harder to give brief answers to the question, "What are the roles of federal executives?", than it is for those local government professionals who identify themselves with city management. Essentially, there are far more federal executives; the functions of most are often more narrowly and deeply specialized; their specialties cover a vast array of activities and organizations; and many do not identify primarily as public management professionals, although most do identify with career public service, often in specialized professions. As a group, federal executives contrast most with city managers in their relatively lower mobility (they resemble private sector executives in that respect).[13] Until the Senior Executive Service, many were more narrowly professional as specialists, often eminent in their separate fields, disciplines, and/or organizations. Most federal executives have functioned at levels somewhat more removed from direct interaction with elected officials but in association with relatively short-term political executives who frequently have lacked professional orientations and commitments to government. Roles of many federal executives may correspond less to those of city managers than to those top staff and program management specialists who report to chief executives in large urban and state governments: those numerous public executives generally ignored in this article, in the pages of *PAR*, and in most of the other literature of public administration.

In July, 1979, when the Senior Executive Service was first implemented, 7,677 executive positions were placed in it, and 1,456 remained in other services or pay plans. The latter included 510 positions at Executive Levels (the top political jobs, including Cabinet and other high officials), 740 positions at supergrade levels in the General Schedule, and 206 executive positions in other pay plans.[14] Other recent statistics on federal executives and information on provisions of the Senior Executive Service and its implementation are included in later sections of this article. The purpose here is simply to highlight who federal executives now are and general perceptions of their roles. More specific information may then be more meaningful later.

One other bit of statistical information on functions performed in the recent past by federal executives is also essential to this initial discussion of executive roles. In a 1974 Civil Service Commission analysis of General Schedule and Public Law executives, occupations of most were distributed as follows:

32 percent were in scientific and engineering occupations.
23 percent were in other professional occupations (e.g., law) and social sciences
40 percent were in administrative occupations (including fiscal and personnel)

Functions of the federal executives surveyed were distributed as follows:

74 percent were primarily managers (among scientists, 70 percent).
11 percent were primarily supervisors (among scientists, 16 percent).
15 percent were primarily individual workers (among scientists, 14 percent).[15]

Other generalizations about roles of this large, diverse group are difficult, but experience of many executives supports some conclusions. Federal Executive Institute participants in the period 1971-1976 tended to identify with four broad roles, as follows:

1. Policy and program implementation, and increasingly, results evaluation.
2. Organizational maintenance and development.
3. Policy, program, and organizational innovation.
4. Conceptual leadership—helping people important to their organizations to make sense of things, bringing a sense of direction to complex, often perplexing situations.[16]

Most federal executives saw themselves as managers even before the advent of SES, as shown by the 1973 statistics. At the same time, however, they lacked mobility opportunities and identification as a corps of professional executives in the sense demonstrated by city managers. Most strongly identified as professionals, but primarily in substantive fields or disciplines like engineering, physics, or law—and/or as career civil service employees of particular organizations in which they had served with high success for many years. If the question was asked, "Commitment to what?", basic program and organizational identifications were generally clearest, since mobility was limited. In the survey noted above, 62 percent of executives *with no mobility in employment outside of the federal government* had been employed in only one agency at Grades GS-13 and above, and 44 percent had spent all their governmental service in one agency. Career federal executive opposition to the Senior Civil Service proposal in 1955 and to all succeeding like-proposals included skepticism about mobility provisions, as illustarated in the article by Earl DeLong in this collection. From the beginnings in 1947 and 1949, the Public Law and supergrade executives had been oriented to specific programs, generally scientific and technical, or to distinct organizations and their missions, and these commitments remained strong in 1978 when the Senior Executive Service was adopted.

Commitment to career public service was not lacking among federal executives prior to SES; it was high for most, but it was primarily programmatically and organizationally oriented. Proposed modifications or additions to that orientation were seen as attacks on career service. Professionalism also was not lacking; but it, too, was most related to specialized programs and organizations. Proposed modifications or additions to that orientation were seen as political threats to professionalism. Government-wide perspectives and interorganizational competencies were in short supply among career federal executives outside of such tiny central agencies as OMB, where mobility to provide line management experience, in turn, was often lacking. Responsibilities for growing interdependencies and for general direction in the federal government were thus left largely to political executives, with limited governmental experience and perspectives, and to Congress, often dominated in the 1960s and 70s by single-interest politics. The professional roles increasingly performed by city managers in local governments—providing some professional sense of government-wide directions—were performed by only a few in the federal government: rare career executives like Elmer Staats, who had been elevated by President Johnson to the position of comptroller general of the United States.

## Past and Emergent Public Executive Prescriptions

Two past sets of prescriptions in thinking about and practice of professional public executives are of central importance in current developments and are reviewed here: expertise and professionalism. A chronicle of past institutional developments and ideas is not needed. But perceptions of roles of many at the top in public administration have undergone such major changes since the 1950s that some of the jumble needs to be sorted out in terms of emergent concerns.

Expertise needs to be considered in the 1980s in terms of three historical expectations of public executives: (1) specialized, functional or program capacities, (2) organization management capacities, and (3) brokerage and interorganizational capacities. As interdependencies have multiplied in recent years, the third of these roles has placed unprecedented demands on public executives. Whether executive expertise can be developed and sustained to meet them in the future is a major challenge for public administration.

Professionalism is the second historical concern relevant to present and future demands on public executives. Three old issues of continuing importance are these: (1) the merging of policy formulation and implementation (and the unity and separation of politics and administration), (2) responsiveness and responsibility, and (3) responsibility to what: ethics and ideals. All three of these issues run together, of course. In terms of emergent public administration concerns, the three center on these recurrent questions: To what are professional public executives committed? Does it make a difference that they are *professionals*? Does it make a difference that they are *public*?

## Expertise

In both city management and federal government service, the employment of professional, appointed executives started for the same reasons. First was acceptance of the value of functional, technical expertise to deal with expanding public functions. Trailing that a bit in local government and still lagging in the federal government came recognition of the value of general management expertise to deal with expanding governmental administrations established to perform those functions. Needs for brokerage and interorganizational capacities are now coming to the forefront as the great challenge for professional public executives.

*Specialized Technical Expertise.* City management started as a marriage of civil engineering and the short ballot movement, and in the early years the practical results in city halls were engineers as public managers and "the influential" as boards of directors, both groups ideally free of partisanship and concerns of ward politics. Much is made today in public administration about our forebears' supposed naive efforts to separate politics and administration into distinct arenas of those engineers and the political elect, but if naive, the matter went deeper than all that. Both the manager and council were ideally nonpartisan. It was not a great concern to keep the appointed engineer-managers from guiding councils' policy decisions, thus preventing administrative usurpation of political responsibility. Managers were hired from the start to provide such expert direction to city governments. The business corporation was a basic guide in formulation of the city management model. A principal function of the executive in that model, as propounded by such figures as Chester Barnard, was to formulate and define the objectives or purposes of the system.[17] In municipal corporations, those executives were engineers—77 percent of city managers in 1934 held bachelor degrees in the field, as noted in Richard Stillman's article. They were experts in technical functions (neutral experts in technical functions or experts in neutral functions?) that were then new to many local governments: street paving (could asphalt or concrete serve best? ... with what base?); sanitary and storm sewers (might the systems be combined and channeled downstream together? ... with or without treatment?); water systems (where upstream should the intake be?); construction codes, and so forth.

Federal government executives were similarly brought forth in immaculate conception (free of political sin) in 1947, some 38 years after Staunton, Virginia employed the first city manager. Professionals served as federal executives long before then, of course. Donald Stone, whose 1945 essay is the first in this collection, was already a distinguished executive in what was then a leading center of professionalism in public administration, the U.S. Bureau of the Budget. He and some other leaders of that time were clearly professional public managers who knew that they were functioning at vital junctures of administration and politics. Federal executives, professional and otherwise, were not new.

*It was the immaculate conception of 45 federal executives in 1947 that was significant.* Like the jobs filled by engineers in the early days of city management, these positions were not to be filled by merely "neutral professional managers." They were to be staffed by experts in "neutral fields." These new "executives" were to be scientists and research professionals, not managers. Public Law 80-313 authorized the Secretary of War to fill 30 positions and the Secretary of Navy to fill 15 at negotiated salaries higher than the maximum allowed for the then highest grade. Although supergrade ranks were authorized two years later, these 1947 "Public Law Type" executive positions were continued and multiplied over the next 30 years to a total of over 1200—some 11 percent of all federal executives prior to creation in 1978 of the Senior Executive Service. These positions continued to be oriented to scientific and technological responsibilities. Professional attachments of incumbents tended to be in scientific disciplines and the field of engineering. They also identified closely with their defense-related organizations. Most were project and program managers or supervisors, but many perceived their roles as those of neutral specialists.

Much of the strongest opposition to Civil Service Commission proposals in the Nixon years for a Federal Executive Service with mobility features came from this group. Many feared that such service would not only diminish essential expertise in crucial science management, but that it also would politicize what they perceived to be professional service in politically neutral scientific and technical activities.

With respect to politics, these executives were the most immaculate over the years—in the same professional sense as the early engineers in city management. Their first professional commitments were to their fields and disciplines; others were to their organizations. Professional perspectives generally ended there. These were experts, the sort of people discussed by Frederick C. Mosher in his book, *Democracy in the Public Service*,[18] devoted to disciplined specialties and to their professional excellence in the federal government.

*Management Expertise.* Next, closely after needs for functional, program specialists—engineers and scientists in particular—came recognition of needs for professional managers. Initially, however, this need was identified with internal organization management—"running" a city administration or directing a federal program division.

Management expertise came to be valued for "getting things together" as well as for efficiency and economy. In terms of Chester Barnard's functions of the executive, needs were recognized early in cities to provide a system of communication for cooperation and coordination, and to bring together the efforts and the resources needed to get things done. Richard Childs' short ballot campaign did not stem from a necessary identification with engineering. As a young business person, he wanted "to get it together" in two respects: a ballot amenable to popular comprehension for civic responsibility and a professionally managed organization for responsiveness. It was simply that engineering was at first the job perceived to be needed in most cities, and the practical had the margin on theory, even when ballyhooed, in most places.

General management moved to the forefront over engineering in demands for professional executive expertise in council-manager cities after World War Two. By the end of the seventies, more than three-fourths of all city managers with advanced degrees held them in public administration; less than a fifth of managers held bachelor degrees in engineering.

Pressures arising from increased size and complexity of the U.S. national government also culminated after World War Two in some acceptance of the value of professional management expertise at executive levels, although, as noted above, recognition of scientific and technical expertise needs came first in 1947.

The Classification Act of 1949 created the supergrades, marking what most people soon came to take as the beginning of a career federal executive workforce. It was something of a beginning: executive positions oriented to management responsibilities were authorized, although some of these General Schedule executives, like the Public Law positions, were oriented to scientific and research personnel. Three new grade levels were established, and 400 positions were initially authorized: 25 GS-18s; 75 GS-17s; and 300 GS-16s. Civil Service Commission approval was required of the qualifications of individuals proposed for supergrade positions, and the Commission also had approval authority initially over establishing GS-16 and 17 level positions, with authority over level 18 positions added later.

The 1949 "beginning" had the markings of an integrated and centrally manageable executive work force system, except that the earlier beginning—the Public Law 313 authorizations of executive-level positions—was continued, and senior foreign officers and some other groups remained in separate systems. Exceptions became the rule almost from the start as varied authorizations of more executives were made over the next three decades—often with specific allocations to organizations written into statutes. The "initial 400" provisions became a "government-wide quota" under general oversight (some management authority) of the U.S. Civil Service Commission, and it grew to more than 2,700 positions. More hodgepodge than system characterized federal executive work force provisions after a few years. The resulting "structure" in the mid-1970s is shown in Table 1.

General federal executive work force management concerns and profiles are considered further in a later discussion of the Senior Executive Service. With respect to the topic here—expectations of executive expertise—the 1949 executive provisions and the hodgepodge built on and around them are important in

Table 1

United States Government Executives
1976

| Personnel System | Number | Percentage |
|---|---|---|
| Executive Schedule I-V | 717 | 6% |
| General Schedule, GS 16-18 | 5,954 | 53% |
| Government-wide Quota | 2,754 | |
| Non-Quota | 1,704 | |
| Special Authorizations | 1,247 | |
| Administrative Law Judges | 249 | |
| Public Law Type | 1,238 | 11% |
| Other Salary Systems | 3,377 | 30% |
| Foreign Service | 1,967 | 17% |
| ERDA | 367 | 3% |
| TVA | 90 | 1% |
| DMS (VA) | 220 | 2% |
| Other | 733 | 7% |
| Total—Less than one-half of one percent of all full-time federal employees. | 11,286 | 100% |

*Source*: Compiled from information in: Bureau of Executive Personnel, U.S. Civil Service Commission, *Executive Personnel in the Federal Service* (Washington: GPO, November, 1977).

two respects. For many, they continued an orientation to program specializations and narrow organizational identification. For others, they encouraged staff expertise and/or management orientations, but also within relatively limited organizational contexts. The entire structures of the General Schedule and Public Law systems were position oriented. Mobility incentives and opportunities were severely limited.

The new supergrades were created in part to satisfy growing needs for professional federal management expertise, but few would be generalist managers. Their commitments were to specific programs and organizations and to career service related to those often-demanding specializations. Most lacked broader experience and government-wide perspectives for generalist management. Many were expert managers, but nearly all were confined to narrow specializations in specific organizations.

*Interorganizational Brokerage.* By the 1970s, interorganizational and interest brokerage were the heaviest demands on leading city managers, and as noted earlier, many had risen to the challenge. At program and discreet organizational levels, many federal executives performed similarly challenging roles, but the federal government employed few professional executives with opportunities for broad government-wide experience, perspectives, and responsibilities.

Three sorts of related demands for interorganizational brokerage expertise confronted local, state, and federal executives in the 1960s and 70s: citizen interests, intergovernmental, and private/public sector.

The protests of the 1960s were the tip of a citizen participation iceberg for local governments, and it had not melted away by the 1980s. Federal statutes and court decisions froze new populist forms into local implementation processes as well as traditionally perceived policy processes. On the "administrative side" now, affected and/or interested citizens must often be consulted or negotiated with before mandated policies and programs may be initially implemented and at later stages. Also, through increased access, courts may intervene to halt, redirect, or attempt to manage activities. On the "policy side," election at large of city councils is still common, but in states covered by the Voting Rights Act, mandated single-member districts have brought more diverse and geographically based interests to some council chambers. Such changes require more of managers in looking out for general city interests while responding to individual councilmembers.

State and federal administrators have been similarly impinged by changed citizen participation modes, but to lesser degrees in most activities both because of less direct implementation involvement and because these governments have exempted themselves from many requirements imposed on local jurisdictions. Freedom of information, sunshine, and privacy rights provisions (sometimes in conflict) are examples, however, of devices of the 1960s and 70s which now have an impact on public management at all levels. Also, the impacts on federal and state administrators of litigiousness and of enlarged single-interest orientations in politics, Congress, and legislatures are similar to those at local levels.

Intergovernmental dimensions of public management are too well known for review here. They, too, have an impact on executives at all government levels, of course. From the perspectives of cities, the situation is generally perceived to constitute a problem of central government domination which contributes to powerlessness to bring balanced direction to governmental activities. The ICMA's Future Horizons Committee viewed the situation as follows: "The result now is that few local decisions or initiatives may be undertaken without close attention to central government regulations, dictates, policies, and opinions—which are frequently inconsistent and conflicting."[19] From central government levels, intergovernmental relations perspectives vary from capacity building, as through Intergovernmental Personnel Act efforts, to forced compliance with federal provisions.

Public/private organizational interrelationships have always placed significant demands on public managers, but some new dimensions of what is public and private now compound demands on executives generally, public and private. Business and government shade into one another today in some different ways than earlier. Distinctions at the margins of public and private activities have always been unclear. Old charges that council-manager government was sometimes more business (rather than public) administration in support of estates of the privileged had some justification in fact. Some of that early day "neutrality" was, in fact, deeper than the theroy of separation of politics and administration, and it was scarcely deep naivete. At state and federal levels, regulatory administration is even richer (or poorer) with shaded and shady experience. Given all that, however, the new shadings of gray are significantly different. Business and governmental organizations become as one today in a vast range of activities from local through international levels. The "state" and the "estate" often become one again, but in a different sense than in Western Civilization's ancient times (or as in contemporary sheikdoms of the Middle East).[20] Demands on executives today are somehow to keep these interorganizational relationships sorted out and working together.

Some authorities, notably Harlan Cleveland and Frank Sherwood in the *PAR* articles in this collection, are cautiously optimistic that the interorganizational future can be dealt with successfully. Others are more pessimistic. Writing in 1979 about top organizational leaders, private and public, William G. Scott and David K. Hart concluded as follows: "The crises of interdependency are unprecedented and represent the largest, most dangerous crises facing the significant people."[21] Scott and Hart were pessimistic that executives can handle these challenges. They viewed future prospects even more dismally because of related forces which they saw in *Organizational America*. Those perspectives relate more, however, to the second category of expectations of public executives to be discussed here: professionalism to match expertise.

## Professionalism

Not much can be added to what Frederick C. Mosher wrote about professionals in government in his award-winning book, *Democracy and the Public Service,* and in two *PAR* symposia, with Richard Stillman, II, published in 1977 and 1978. In his 1968 volume, Mosher said: "the characteristic of the public service—and indeed of a great part of the rest of society—which seems to be most significant today is *professionalism.*"[22] He raised the issue which is most relevant here: "how can a public service so constituted (of professionals) be made to operate in a manner compatible with democracy?"[23]

The oldest questions, like Mosher's, remain the newest in public administration. Some answers with respect to public executives have nuances which are different today, however, because of new complexities of society, changed roles among local public managers, and such developments as the Senior Executive Service in the U.S. government.

Many public executives, city managers in particular, now see themselves as primarily professional public executives—specialists in being public service generalists. They do not function as managers or otherwise in the "reasonably clear-cut occupational field(s)"[24] about which Mosher wrote, except as local public management is such a field. Many have embraced responsibilities which are different from specialized program and intra-organizational management which continue as vital functions of other public executives. As shown above, many now perceive their roles to be at the junctures of politics and administration and in interorganizational arenas which increasingly characterize society and the problems and resources of its governance.

It is in that context that the time-worn questions have much continuing and urgent relevance into the future. To what are these professional public executives now committed? Does it make a difference that they are *public* administrators in orientation? Emerging responses to these questions are briefly discussed here under these three headings: the mingling of policy formulation and implementation, responsiveness and responsibility, and ethics and ideals.

*Policy and Implementation.* Dwight Waldo wrote in 1979: "*it is the area in which politics/policy and administration/management mingle that the crucial problems of the large modern polity are to be found.*"[25] These processes not only mingle but often blend and become one at levels of government occupied by many professional public executives.

Public administration academics have, at times, glorified the generalists at the expense of the specialists, and politicians have often tended in the other direction in writing laws and employing executives. Politicians, after all, are the generalists from that perspective. Even in the cities, about half of chief executive officers are elected and half are appointed.[26] In the largest governments, it is certain for now that the president of the United States, governors, and mayors of some giant cities are not about to be displaced by appointed CAO's. Both politicians and professional administrators are needed for American democratic government to function, and it would probably perform better if both groups could act on that reality. In that sense, it is clear that the old politics/administration dichotomy is not only real but desirable. Politics and administration often merge as one in policy formulation and implementation, but in responsible politicians and professional administrators role distinctions are present which are essential to democratic governance. Just as both politicians and professional administrators are essential to governments, both generalist and specialist professionals are essential to high executive levels to deal with today's complexities. Council-manager cities rely heavily on professional specialists also, not simply generalist managers. Otherwise the complex operations of local governments would not function well. It should not be taken as denigration of specialist executives in the federal and state governments to note the great needs there also for some generalist executives with public and professional orientations.

Present complexities of governance involve meshing of policy formulation and implementation at all levels, including levels of service delivery to citizens. Some differences do exist between those words, politics and policy, and those other words also, administration and implementation. *Those differences reveal some of the reasons that politics and administration increasingly mesh: because now policy formulation and implementation almost always do.* Today's administrators are often responsible for implementing legislation which sets forth broad goals and which leaves to them much of the task of spelling out specific policy in regulations. At delivery levels, they are also required to involve citizens in implementation, often including decisions on specific objectives and actions to accomplish them. In short, many administrators below top executives have been converted into public implementers, just as top executives have been transformed into facilitators (a term appropriately expropriated perhaps from agriculture, where it refers to those who help the bulls and heifers to mingle).

*Responsiveness and Responsibility.* Since many professional public executives now function at critical junctures of creation, old questions of responsiveness and responsibility take on new meaning. Because of the implications for democracy, Mosher was rightly concerned in 1968 that professionals, largely as specialists, were then responsible for much of our governance. He wrote that "The choice of these professionals, the determination of their skills, and the content of their work are now principally determined not by general governmental agencies, but by their own professional elites, professional organizations, and the institutions and faculties of higher education."[27]

Responsiveness was the issue, as much as any, that gave impetus in the Eisenhower administration to the Senior Civil Service (SCS) proposal of the Second Hoover Commission.[28] The SCS proposed to solve the problem primarily through the old separation of politics and administration. The Hoover Commission recommended an expansion in the number of political appointees at departmental levels to give agency heads control: to secure responsiveness. Career *administrators* (the political appointees would have been called "executives") would have been politically neutral, avoiding strong attachment to the policies of any one administration. Earlier, the Brownlow Committee had also recommended grouping all top executive positions into two categories, one specifically political and policy making and the other nonpolitical and administrative.[29] When the Eisenhower administration entered office, however, it found the Public Law and supergrade positions started in 1947 and 1949 largely filled with career protected appointees who were perceived by some to be wrongly functioning at policy levels and unresponsive to administration policies. It found fewer positions than it wanted for its own political appointees and set about to change that.

The 1955 SCS also proposed to generate responsiveness by stressing *generalist administrators*, with mobility obligations, instead of functional specialists: "The men commissioned as senior civil servants should have substantial areas of transferability; they should be more than narrow specialists."[30] These generalist public administrators, hopefully, could escape orientations of specialists, wed to single organizations or to narrow professional perspectives which allegedly limited their responsiveness to government-wide concerns and responsible political officials.

The Second Hoover Commission proposals were not successful in Congress. Values of professional specialists were strongly defended, and the Eisenhower administration was denounced by many for seeking to make political incursions into the merit system.

Federal executive work force developments turned in other important directions toward the end of the Johnson administration, as explained in the article by Roger W. Jones in this collection. A Bureau of Executive Manpower was created within the U.S. Civil Service Commission in 1967, and the president also directed CSC Chairman John Macy to establish "a center for advanced study for executives in the upper echelons of the Civil Service." That led to creation of the Federal Executive Institute (FEI), with the mission to "heighten responsiveness to national needs and goals, to increased appreciation of the totality of the governmental system, and to improve kowledge of managerial processes." Frank P. Sherwood was selected to direct FEI, and John Macy inaugurated the Institute in October, 1968, with remarks later published in the *Public Administration Review* and included in this collection. Macy quoted Roger Jones, Sr., the strongest force behind FEI's creation, and one of his often-stated views on responsiveness and responsibility: "The Federal career executive should be just as much a representative of the people as a legislator."[31]

The Nixon administration, through CSC Chairman Robert Hampton, was supportive of executive education at the Federal Executive Institute, but it also attempted some new approaches to issues of executive responsiveness and expertise. A Federal Executive Service (FES) proposal of 1970 called for renewable, fixed-term employment contracts of three years for career executives. An executive whose contract was not renewed would have had retreat rights to a GS-15 level position with two years saved pay, or retirement if eligible. That proposal, combined with controversial ratios of political and career executives, brought a storm of criticisms of perceived threats of politicization of the career service.

The FES proposal, like the SCS of 1955, would have designated executives as career or noncareer, but no distinctions would have been made between positions or assignments. Career and noncareer executives could have been used interchangeably, and agency heads could have assigned executives to any duties within the scope of FES. That got away from the rigid policy/implementation dichotomy while accepting differences between political and career executives. The mobility feature threatened the functional/organizational specialists, however. Strong opposition resulted in defeat of FES in 1972.

Another proposal to deal with these issues—an Executive Personnel System— was sent to Congress in July, 1974. By then Watergate was an overriding concern, and problems of the federal executive work force were left for the next administration and the creation in 1978 of the Senior Executive Service, to be discussed shortly. In the interim, Hugh Heclo's important book, *A Government of Strangers*, was published in 1977. It was a major study of political/career executive relationships in the U.S. national government. The main thesis was that political appointees in the executive branch are "a government of strangers" without group commitment to political leadership. One recommendation was for creation of a new "Federal Service" of 1800 career "Federal Executive Officers: in grades GS-17, GS-18, and Executive Level V." Heclo proposed that the appointments be made by a new central agency located in the Executive Office of the President. He sought a system that would balance needs of responsiveness and continuity: "a group of high-level officials who are more changeable and mobile than bureaucrats but more institutional and enduring than political appointees."[32]

Responsiveness and responsibility of professional public executives were issues to which city managers contributed most significantly in the 1970s while the attention of the larger public administration community was fixed primarily on U.S. government efforts. The city managers and their professional association, ICMA, moved steadily toward more rigorous enforcement of a long-standing professional code of ethics and, by 1980, were energetically developing a code of professional ideals to deal with these issues of responsiveness and responsibility.

*Ethics and Ideals.* The issues of responsiveness and responsibility pose the question: "To what?" As an answer, Mosher's perceptive analysis in 1968 focused on the importance of standards set for public executives by their professions and by the educational institutions and faculties which help to foster them. The medical, social work, legal, and other professions, for example, define the work content, knowledges, skills, and behaviors required of their members. Those criteria established by those elites become the standards of practice of those professions in government as elsewhere in society. Thus, whether or not they have conscious public responsiveness or responsibility dimensions to their professional standards, these elites largely define what in fact is done in governments in their specialized fields. They determine many aspects of public policy and implementation.

Mosher urged that the education of these professionals offers the best hope of instilling in them "a philosophy of a public service which is both consistent with and supportive of democracy."[33] He suggested a construct of responsibility and morality drawn from experiences of Chester Barnard, Paul Appleby, and Stephen Bailey. It stressed (1) the ethical content of significant public decisions, (2) differences between private and public ethical standards, (3) that public choices are seldom clearcut between good and evil, and (4) that politics and administrative organizations, if open and public, "are themselves the best protectors of administrative morality."[34]

As noted, city management has gone further in developing and implementing professional public service responsibility standards. They are reflected, in part, in a "City Management Code of Ethics" originally adopted in 1924 and amended five times—in 1938, 1952, 1969, 1972, and 1976. Even more relevant to emergent concerns are the conclusions of the Future Horizons Committee, discussed in the first section of this paper. These merit further note here, before a comment on current implementation of ICMA's ethics code.

The initial 1979 Committee report stressed democracy as the key dimension of public service ideals, as in the quotation cited earlier in this paper. This was also stated forcefully in these words, projecting into the future:

> The next 20 years will be years in which the concept of representative democracy will be greatly challenged. People will try to tinker with it in the interest of expediency. People will tend to lose confidence in their own ability to participate in democratic decisions.
>
> Yet democracy is the very foundation of professional local government management. Indeed, in many respects the job of the administration reduced to its basics is to make democracy work.
>
> This means that the managers' jobs will be to help the elected representatives of the people. This means helping assess and interpret public opinion. This means seeing that they have the best information on local programs, that they have available a sound process of making decisions, and that they can best communicate these decisions to the public....
>
> This representative democracy is one of our ideals.[35]

Responsiveness to responsible elected officials and the public is a principal dimension in this ideal, but large professional leadership responsibilities are also stressed. Informed perspectives about alternatives, resources, relationships, scope, history, and prospects, for example, must be shared with political officials and the public. It was described at one point as follows by the ICMA Committee: "The leadership of the profession ... will call on the ability to help people see more clearly their own desires and goals, and unobtrusively to help them satisfy those desires and goals. Leadership is continuing quietly to instill in people the belief that they can successfully contend with the future."[36]

That affirmative assertion by city managers goes well beyond where most other groups of government executives are in their perceptions of professional public responsibility for implementing and advancing democratic ideals. Most professionals do well to identify with a code of ethics with some dimensions of public responsibility. ICMA started in that way also, and the profession has attained sufficient stature that its ethical provisions are now applied not only as goals but as enforced standards.

Keys to ICMA membership are "Agreement to abide by the City Management Code of Ethics and service in a professional position . . . recognized by ICMA as providing for overall management responsibilities."[37] By the late 1970s, 20 to 25 ethics cases were handled annually by an ICMA Committee on Professional Conduct, composed of three association board members. Expulsion from membership was imposed where evidence was found to warrant that, and the process also cleared some of unfounded charges. Behaviors investigated as unethical have involved conflicts of interest, falsifying an application, failure to show after announced acceptance of a position, job-hopping (short-service), felony convictions, and partisan political activity. Based on practical experience, a set of guidelines to behavior relates to Code provisions. It provides guidance to managers on such matters as: advising municipal officials, giving impressions of improper influence, length of service, seeking a non-vacant position, meaningful equal opportunity action, gifts, investments in conflict with official duties, and commercial endorsements.

Much of the reason that city managers are now able to move confidently toward a positive code of professional ideals is that they have successfully acted for a long time, through their association, to promote and enforce a public service oriented code of ethical responsibilities. For more than 50 years, that ICMA Code has stressed democracy as the essence of public executive professionalism, as follows: "Be dedicated to the concepts of effective and democratic local government by responsible elected officials and believe that professional general management is essential to the achievement of this objective."

Outside of city management, issues of professional standards for service of much-needed experts at executive levels remain an urgent agenda of public administration. In part because it is a field which draws on many other fields and disciplines, public administration has been impeded in responding generally to needs which are basic to it.

Throughout American government, specific codes of conduct—only one negative dimension of professional standards—were enforceable on employees up to the late 1960s under the former legal doctrine that public employment is a privilege. Pursuant to that, civil service systems required behavior consistent with the "good of the service."

Within the U.S. national government, more general and affirmative standards were set forth in a "Code of Ethics for Government Service," agreed to during the Eisenhower administration by a concurrent resolution of the 85th Congress. The Code had no legal sanctions, and it remained generally unknown. During the Johnson administration, Executive Order 11222 on ethical conduct was hurriedly issued after an assistant secretary for administration who was responsible for ethical conduct standards in a cabinet-level department used official information to play the stock market.[39] That executive order imposed personal financial reporting (but not public disclosure) requirements on mostly higher-level federal employees. It was only after the agonies of the Nixon administration that much general attention was turned to ethical considerations at national levels. Dwight Ink, then president of the American Society for Public Administration (ASPA), summarized the situation in these words in 1979: "In the aftermath of Watergate widespread attention was focused on professional ethics and standards, a subject which had been accorded little attention in the previous years."[40]

Congress enacted an "Ethics in Government Act of 1978" in response to post-Watergate reactions.[41] The Act expanded financial reporting obligations of senior federal oficials and employees and added public disclosure as a requirement. It also enlarged and added new post-employment restrictions on dealings with government; restricted outside earned income of presidential appointees at GS-16 equivalent levels or above who require Senate confirmation to no more than 15 percent of their salary; provided for appointment of a special prosecutor on charges of criminal activity of top presidential appointees, the vice president, or president; and created an Office of Government Ethics within the Office of Personnel Management to oversee the ethics program in the executive branch. Criticism by top political appointees of this act's post-employment restrictions led to immediate amendments to moderate their impacts in "in-and-outers," but the act remained as the principal general standard for ethical conduct for U.S. government executives.

A Committee on Professional Standards and Ethics was created in ASPA in 1974 to deal with broader public administration concerns. That committee took as its mission the development of "constructive guidelines to help individuals and organizations achieve high standards of public service."[42] With leadership of Chairperson Nesta M. Gallas, the committee produced a workbook published in 1979 for that purpose.[43] That short workbook contains self-diagnostic questions concerning knowledges, skills, and responsibilities of public administrators. That ASPA publication was the most succinct, generally applicable guide to professional standards and ethics of public administrators at the beginning of the 1980s.

## Senior Executive Service

The Senior Executive Service is the crucial arena of federal executive workforce agendas of the 1980s and probably beyond. As such, it warrants major attention of the public administration community. Alan K. "Scotty" Campbell, as chairman of the U.S. Civil Service Commission and later as the first director of the U.S. Office of Personnel Management, was the principal figure in adoption and initial implementation of the Civil Service Reform Act (CSRA) of 1978. He often characterized the SES, created by the act, as "the cornerstone of our efforts to improve the Federal personnel management system."[44] Principal SES provisions are summarized here under five headings. Those provisions are then briefly analyzed in terms of the traditional and emerging expectations of public executives reviewed in the preceding section of this paper: expertise and professionalism.

The SES features noted here, as instituted in July, 1979, are these: (1) appointment authorities and position types, (2) mobility, (3) compensation and other benefits, (4) performance requirements, and (5) protections.

## Appointment Authorities and Position Types

As noted in the first part of this paper, not all employees at federal executive levels are included in the Senior Executive Service. The General Schedule grades 16-17-18 were not abolished; they continue to function, largely for non-managerial specialists who, in the past, have been "executives" in name only while performing as high-level professional experts outside of management. Also, when the new system was inaugurated, executives in positions designated for the SES had an option not to enter, and 81 (1.4 percent) declined. A total of 740 positions continued in the General Schedule in July, 1979. At that time, the SES took in 7,677 positions which had formerly ranged from GS-16 up through Executive Schedule levels V and IV. The Executive Schedule was also continued, and 510 positions remained in it. Some agencies, the FBI, CIA, and GAO, for example, and the Foreign Service were excluded from SES coverage, and they continue to function separately.

Table 2, published by OPM, shows the SES appointment authorities and

### Table 2

### Senior Executive Service
### Appointment Authorities/Position Types

| Government-wide Proportion | SES Appointment Authorities | SES Position Types | |
|---|---|---|---|
| | | General (about 60%) | Career-Reserved (about 40%) |
| No less than 85% | Career | X | X |
| No more than 10% | Noncareer | X | — |
| No more than 5% | Limited<br>• Term<br>• Emergency | <br>X<br>X | <br>—<br>— |

*Source*: U.S. Office of Personnel Management, *SES: Senior Executive Service Conversion Information for Federal Executives* (Washington: OPM, February, 1979), p. 4.

position types.[45] When inaugurated in 1979, career appointments actually accounted for 92.4 percent of all SES executives, whereas the law provided for no less than 85 percent; noncareer totaled 7.1 percent, as against a legal maximum of 10 percent; and limited appointments were about one-half of one percent, as against a five percent maximum.[46]

The SES, for the first time, places fixed limits on the percentage of noncareer executives. Although the government-wide total in SES may not exceed 10 percent, within any particular agency the maximum is 25 percent (unless it had a larger percentage in 1978 when the CSRA was adopted).

### Mobility

SES provisions represent an effort to balance values of mobility and generalist expertise with those of continuity and specialization. Both values are prized in CSRA provisions. An SES member may be reassigned to any position for which qualified within an agency, but involuntary transfers between agencies are not authorized. OPM is to assist those who wish to transfer to an SES position in another agency.

Intra-agency involuntary transfers may not be made within 120 days after appointment of a new agency head or new noncareer supervisor. Fifteen days' notice is required of reassignment to another SES position within an agency.

Career SES executives may accept presidential appointment without sacrificing their status and benefits. A person could leave SES for a position as high as cabinet-level, for example, carrying all benefits and with entitlement to reinstatement into an SES position.

### Compensation and Benefits

Executive compensation under SES includes base pay, performance awards, and stipends. Two other benefits are also authorized on top of retirement, annual leave, holidays, and other "fringes" which are equally applicable to federal employees at other employment levels.

Congress provided that at least five SES pay levels had to be created, and six were established, as follows (with pay levels shown for October 7, 1979): ES-1 = $47,899; ES-2 = $49,499; ES-3 = $51,164; ES-4 = $52,884; ES-5 = $54,662; and ES-6 = $56,500. On October 12, 1979, Congress placed a pay ceiling of $50,112.50 on most SES and General Schedule salaries, continuing past patterns of pay compression for executives. In the initial SES conversion on July 13, 1979, most executives who had been in the first two steps of GS-16 or equivalent were converted to the first three SES pay rates—17.5 percent of all SES executives. Those who had been at the previous GS pay ceiling (the pay compression asterisk) were generally converted to ES-4—49 percent of all in SES. Just over 10 percent of the total were converted to ES-5, and 3.3 percent were placed at the highest level, ES-6.

Career SES members whose performance is evaluated as "Fully Successful" or better may qualify for an annual lump sum award of up to 20 percent of base pay. Total awards may not exceed 50 percent of the total SES positions in an agency. Exceptional performance may qualify a career executive for award of one or two presidential ranks: Meritorious Executive, which carries a $10,000 payment, may be awarded to no more than five percent; and Distinguished Executive, which carries a $20,000 payment, may be awarded to no more than one percent of the total number of SES members. The maximum total of base pay and awards for which a career executive is eligible may not exceed the salary of Level I Executive Schedule positions (cabinet level, etc.), which was $69,630 on October 7, 1979. Only base pay is figured in retirement pay computations.

Beside executive schedule compensation and fringes provided to employees generally, two other benefits were authorized for members by the CSRA of 1978. SES members may now accumulate annual leave without limit instead of forfeiting it annually as in the past. They may take that benefit in cash upon leaving federal government service. Sabbatical leaves with full pay may be granted once in any ten-year period. Other developmental opportunities are also provided for.

## Performance Requirements

Performance and its improvement are central thrusts of the entire CSRA of 1978. Performance appraisal in the SES parallels that emphasis. Performance objectives must be set annually, in a collaborative process between each executive and his or her supervisor. Assessment of accomplishment must be made in terms of established objectives, initially by the supervisor and then by an agency-level Performance Review Board. For career executives, a majority of board members must also have career status. Agencies may have several boards with membership appropriate to those being rated.

An appraisal of "Fully Successful" or above makes an SES member eligible for the performance awards explained above. If rated "Unsatisfactory," an executive must be reassigned. Two unsatisfactory ratings in five years or two less than "Fully Satisfactory" (a person may be rated "Minimally Satisfactory") ratings within three years require removal from SES. If removed, a career executive must be given a position at no less than a GS-15 level, with salary saving.

## Protections

Besides fallback rights if removed from SES based on performance, career executives have many other protections under the 1978 CSRA. Some have been identified above, but others are also important.

Performance cannot be evaluated within 120 days after the start of a new presidential administration. Performance appraisals must be fully documented, and executives must have opportunities to respond to them. A person may not be reassigned to a position for which he or she is not qualified. An executive may have an informal hearing (not an appeal) before an official designated by the Merit Systems Protection Board (MSPB) if removal from SES is set for performance reasons. Removal from SES for poor performance is not an adverse action.

If removal from the federal service is set for misconduct, neglect of duty, or malfeasance in office, that is an adverse action, and a 30-day advance notice is required. An executive may appeal such removal to the MSPB. If a personnel action is alleged to be taken for political reasons or in retaliation for "whistle-blowing," the matter may be taken to the special council of the MSPB. It is the MSPB, an independent agency, not OPM, which guarantees entitlement to these protections.

If a personnel action is allegedly discriminatory, it may be appealed to the Equal Employment Opportunity Commission.

### Executive Expertise and Professionalism

The Senior Executive Service and related CSRA provisions represent results of an informed effort to balance values identified during over two decades of work to create a basic charter for a distinctive federal executive work force. They are the product of the late 1970s also, of course, and of the give and take of political processes, but Title IV provisions of CSRA came through adoption with unusually high integrity. With respect to traditional and emergent expectations of executive expertise and professionalism, the results as a whole are promising, although much remains to be accomplished.

*Expertise.* The old battle of speicalists versus generalists in government wes not fought much in the CSRA struggles. Values of both were recognized instead, and some practical compromises were made. Many gains and a few losses resulted. As explained above, the General Schedule supergrades were retained for non-managerial specialists. Executives are protected from involuntary moves to other agencies, permitting them to continue to specialize in given organizations. On the other hand, SES rank is no longer position oriented, and increased mobility within agencies is easier to accomplish. SES members may be voluntarily moved from one agency to another, and OPM is supposed to assist executives who wish to transfer.

In short, SES stops short of creating a government-wide generalist executive corps, but it provides a framework within which professionals with that sort of public service orientation may have somewhat greater opportunities to create such a corps through their own efforts.

*Professionalism.* SES provisions deal head on with old politics/administration issues, but not by attempting to strike some artificial distinction where none exists. Instead, SES sets a clear minimum percentage of required career executives and permissible percentages of others; it reserves some positions, as in IRS, for career people only; and it permits flexible utilization of executives generally in other positions. Career executives may now move into presidentially appointed positions without giving up SES career status, and as a result some may be able to do that, not as partisans, but as professionals.

Time-worn issues of political placement of partisans in SES with career status are probably inescapable. Violations occurred under the former hodgepodge executive work force provisions, and it would be naive to imagine that some will not happen at times in the future. Nevertheless, the SES, at least at its inauguration, is a more visible and understandable system than the earlier mess of provisions which it replaced, and that may militate some against improper personnel actions. Also, the MSPB is an indepedent agency with authority which may be effective in minimizing abuses. Most importantly, SES at least avoids tying the hands of all to prevent abuses by a few. It provides an arena in which career executives may themselves create professional standards and processes of responsibility whereby the federal government may be hampered less by illegal and other unprofessional actions and turned on more to positive accomplishments and opportunities for improved public service. While SES can and does set aside the vast bulk of the federal executive service for career people, however, it can only facilitate actions to help them to improve themselves individually or as a group. Ultimately, federal executives must exercise leadership for high perofessional excellence, using SES and other resources. Many are presently outstanding professionals, and that is the richest resource for further improvement of the Senior Executive Service.

## Public Administration Agendas

Four statements in the first paragraph of this paper related issues concerning professional public executives to basic agendas of public administration. PA agendas have not been discussed in a discreet sense. Major executive issues and developments related to them have been, however. The thesis here is that much that is distinctive and most fundamental to public administration exists among these professional public executives. If so, some of the discussion of issues above may approach some basics of the field.

For example, the questions were posed: Does it make a difference whether these executives are professionals? Does it make a difference to what they are committed as professionals? Does it make a difference that these are *public* executives and that the field is *public* administration?

It is certain—Mosher made it clear, for example—that professionalism makes great differences in government, for good and ill. Professionals are governed by standards and codes of their disciplines and fields, and in public positions they tend, in turn, to govern by those. It makes a crucial difference then as to what is in those professional standards and codes. Professions in name only may commit some, quite simply, to narrow interests of elites. Or, more likely, professions may commit members to narrow or elitist perspectives of "the public interest."

Or they may comit them to disciplined excellence and to values and processes of democratic governance—in short, to a distinctly public administration orientation, in the contexts of constitutional democracy.

City managers, as generalist executives in local government, have demonstrated that professional public service ethics and ideals, oriented to democratic values and processes, are not only eminently practical but of the essence of public administration in the United States. This is not simply due to city managers being generalists, although that is important to their perspectives. It is in part because they function at levels of constant public and political contact. Also, today, three-fourths of those who have master's degrees have them in public administration, and, true to Mosher's thesis, they are doing as they were taught. They are *public* in their commitments.

A focus on city managers is not to value *other* specialists in government less. Probably no group values other public service specialists more, as demonstrated in how they go about their specialty of facilitating excellence in responsible, democratic, local government. Public executives in other specialties are far more numerous and similarly of crucial value in local governments as well as at state and national levels. It is merely easier to identify some of the fundamentals of public administration among city managers—they are all over and in microcosm, and they see themselves as public service professionals. But it may be a more urgent agenda today, though less easy in some ways, to examine public executives at other levels, their roles, their administrative/political environments, and how they do their jobs. The inauguration of the Senior Executive Service in the national government, combined with encouragement by the U.S. Office of Personnel Management of basic and applied research, may help to produce some of that.

Examples have been noted in this paper of public executives functioning today at the junctures of public affairs where politics and administration merge or are one. Dwight Waldo, as quoted earlier, seems correct in the observation that that is the area where "the crucial problems of the large modern polity are to be found." Much that transpires at professional public executive levels is revealing about the old politics/administration dichotomy. At that level, the political and administrative systems are both differentiated and merged. The dichotomy is valued in the differentiation of roles of responsible politicians and professional administrators. On the other hand, the political and administrative systems often mesh in policy formulation and implementation processes with politicians and professionals performing differentiated functions in a merged set of processes. In the absence of some balance between that differentiation and merger, politics and administration fail to mesh, clash, and destabilize one another. Where some balance is achieved, more of what is wanted may get done.

A related dimension of what is basic to public administration is how the roles of politicans and professionals are differentiated at executive levels. The information in this paper on the ICMA's code of ethics and emerging code of ideals is relevant to that. Basic theory is found in practice in conscious efforts there to reconcile disciplined professional excellence and processes of constitutional democracy.

Brokerage and interorganizational capacities, like those practices where policy formulation and implementation mingle, are increasingly required of professional public executives. This is true for both functional specialists and general managers because of a multiplication of interdependencies within the United States and worldwide. Some authorities, particularly William Scott and David Hart, as quoted in this paper, are pessimistic about prospects that "the significant people" have capacities for the challenge. Among public executives, many examples of highly mobile individuals with superior interorganizational competence provide bases for some optimism, contrary to Scott and Hart's views. More basically, they argue that the problem in America is that values have changed from individualism to a form of organizational collectivism, and that "the drift inherent in this value change will carry us into a totalitarian society."[47] They argue that hope lies in professionals leading organizational reform in a change of values in the direction of an individual imperative. Whatever the force of facts in private organizations, many public ones demonstrate high regard for democratic values of human dignity and reasonable processes. Yet, some public organizations do demonstrate imperatives which narrow perspectives of the less mobile people in them. The giant, specialized bureaucracies of the United States government, where deep and intensely disciplined expertise seem essential, may especially suffer in this respect. That does not support the conclusion that functional specialists should not be valued at executive levels. It does argue for other sorts of executive expertise also—generally brokerage and interorganizational skills and some government-wide perspectives that mobility in varied organizations may produce. It argues even more that both groups, functional specialists and those who specialize as generalists, need to be professionals with a conscious value orientation. In government, that commitment needs to be *public* values and democratic governance.

What is most basic to public administration is present there. At public executive levels, it is apparent that the significant distinction among experts in the field is not the old one of specialists and generalists. It is, rather, between primary commitment to *public* values, in the sense of constitutional democracy, and first commitment to some other values instead.

Examples of executive excellence in the performance of diverse and challenging public responsibilities need to be high on future agendas of public administration. The field exhibits an unhealthy preoccupation with what does not go well, as if dominated by journalists. (In some respects it is, and that is a principal challenge for public administration.) When public executives perform well, and many do much of the time, that merits recognition, if only for the practical reasons that it is easiest to learn from examples and to build on strengths rather than the reverse. The SES should help to give needed prominence to outstanding executive performance.

This paper was introduced with examples of high excellence among local public executives. Examples of outstanding professional public service are also numerous among executives at other levels of government. Along with Donald Stone, whose 1945 paper is the first in this collection, another of the most eminent of career (and politically appointed) national government executives may serve here as a concluding example of excellence. Roger W. Jones, who wrote one of the articles in this collection, was quoted earlier via John Macy. Drawing on more than 40 years of public service experience, much of it at demanding federal executive levels, Roger Jones developed ten commandments for public executives. They included these two: "Be a part of the society in which you live"; "Study democracy."[48] Those experienced executive perspectives say much about what is most basic in American *public* administration.

### Footnotes

* The views expressed are those of the author and do not necessarily reflect positions of the U.S. Office of Personnel Management. This paper was completed while the author was a professor of public administration at the University of Southern California.
1. ICMA Committee on Future Horizons, George R. Schrader, Chairperson, *New Worlds of Service* (Washington: ICMA, October, 1979).
2. Robert A. Kipp, "Mayors and Councils—the New Breed," *Public Management* 59 (September, 1977), pp. 2-4.
3. ICMA, *Directory of Recognized Local Governments: 1980* (Washington: ICMA, 1980), p. 11.
4. An excellent article of COGs and related developments, not in this collection, is: Walter Scheiber, "Regionalism: Its Implications for the Urban Manager," *Public Administration Review* 31 (January/February, 1971), pp. 42-46.
5. Thomas W. Fletcher, "What Is the Future of Our Cities and the City Manager," *Public Administration Review* 31 (January/February, 1971), pp. 14-20.
6. Kipp, *supra.*, p. 2.
7. This NLC program was discussed in an article by Robert J. Saunders, "Improving Policy-Making Skills," *Public Management* 61 (July, 1979), pp. 2-5.
8. Editorial staff, "Political Problems: An International Concern," *Public Management* 61 (July, 1979), p. 8.
9. George R. Schrader, "A Glimpse into the Future," A progress report to the ICMA Executive Board (Quebec City: July 27, 1979), pp. 4-5.
10. *New Worlds of Service, supra*, p. 1.
11. *Ibid.*, pp. 14-15.
12. *Ibid.*, pp. 32-33.
13. On limited mobility of private sector chief executive officers, see: William G. Scott and David K. Hart, *Organizational America* (Boston: Houghton Mifflin Co., 1979), pp. 172-174.
14. "Statistical Report on Inauguration of the Senior Executive Service," An

unpublished, three-page paper prepared by the Executive Personnel and Management Development Group, U.S. Office of Personnel Management, Summer, 1979.
15. Bureau of Executive Manpower, U.S. Civil Service Commission, *Executive Manpower in the Federal Service* (Washington: GPO, September, 1975).
16. Chester A. Newland, *The Bicentennial Era Public Executive* (Charlottesville: Federal Executive Institute, 1976). Principal essay reprinted in *Current Municipal Problems* 20 (Summer, 1978), pp. 1-13.
17. Chester I. Barnard, *The Functions of the Executive* (Cambridge: Harvard University Press, 1938).
18. Frederick C. Mosher, *Democracy and the Public Service* (New York: Oxford University Press, 1968). Also, see Mosher's symposium, edited with Richard J. Stillman, II, "The Professions in Government," *Public Administration Review* 37 (November/December, 1977), pp. 631-685, and 38 (March/April, 1978), pp. 105-150.
19. *New Worlds of Service, supra*, p. 6.
20. Dwight Waldo, both as past editor of the *Public Administration Review* and in other roles, has long urged attention to new public/private relationships. He touched on this matter thoughtfully in a conference paper: "Public Management Research: Perspectives of History, Political Science, and Public Administration." The meeting was sponsored at The Brookings Institution by OPM/GAO/OMB/GSA, as a Public Management Research Conference, November 19-20, 1979.
21. Scott and Hart, *supra*, p. 170.
22. Mosher, *supra*, p. 101.
23. *Ibid.*, p. 3.
24. *Ibid.*, p. 106.
25. Waldo, *supra*, p. 15.
26. *Directory of Recognized Local Governments: 1980, supra.*
27. Mosher, *supra*, p. 132.
28. Commission on Organization of the Executive Branch of the Government, *Task Force Report on Personnel and Civil Service* (Washington: GPO, 1955).
29. The President's Committee on Administrative Management, *Administrative Management in the Government of the United States* (Washington: January, 1937), p. 122.
30. *Task Force Report on Personnel and Civil Service, supra*, p. 6.
31. John W. Macy, Jr., "Executive Preparation for Continuing Change," *Public Administration Review* 29 (September/October, 1969), p. 503.
32. Hugh Heclo, *A Government of Strangers: Executive Politics in Washington* (Washington: Brookings, 1977), p. 249.
33. Mosher, *supra*, p. 214.
34. *Ibid.*, p. 215.
35. *New Worlds of Service, supra*, pp. 14-15.
36. *Ibid.*, pp. 16-17.

37. ICMA, *Directory of Members, 1978-1979* (Washington: ICMA, 1979), unnumbered introduction.
38. ICMA, *City Management Code of Ethics* (Washington: ICMA, 1976 ed.), one page.
39. Chester A. Newland, "Federal Employee Conduct and Financial Disclosure," *Record of the Association of the Bar of New York* (March, 1967).
40. Herman Mertins, Jr., editor, *Professional Standards and Ethics: A Workbook for Public Administrators* (Washington: ASPA, 1979), p. ii.
41. *Ethics in Government Act of 1978*, Public Law 95-521 (October 26, 1978).
42. Mertins, *supra*, p. iii.
43. *Idem*.
44. U.S. Office of Personnel Management, *SES: Senior Executive Service Conversion Information for Federal Executives* (Washington: OPM, February, 1979).
45. *Ibid.*, p. 4.
46. "Statistical Report on Inauguration of the Senior Executive Service," *supra*.
47. Scott and Hart, *supra*, p. 223.
48. Roger W. Jones, "The Executive's Responsibility," in Patrick J. Conklin, editor, *Ethics, Leadership, and Interdependence* (Charlottesville: Federal Executive Institute, 1975).

DONALD C. STONE

# Notes on
# The Governmental Executive:
# His Role and His Methods*

THE FIRST *Public Administration Review* article on public executives was written by a distinguished executive, researcher, and teacher who had already served in several administrative capacities when this article was published in 1945. The perspective was largely from Donald Stone's extensive practical experience, and therefore his background is especially relevant for understanding it.

Donald Stone entered the U.S. national government in 1939 when the Bureau of the Budget was moved from the Treasury Department to the Executive Office of the President. He served as an assistant director in charge of administrative management during the Bureau's great era until he became the director of administration of the Marshall Plan (ECA) in 1948. He also served with the Mutual Security Agency, 1951-53. Before entering federal service, Don Stone was the executive director of the Public Administration Service, 1933-1939. He entered public service as an assistant to the city manager and a staff member of the Bureau of Governmental Research in Cincinnati, 1926-28. Following governmental service, Don Stone became president of Springfield (Mass.) College, 1953-57, and then Dean of the Graduate School of Public and International Affairs, University of Pittsburgh, 1957-69. He then continued his leadership in public administration as a professor and in worldwide professional activities.

From a 1980s perspective, the orientation to men alone as public executives, as reflected in the article's title, suggests both how greatly some things have changed and how much they remain the same. A woman, Sally Greenberg, became the first executive in charge of the U.S. Office of Personnel Management's Senior Executive Service responsibilities when that new system was started in 1979. But, as reflected in several later articles in this collection, the assumption that most public executives are men continued to dominate more than the language for three decades. That reflected reality--not

---

*"Notes on the Government Executive: His Role and His Methods," Donald Stone, from *New Horizons in Public Administration*, copyright © 1945, The University of Alabama Press.

necessarily advocacy. Even at the inauguration of the SES in July, 1979, only 4.8 percent were females; only 5.6 percent were minorities.

On executive roles and methods—the subject of Don Stone's reflections—the perspectives have great continuing value. They focus on organizational leadership responsibilities at the highest levels, just below elected officials. They are a principal source of the beginnings of conscious study and teaching about roles and performance of professional public executives. Contrasts with the ICMA's Future Horizons conclusions of 1979-80, discussed in the opening article of this collection, are instructive about changes and continuities in the field over 35 years. In that respect the title of the University of Alabama book in which this *PAR* article was published in 1945 is important as it was then: *New Horizons in Public Administration.*

GOVERNMENTAL executives—what they do and don't do and what they should and shouldn't do—have received their full measure of popular attention in recent years. They have been pulled apart and discussed pro and con. They have been demolished vocally; sometimes they have been given the stamp of approval. More often than not, however, these oral onslaughts have failed to take cognizance of the essential character of the executive job in large establishments. In the public press, and even in the textbooks, such phrases as "delegation of authority," "sharply defined responsibilities," "elimination of duplication and overlapping" are worked over repeatedly to the point of weariness. In the public administration societies it is the old stand-bys of organizing, coordinating, analyzing, budgeting, controlling, *ad infinitum,* that get the spotlight.

Discussion focused in these directions often misses the crux of the problem the executive must solve if he is to be able to guide and direct his organization so that it can carry out the program for which he is made responsible. What does the executive have to do if his leadership is to be effective? How does he meet the limitations and obstacles that are inherent in most management situations? It is with this point, the position of the executive and how it is implemented, that I am here concerned. It is not the planning, development, and execution of program that I propose to discuss, but rather the conduct of a large organization in discharging its assignment.

There is, of course, no standard prescription, no patent medicine that can be given to the executive, guaranteed to solve all his problems and leave him free of frustration and dismay. The differences in individuals who find themselves in executive positions and the variations in the life cycles of organizations produce practically limitless permutations and combinations. The pattern is never the same, and only after penetrating inquiry of the circumstances in each case would a wise man undertake to suggest what might be required to assist the executive in establishing reciprocal relationships with his organization.

A new organization set up to perform an emergency function—a War Production

Board, an Office of Price Administration—puts very different demands upon its executives than an organization that has had time in which to mature its program and develop its precedents and traditions—for example, the New York State Department of Education, the U.S. Forest Service, or the Cincinnati Public Works Department. Similar contrasts run through the entire catalogue of agency characteristics. Requirements differ in an organization rendering a routinized service or engaged in a paper processing job such as the Postal Service or a dependency benefits office, from requirements in a planning or development commission. They differ within the life of an organization, between the time when it is moving in an accustomed pattern and the time when external pressures or events are forcing drastic changes—the Department of Agriculture in the early years of the century and in the 1930's. They differ between an organization in which activities are conditioned to a large extent by outside circumstances and one in which the product to be developed is relatively definitive and tangible—the U.S. State Department vs. the Railroad Retirement Board.

When the variations in the personalities of executives are intermingled with the kaleidoscopic aspects of organization, the possible results become almost infinite. On the one hand, there are those who function by giving their staffs full rein and, on the other, those who believe in relying more on executive drive and push; the idea men and those whose expertness lies more in salesmanship and negotiation; the men skillful in legislative and public relationships and those whose forte is internal management; those with a great fund of administrative experience and those without. Both institutional and personality factors affect the sum total of what any organization is and both must be taken into account in estimating what is needed to make the thing work.

We have had sufficient experience in analyzing the variables, however, to have acquired some useful benchmarks. We have learned enough to know in a general way what is required if the executive is to be able to fulfill his role and what may stand in the way of success. It is in this context that I have assembled these notes in the hope that they might illuminate in some degree a few of the many facets of the problem of large scale public management.

By large scale, I mean organizations of such size as to preclude face to face dealing by the executive with all of the constituent elements. Although there will be many modifications in the method of executive leadership between an organization of 500 or 1,000 employees and one of 10,000 or 20,000 employees, the variations are not crucial for the problem with which I am concerned: How results can be achieved when the activity is of such scope that it is beyond the ability of the executive to keep personally in touch with all of its aspects or to apply his personal efforts to very many of its problems.

Much of what I have to say is true of any large organization, public or private. In this discussion, however, I am directing my attention more specifically to the executive in the environment of the public service. By this I do not mean the Chief Executive: Mayors, Governors, the President, although many of my comments apply also to these top officials. What I am concerned with primarily is the number one man in an agency or department, or bureau or other major subdivision which presents the problem of leadership through an institutional framework.

The specialized conditions surrounding governmental programs put extraordinary demands on their directors in terms of knowing how to weave the competing and disparate elements into a unified whole and producing an organization capable of accomplishing its mission. Public pressures, the need to adjust to the views of legislative bodies, the rigidities in procedures attendant upon management according to law and executive regulation are elements present in any public service enterprise. All of these are related to that central characteristic that distinguishes executive positions in the public service from those in private management—the fact that the government executive is the guardian of the public interest and is accountable to the electorate, directly or indirectly, for what he does. This is very different from the concern for the public which the private executive has in relation to the marketability of his product and the good name of his firm.

### The Executive's Role

This discussion of the job of being a successful governmental executive is predicated on the assumption that the product of any organization is an institutional product, not the executive's personal product. What the executive can accomplish—his impact on the organization—at any one point in time is conditioned by the state of his organization, and what he achieves is largely the product of his influence rather than his command. Therefore, in long range terms, the job of an executive is to create an environment conducive to concerted effort in pursuit of the organization's objectives. In short run terms, his job is to know what is going on in the organization and to be in a position to act on the issues which require his personal attention and still to retain sufficient freedom to deal with those outside his organization—superiors, legislators, public. Stated differently, the executive's job is one of maximizing his influence throughout his organization as distinguished from relying exclusively upon his formal authority and the power of command. A good many aspects of these propositions have been probed by others, notably by Mr. Chester Barnard in his numerous writings on executives and their work, and perhaps require no further comment. In many quarters, however, these concepts seem to be insufficiently understood.

Whatever may be the notions of what executives do and how they do it, the bedrock fact is that the executive must rely on his staff for the achievement of his objectives. Most issues in his organization will be settled without ever reaching him. And on those that do reach him his choice will generally be a restricted one. By the time a report or instruction has been developed, worked over, revised, reviewed, level by level, what finally remains for the executive to say in most cases is "OK." He may be inclined to make some changes, but he will soon learn that something else will demand his attention before he is through. Unless what comes to him involves an issue of great importance, he will, therefore, frequently have to accept what he considers to be an inferior product. When the issue is a crucial one for the organization's program and involves high level judgments on the consequences of a given course of action, the executive may be called upon to choose among two or three alternative solutions, but secondary questions are likely to have to go by the boards. Consequently, unless the executive's objectives are wholeheartedly accepted by his organization, the chances that they will be achieved are problematical.

Failure on the part of the executive to seek aggressively his organization's support may leave him in a precarious position. The forces militating against an effective working together toward a common goal are many and powerful in any large organization: Unreconciled points of view, tradition and routine, inertia, the distortions that grow out of specialist interests, personal ambitions. These internal resistances singly or in combination can cancel out the executive's efforts. To be sure, some of the drives in any established organization represent forces of stability that will keep the organization running when there is no leadership and will save the new executive from many mistakes. Furthermore, the necessary adjustment of the executive to the facts of his environment can contribute to his development by increasing his understanding of how he can function in relation to what goes on around him. On the other hand, if the executive is entirely unsophisticated in the ways of institutional behavior and does not consciously and continuously take steps to offset the divisive elements in his environment, he will find himself dominated by rather than dominating his organization.

The executive is often seen as the man sitting at the top of the organization possessed of a dangerous amount of authority, hiring and firing at will, whose every suggestion or order is responded to promptly and completely. This view reflects one of the greater misconceptions about the nature of executive work. The government executive may have a large grant of legal authority, but he will find that, in actual fact, it must be used in an economical fashion. If he lacks discrimination in the use of his power, he will debase its value and perhaps find himself impotent at a moment of crucial importance. He must guard against destroying the organizational support on which he must depend in executing his program. As Paul Appleby has often remarked, the new executive in an organization may fire a few persons but not very many. Reducing the point to an absurdity, he can't issue an order, "Now and henceforth all employees shall wear red neckties," and expect to get a response. By persuasion, by indoctrination, by leadership—in other words by influence—he may, however, be able to accomplish what he cannot accomplish by fiat. This is by no means a universally understood truth. There are too many executives who fail to recognize that because the members of their organizations are creatures of reason their positions would be strengthened if they bolstered their formal authority with the support that comes from conviction.

I do not mean to suggest, however, that awareness of the importance of influence as a method of reaching institutional goals is strictly a milk and honey proposition of dubious effectiveness in moments of crisis. If the executive is skillful and knows how to establish his position, he can be the decisive element in determining the character of the organization, and he can exercise his authority with telling effect when the occasion demands it. The point is he cannot "bull his way through" any and all situations; he cannot run against the tide of organization opinion. He may buffet his way by sheer force on occasion or on specific issues, but if he does it too often he may pay for his gains by failure to carry his organization with him over the long run.

I have already commented that the executive's job has to be viewed in long range terms as well as on a day-to-day basis. His aim will be to use his own time and talents on the activities and issues that will contribute the most to the organization's forward movement and to develop a supporting team to the point of optimum production. His success in reaching it will be, in important measure, determined by his success in developing a body of commonly shared ideas. This is a prerequisite if his staff are to have guide posts against which to judge their general direction and their specific actions and if he is to have some assurance of reliable performance. Without this kind of institutional environment, the executive will be unable to mold the organization into something more than the sum of its parts. Furthermore, cultivation of such an atmosphere is essential if the members of the organization are to have a sense of participation in an enterprise bigger than themselves and secure the satisfactions necessary to good staff work. Only then do the fragmented jobs that are the lot of most people in large organizations become a source of stimulation.

The importance of an institutional environment and of indoctrination in its meaning has long been understood by the Army and Navy, but in large part has been neglected by civilian governmental organizations. It has often been observed that indoctrination permits West Point and Annapolis trained men to function, and function well, even though the commonly accepted rudiments of good organization may be missing in a given situation. Some of the civilian organizations such as the Farm Credit Administration, the New York City Police Force, and the Tennessee Valley Authority are conspicuous for their high morale—the natural by-products of a consciously fostered environment. More often than not, however, this basic source of organization strength has been given too little attention by governmental executives in this country.

Whether the executive's job is viewed in long range or short range terms, the ways in which he can seek to maximize his influence and close the gap between present reality and the ultimate ideal of smoothly integrated activity are the same. It is on these that I shall comment briefly for the remainder of this discussion.

### How He Spends His Time

The executive's concept of what his job is and the way this affects the scheduling of his time and talents will be a primary factor in the results he secures. In large part this can be encompassed under the head of "operating at his proper level." In his forthcoming book, *Big Democracy,* Paul Appleby develops the point at some length. By this he means that no head of a government department or other subdivision should do work or make decisions that should be the responsibility of officials at a lower level in the organizational hierarchy. Not only does this disrupt and confuse his subordinates but it prevents the executive from doing what is properly his job.

### Dealing with People

The executive job is one of dealing with people, of judging, adjusting to, and working around personalities both inside and outside his organization. This is at the core of the business of getting people to apply their energies in harmony with each other and getting things done. I recall the case of a city manager who was extremely unpromising at the time of his appointment. He had no apparent experience or interest in such matters as working out arrangements for delegations of authority or subdivision of labor, he probably had never heard of the follow-up principle, and he was completely baffled by theoretical discussions of management. He had, however, an abiding interest in people. He attracted people, and he had an uncanny sense of whom he could trust. Anyone looking at his organization and how it functioned would say it couldn't work. But it did. He had a feeling for what it took to provide the cohesion and the central pull necessary for turning out services to the community.

This is in part a reflection of the fact that the executive should use a major portion of his time and talents in being the catalyst who assimilates and draws together the ideas of others, resolves lines of action, gets agreements nailed down, sees that action gets taken. He must develop and rely on his staff for the carry through on the specific elements of his program and must carefully restrain himself if tempted to dip into technical work.

The public arena character of the executive's responsibilities will draw upon his resources day and night, and he will find that in varying degrees, depending upon his status in the governmental scheme of things, he will not be able to live his life according to his personal choice but must govern himself in the light of the demands upon him. Nor will he be able to compensate for this by pointing at the end of the day to specific accomplishments and saying, "I did such and such." He may be able to think of a number of things that his organization did and how he tried to influence his organization and perhaps provide the capstone to some enterprise, but he can't look upon the results as his own.

### Not as a Technician

The need for the executive to eschew the technical and stick to the level where adjustments get made and judgments about the implications of surrounding circumstances are applied is one of the oft repeated dictums of the public administration fraternity, but the point too frequently is oversimplified. For one thing the dividing line can never be determined with finality. The extent to which the executive concerns himself with specific issues will always be affected by such factors as the age of his organization, outside circumstances, and the extent to which he may have to compensate for failures at lower levels.

In any event, the executive must know enough of the general field not to get lost in the labyrinth. If he does not know the program at the outset, he must master quickly its major substantive elements. Otherwise he will be unable to command the loyalty and respect of his specialists and weld them together as a team. He must have sufficient understanding of the basic issues involved in his program to be able to judge whether the necessary steps have been taken to arrive at a proper conclusion.

### External Affairs

It is the executive's job to cultivate relationships with the heads of other government agencies, with members of legislative bodies, with private institutions, and with the public so that his staff will have a favorable climate within which to function. In this way, he can increase his awareness of the ways in which programs and ideas must be carried out if they are to be accepted. The job of running interference for his organization is one that only the executive can do, and the effectiveness with which it is done will be a significant determinant of what his organization can accomplish.

His success in this part of his job will be affected in part by whether the executive confines his contacts to those that come to him or whether he consciously seeks to direct the character of these relationships. The government executive too often restricts himself to persons of his own social background or of the particular group with which his agency deals. He needs to mix with those who are against as well as for his program. If his agency's function is concerned with aids to business, he needs to understand the viewpoint of labor; if it is social welfare, he needs to mingle enough with the rugged individualists to see life from their angle. If his outside contacts are not well rounded or if he neglects them altogether, he may find that he will end up with a distorted view of the outside environment.

The executive's success in meeting these outside responsibilities will also be in part a by-product of his reaction to what his job demands of him as an individual. The broader and more generalized it is, the more important it will be for him to know what is going on not only in his general field, but in the community, in the nation, and in the world. He will need to broaden his own horizons, stretch his mind, and develop new ideas from which his whole organization can benefit.

### How He Saves His Time

I trust these comments on the level of activity on which the executive's energies should be focused do not give the impression that all the executive need do is have a bit of insight into what is demanded of him and proceed forthwith. It will unfortunately be an inevitable part of his lot that people and things will press for his attention far beyond his capacity to deal with them. His life will be a succession of meetings, telephone calls, documents. He cannot escape spending appreciable time handling many problems which will seem small in themselves but which may have serious implications for the status of the organization; persons who are not performing, staff troubles and worries, some aggrieved citizen, a press release. Many persons outside his organization will seek him out—citizens, legislators, newspaper men, old friends, *ad infinitum.*

Although he will need to take the greatest care not to appear inaccessible either to his staff or to those outside his organization, he must face the very practical problem of deciding whom he will see and of maintaining a balance among the competing demands for attention. If he holds himself open to deal with any problem that comes to him he will become inaccessible to his operating chiefs and he will neglect his outside responsibilities. Decisions will be delayed. He will lose perspective both on his organization and the world and will fail to provide the upward pull and unifying influence that his position requires. With a little firmness and careful planning, however, there are a number of steps he can take to conserve his time, and he can establish controls that will in reality increase rather than decrease his accessibility.

**Personal Staff**

Judicious use of personal assistants is one of the best of these. In a large department or office, the executive may have several such assistants. The city manager of a city of 50,000 inhabitants, the head of a department of a medium-sized state, or a Federal division chief, for example, may find that a single administrative assistant will be sufficient.

One of the most important uses of the executive's personal staff, including his secretary, is in meeting the problem of seeing people. They can help him arrange his calendar, determine whom he should see, control the length of time he spends with visitors. They can frequently do much to satisfy those whom the executive is not able to see or arrange for their business to be disposed of by other officials. To meet the needs of subordinates they can often secure spot information or decisions from the executive. They can arrange meetings between the executive and persons both within and without the organization according to relative urgency.

The personal staff can also help identify the most pressing problems requiring the executive's attention and can pave the way for their speedy disposition by being sure that all necessary information is at hand and in order. They can sometimes pinch hit for the executive on spot jobs. They can give assistance in writing speeches and articles and can accompany him on trips when they can be useful. They can keep him up-to-date with what is going on. Sometimes one of them serves as an intimate advisor and will help select key officials and evaluate the performance of subordinates who seem to be falling down on their jobs. Obviously, each of the executive's personal assistants is not assigned to all of these tasks, as there will be specialization among them. But until his immediate office is staffed with aides who can do some or all of these things for him, he will be unnecessarily handicapped.

On the other hand, he must guard against overdoing it. A large number of personal assistants may mean that there are deadheads or blanks in the organization for whom the executive is seeking to compensate by increasing his personal staff. This can only muddy up the regular lines of communication and command and cause confusion in his organization. Personal assistants can also be a source of uncertainty if the executive fails to define their jobs so that their roles are understood by the rest of the organization.

An executive's personal assistants must not function as palace princes, accessible in varying degrees to other organization officials and pleading the cause only of favorites. They must be the same to all men, and the executive must kill any tendency to manipulate the organization or to afford an entrance through the "back door." Equally fatal is reliance on them by the executive to the point that his outlook becomes limited and warped.

## Operating Aides

In addition to what the personal staff can do to save the executive time and energy, there will also be need in any large organization for the kind of assistants who can share his principal operating burdens. If the executive chooses such aides judiciously he can compensate for talents which he may not have and multiply several times the impact of his leadership.

If the job of the executive requires a high level of public leadership, extensive dealing with a legislative body, a large number of outside contacts, or the devotion of much time to evolving a program or to negotiations with other executives, or if his talents do not lie in the management of an organization, a general deputy responsible in the line of command for internal administration will be needed. A permanent deputy position is likewise desirable when the executive post is one that changes with political fortunes. To be sure, it is not possible to have such a deputy in all of the situations where one could be used advantageously. In most city manager cities, for example, it is not often feasible for the manager to share his principal duties. The extent to which public attention is fixed on the centralization of responsibility in *the* city manager almost precludes the use of a double, although not other types of assistants.

Short of a general deputy, the executive may utilize a principal assistant either as an operating aide or as a chief of staff, giving him varying degrees of responsibility, or he may divide his managerial duties with one or more such assistants in a manner mutually compatible with the persons involved. The specific arrangements must be based upon the systematic analysis of tasks to be performed and of the executive and the persons that can be secured to perform them.

## Time Saving Procedures

Apart from the help the executive can get by providing himself with staff to supplement or complement his own efforts, there is much that can be done to save his time if careful attention is given to the way in which documents, information, problems, issues are presented to him.

With a little ordinary care the amount of time the executive need spend on strictly informational material can be reduced to manageable dimensions. Summaries can be prepared for reports, lengthy memos can be briefed to one page, papers dealing with related subjects can be brought together. I am currently using a simple device in my own organization which, though small, is one in which the flow of information is enormous. My executive assistant and assistant chiefs provide me daily with a memorandum entitled "daily intelligence" in which they enumerate the things that have happened that I should know about, matters that have come up which they have arranged for others to settle, and steps they are taking to deal with affairs in which they know I have an interest. I in turn use the same device in posting the Director of the Bureau of the Budget on things he should know about. This is a very elementary but useful arrangement.

The way in which this can be done in a vast organization is illustrated by the manner in which information is packaged and presented to the Army Chief of Staff and other principal officers in the War Department. A log of selected, important messages to and from the War Department and points in all parts of the globe is the first order of business each day and takes from 15 to 45 minutes. This is followed by a meeting, attended by the Chief of Staff and his Deputy, the Secretary of War, and the Commanding General of the Army Air Forces, at which material on military operations throughout the world and on enemy developments and capabilities is presented and discussed. The data are organized by the Operations and Intelligence Divisions of the General Staff, and the discussion consumes from one-half to two hours. These daily informational routines are supplemented by a comprehensive system of briefing the Chief and Deputy Chief of Staff on all matters on which they must make decisions or on which they should be informed.

## How He Communicates His Ideas

It will not profit the executive a great deal to be a genius in the management of his time, if he does not take steps to forge strong links between himself and the other elements in his organization. In this connection, the mobilization and indoctrination of his team of key subordinates must be near the top of any executive's agenda. When the executive sees to it that the persons in positions of responsibility have been selected and trained for the function of leadership, the way will be open for securing response to new objectives, policies, and methods. Without such a staff he will have a mob, not an organization.

If there is a free and open channel through which ideas and information can move both down and up, the influence of the executive can be felt all the way through the organization. This is not, of course, a one way process. If the executive is skillful he will take pains to develop to the utmost the ideas and suggestions coming from his staff, both because this is the way to strengthen the net product and because only in an atmosphere where there is mutual respect are the executive's views likely to carry their maximum weight.

The kind of person the executive happens to be also has a good deal of bearing on the amount of influence he has. He is a symbol to his organization, and in the case of the higher posts, to the public as well. His attitudes and actions, both private and public, will have an effect—indirect and subtle perhaps, but nonetheless important—on the attitudes of all within his organization. If his characteristics and actions excite admiration, his staff will unconsciously be motivated to respond to his leadership and ideas. If the contrary is true, the natural reluctance of individuals to adapt themselves to the requirements of organized activity is likely to be thrice compounded.

## Oral Communication

In small sessions with key officials, the executive has his best opportunity for putting over his ideas. The values of such sessions can be multiplied if, when feasible, the officials primarily concerned with the resolution of an issue bring with them a principal subordinate or two, and if appropriate staff officers are included in important discussions with line officers. Any such devices that will increase the likelihood of cross-fertilization of ideas without setting undue obstacles in the way of the expeditious handling of business should be encouraged by the executive. Furthermore, to the extent that the executive makes the most of his opportunities for meeting with groups of people rather than individuals, he will be able to extend the area over which his influence is directly felt.

If as issues come to the top they can be thrashed out by the principals involved, all points can be brought out on the spot and the most effective answer nailed down. This speeds the handling of important business, and through the process of dealing in unison on organization-wide matters, the principals get to know each other and how to work together. The more this understanding is developed, the more readily they will team up voluntarily when special problems confront two or more of them.

## Staff Meetings

General staff meetings, if well planned and confined to subjects that are of common interest and concern, can do much to aid communication. They can bring about fuller recognition by each individual of his relationship to the larger whole, and the executive can use them to bring about a common perspective and to help him in knitting the organization together. Anyone who has attended an effectively conducted meeting has observed how much more readily ideas take shape and are acted upon when an easy means of exchange is developed.

I do not wish to suggest, however, that general staff meetings are of exceptional importance. They are only one of many tools in the management kit. It is often taken for granted that every executive should get his key subordinates together—the department heads of a city or state government—as a cabinet, at frequent, regular intervals. The only useful purpose of group meetings of this character is discussion of matters of common concern. There is no merit in bringing diverse officials together to consider matters that can be settled in the line of command. In a meeting of departments heads with the governor, any discussion of the welfare director's problems would put the director of public works to sleep. If the head of the agriculture department started to bring up his problems, most of the rest would be bored stiff. The reason for calling key subordinates together should be to dispose of issues requiring their collective judgment.

**Written Communications**

Written communications are a generally understood although not too well applied method of conveying the executive's ideas from one level to another in an organization, and they can be an aid to his long range efforts to develop his institution. In many organizations subordinates down the line are deluged with detailed instructions and regulations on every aspect of institutional life. Failure to credit staff with a certain amount of common sense and ingenuity will not generate mutual understanding and more likely than not will lead to complete indifference. In either event, the executive is not helped by the result.

On the other hand, there is only too apt to be a grievous lack of well thought out statements issued by the executive outlining specific objectives, schedules of operating requirements, and definitions of responsibilities. However good a job the executive may do in dealing with his principals and however conscientious they may be about passing on the information they get from the top, this will not cover the situation entirely. Written communications are an important supplement in getting to the entire organization the basic outlines of policies and objectives.

As important as it is that policies, and also programs and methods, be translated into clear, written communications, these should not be relied upon to get an essential thought over without the assistance that comes from personal comment on their application. Furthermore, this is the only way there can ever be assurance that staff members read or at least become aware of the written word. Written communications are useful chiefly as a point of departure and serve their primary purpose, after the actual labor of thinking them through is complete, as a basis for a discussion or series of discussions with staff of the ideas or directions contained therein. They are particularly useful for the orientation and instruction of new members of the organization.

### How He Harnesses His Organization

My comments to this point have been focused on the ways in which the executive uses and extends his personality, ideas, and time. This has largely left out of account the institutional framework through which he must function. None of his personal activities, negotiations, or dealings will amount to much if his institution is not so organized that he can get a firm grip on it at crucial points and at crucial times.

### Keeping Up To Date

Essential number one is that he must know what is going on in his organization. If he organizes for the purpose, he can keep track of the trend of affairs—weak spots and strong spots, emerging problems, bottlenecks, opportunities for progress. If he does not, he is likely to be at a loss in attempting to pursue a balanced program.

In the normal course of events he will be confronted with a vast array of paper: actions or letters requiring his signature, drafts of orders and regulations, proposed plans of work, reports of inspections or organizational studies, program appraisals, reports of progress, statistical summaries and interpretations, personnel documents, budget and fiscal analyses *ad infinitum.* With the help of his assistants in organizing and controlling these materials they can provide him with much grist for appraisal of the organization's operations.

The picture the executive gets in this fashion will be only a partial one and will lack a good deal of realism if he does not supplement these sources of information with others. Many of the gaps the executive can fill in for himself, through conversations and dealings with his subordinates, and in some fields of governmental work, through inspections. The state conservation commissioner can see at first hand what is being done in the way of development and use of state parks and in the management of state forests. On the other hand, the head of an agency engaged in activities having little tangible or physical expression cannot rely very heavily on this device. A commissioner of internal revenue, for example, cannot learn much about the product of his organization by looking at the files of paper in process.

The executive's personal staff can help keep him posted on what is going on by passing on information that he might pick up himself if he could see more people. What I am referring to is spot news that may affect the organization and its work, information on breakdowns in the organization, on personnel maladjustments, reactions of particular persons to actions by the executive, new proposals or ideas in the making, complaints with which the executive may have to deal. They may learn of these things informally by contacts below the upper crust of the organization, and they may pick up some of it from conversations with or reports by both staff and line officers. The executive needs to differentiate between the significant and unimportant in this kind of stuff which may often be little more than rumor or gossip. He must keep a check rein on it, and not let it offset the solid help which his general staff divisions can give him directly.

**Staff Divisions**

Perhaps the most important single tool the executive has in harnessing his organization and keeping it in focus is his general staff—the budgeting, program planning, personnel, organization and methods planning divisions. I do not include here service or auxiliary units such as statistical, procurement, and office services, as important and necessary as these may be. Neither do I include here accounting and legal services which, while providing control mechanisms for the executive, are otherwise more akin to the service units than they are to the general staff divisions. It is true, however, that because of personal competence, as well as the fact that they engage in some general staff activity, the accounting and legal chiefs are often used by the executive for a variety of general staff responsibilities.

The staff divisions provide resources for the analysis and development of solutions of problems common to the whole organization. They provide a source of highest counsel and advice on matters about which the executive is uncertain or has reason to doubt the solution offered by an operating subordinate. They provide a general rather than a specialized viewpoint in review both of proposals made by the operating subdivisions and of evaluating the results of the work of such subdivisions. They can do much to help the executive bring the objectives of the organization into focus and get consistency of action. In addition, the employees of such divisions circulate around the entire outfit and provide one of the most fruitful means of gathering information and of securing understanding and acceptance of policy.

The executive needs the benefit of a group of staff advisers functioning in this fashion to help him in anticipating tasks to be done, in planning to meet contingencies that may be around the corner, in mapping out policy and program, and in working out fundamental organization and methods. Their value depends, however, on the way in which they function. They must stay in the staff role of advising, consulting, and coordinating and must avoid imposing their personal judgment on line officials on operating matters. Staff divisions can become a burden rather than a help if they diffuse the executive's line of command by dipping into operating work and if they insulate the executive from other sources of counsel. That the temptation to move outside the staff realm frequently is not resisted is reflected in the common practice of having a large number of detailed transactions referred to the budget office or personnel office for review, transactions that involve no new policy questions. Perhaps the reason staff officers often insist on this is because it is easier to review the activity of others than to do creative work or because they do not have the capacity to do staff work, or because they have never learned what real staff work is.

The staff divisions cannot fulfill their roles to the maximum if they move off on their own in separate directions. It is, therefore, essential that general staff activities be coordinated with each other. The executive or his general deputy may be able to supply this coordination. Sometimes this can be more readily achieved by placing the staff units under an executive officer or a chief of staff. The various staff elements can in this way be brought into focus by someone concerned with the management of the organization as a whole, and the total resources are more available to the executive. Furthermore, there will then be less likelihood of nonproductive competition for the attention of the executive, and the number of organizational units the executive must keep track of personally will be reduced.

But regardless of the arrangement, general staff functions must be directed by high level officers who have a considerable amount of free access to the executive, with the executive officer performing a facilitating function and providing the environment in which the executive can most easily tap the reservoir of ideas of the individual staff officers.

### Arrangement of Line Units

The way in which the executive arranges the subdivisions of his agency or bureau will also have a lot to do with whether he is on top of or at the mercy of his organization. There is much common knowledge of how to organize operating subdivisions, and I shall not go into the question in detail. I should like to comment particularly on the relationship between the way in which the organization is put together and the executive's opportunity to act on significant issues.

For example, a small number of operating divisions will not necessarily mean that the executive is sufficiently free of detail that he can contribute the element of overall perspective and influence. When there are so few or the establishment is so arranged that the executive is walled off from operations by many layers of supervision or the job of harmonizing and coordinating on major issues is pushed down to a subsidiary level, he may become the slave rather than the master.

Related to the question of too few operating units and the layers of supervision that this may entail, is that of the excessive independence that statutory provisions often give subordinate operating officers. When the functions of major division heads are defined by statute, the top executive is placed under a severe handicap in trying to manage what frequently become independent principalities. I recall the vivid comment of a Federal executive who complained that he had the impossible task of administering a federation of bureaus rather than a department.

In a different category are the complications that may ensue if there is too fine a breakdown of activities. Not only is he unable to hold the separate units within his span of attention, which leaves them floating on their own, but those issues that do reach him may get one sided or unbalanced consideration. Functions need to be so arranged that, to the maximum extent possible, varied points of view will be brought to bear and reconciled at points along the way.

There is another disadvantage in agencies or units set up with relatively narrow functions. If the agency commands the support of a specialized or single purpose type of interest or pressure group, undue influence in one direction may be exerted on the executive, and it will be more difficult for him to keep his organization in proper focus.

### Is He a Success?

This discussion has touched on some of the things that the executive can do to harmonize and get the most out of the other elements in his organization. I have emphasized that this is the way that he builds up his influence in his organization and guides it toward its objective. In closing, I should like to reiterate my earlier point that although the executive is not likely to succeed if he approaches his organization as something that is his own to command, he is at no disadvantage as he takes up the role of leadership.

The fact that he is the repository of formal authority in his organization is a powerful asset in the business of developing his titular position into one of genuine force and strength. Furthermore, it is up to him at any one point in time to determine the issues which he wants to have referred to him for decision. Although he may not decide much in his organization, quantitatively speaking, his choice of the decisions that he should make will determine how his organization meets its major difficulties. The point is that for the most part, he must depend upon others; therefore to the extent that the entire organization moves within a commonly accepted framework will it develop some speed and assurance in its forward movements.

My comments have been directed in large part toward some of the methods by which this team relationship can be developed. I trust that these may have proved helpful by suggesting some of the aspects of the business of managing a government enterprise beyond those generally taken for granted. All of these devices and suggestions, however, will not prove any substitute for general aptitude in the business of getting people to pull together. The real leader does not consciously rely upon any pat method of exercising leadership and influence. This is something to which he will be sensitive by his very makeup. He will feel the pulse of his organization and will understand it as a whole rather than as a lot of separate segments. He will know whether he understands it by whether it is responsive to him. If he has this sensitivity, even if he is a neophyte, he will soon learn the tricks of the trade. If he doesn't have it, no amount of boning up on what experience has taught us will help him much.

This can perhaps be illustrated by an analogy that is more suggestive than it is accurate. A person making his first public speech has little impression whether or not he is carrying his audience. By his 100th speech he should know. If he doesn't, he is not a real public speaker. If he does, he will adjust his performance in many ways in order to bring the audience and himself into harmony. And so it is with the executive in relation to his organization. A good executive gets the feel of situations by the way in which those with whom he deals respond to him, and adjusts himself and his staff arrangement accordingly.

LEONARD D. WHITE

# The Senior Civil Service

THIS ARTICLE, by the first editor of the *Public Administration Review*, contains a brief but definitive first-hand account of early efforts to create a senior civil service corps in the United States government. It was Leonard White who first worked out details of such a service in 1935. Two ideas were dominant then, and they were reflected in the 1955 proposals of the Second Hoover Commission, presented in this article. Those ideas were (1) a sharp distinction between top political and nonpolitical positions, and (2) a permanent administrative corps to provide non-partisan expertise and continuity at high executive levels of government.

The focus here was on creation of a federal executive work force system, and Professor White was attentive to needs for both partisan political and nonpartisan administrative capacity for governmental leadership and management. The role distinctions drawn and the institutional provisions recommended to sustain them are important in this article. But continuities in policy processes where the political and administrative were recognized as meeting were also central to the ideas here, and they merit recognition.

Leonard White was Ernest DeWitt Benton Distinguished Service Professor at the University of Chicago when he wrote this article.

THE PROPOSAL for a senior civil service in the federal government, launched by the task force on personnel and civil service of the second Hoover Commission and endorsed by the commission, has antecedents stretching back nearly a quarter century. The issue was first raised in the Report of the Commission of Inquiry on Public Service Personnel in 1935. This able but unofficial body turned the course of discussion from the technical details of personnel management that had occupied the previous decade to the grand strategy of the public service. Its members recommended an administrative service firmly set on career foundations: "... to make public employment a worth-while life work, with entrance to the service open and attractive to young men and women of capacity and character, and with opportunity of advancement through service and growth to posts of distinction and honor."[1] The projected administrative service was intended to include all the nonpolitical top positions, "posts of real eminence and honor." The details of such a service were not worked out by the commission but shortly thereafter were stated by the present writer, in *Government Career Service*.[2] Neither of these proposals struck fire, offered as they were in the midst of the Great Depression.

The problem of a permanent administrative corps was tackled anew by Floyd W. Reeves and Paul T. David in their report, *Personnel Administration in the Federal Service*, addressed to the President's Committee on Administrative Management in 1937. Reeves and David declared:

> ...few if any changes in personnel administration could do more to invigorate the public service than a sharp demarcation between the high political and the highest nonpolitical positions, with the reservation of a number of high posts immediately below the Cabinet rank for nonpolitical career administrators.... A corps of career administrators immediately subordinate to policy-forming officials should therefore be regarded as indispensable to the successful functioning of the Executive Branch.[3]

Reeves and David found, indeed, that a *de facto* administrative service had come into existence, although its function was not generally understood and its status was undefined.

> ...they [the corps of career administrators] do not receive the recognition in dignity of office, emoluments, or security of tenure to which their actual contribution to the business of government entitles them. They are thus handicapped in their work, and the positions they occupy do not hold out the incentives and opportunities to the lower grades of the service that are so necessary to attract new talent to the service and to improve the morale and performance of that already present.[4]

To improve this situation Reeves and David recommended a nonpolitical career group comprising executive officers equivalent in rank to an under secretary; assistant executive officers; the persons responsible for personnel, budgets, accounts, and procurement; and the heads of the various bureaus. These recommendations were forgotten in the general excitement over "packing the Supreme Court" and the "dictator bill" designed to carry out the proposals of the Committee on Administrative Management.

The other effort to strengthen top management occurred before World War II broke out, the recommendations of the President's Committee on Civil Service Improvement, popularly known as the Reed Committee from its chairman, Mr. Justice Stanley Reed of the Supreme Court. The primary concern of this committee (1939–41) was the status of federal lawyers. In addition, the committee recommended the creation of an administrative corps to include all administrative positions in CAF-11 or P-4 and above. Each department was urged to develop an effective and orderly means of training junior executives for eventual promotion into the new corps. This plan was quickly lost from sight in the turmoil and anxiety of World War II.

Despite a decade of discussion, therefore, little actual progress was made. Some agencies began to develop training programs and the Civil Service Commission began to recruit young college and university graduates for a type of public service opportunity that was yet hardly understood within the federal government. More progress was probably made in the new emergency agencies of the 1930's than among the old-line departments, but the general advance was partial and limited.

Change comes with crisis. The economic crisis of the 1930's demonstrated that government was likely to play a more active role in human affairs than ever before, and that it would need a more imaginative type of executive leadership. The annual Junior Management Assistant examination and its predecessors were a half-intuitive recognition of this need. The war crisis of 1941-45 was met, necessarily, by improvisation and a desperate search for such business, industrial, and academic talent as might be available. The post-war executive crisis was hardly visible to the first Hoover Commission's personnel policy committee, but it occupied the central place in the thinking of the second commission task force.[5]

The contemporary managerial crisis, insistently demanding radical reform in the public service, is deep-seated. The government cannot withdraw from the task of ensuring, so far as possible, stability in the national economy. The government cannot escape the obligation of maintaining a monopoly of atomic energy, perhaps destined along with water power to be one of the principal sources to supply the needs of the American people for primary power. The federal government, it now appears certain, cannot release any of its complex activities to the states. They appear both unable and unwilling to carry more of the governmental burden. The great constructive tasks of research, military and civil, raise new problems of the adjustment of management to science. Every quarter of the official compass reveals problems, urgent and complex, with which only the federal government can cope. It is against this pressure of need for the indefinable future that the proposal for a senior civil service must be measured. It was designed not for a temporary palliative but as a permanent force progressively making ever more significant contributions to the management of a huge organization and to the analysis of the great issues of public policy with which the government is obliged to deal.

## The Plan

**Membership and Functions**

The senior civil service is designed to include initially about 1,500 men and women in the permanent career service with at least five years of government employment, drawn primarily from present grades GS-15–18. Selection would be made on the basis of demonstrated competence for the highest level professional administrative work, whether line or staff. The size of the corps might increase eventually to about 3,000, depending on the needs of the service and on the availability of candidates of the highest quality. Not all present members of the GS-15–18 groups would necessarily be selected for the senior civil service; some of them are scientists who have neither taste for nor interest in administration; some of them are specialists whose talents are different from those expected in the senior civil service; some from age or other circumstances might prove not to have the necessary qualifications.

Selection for membership in the senior civil service would be the task of a senior civil service board. It is proposed to establish a board of five—three distinguished citizens with suitable experience appointed by the President, and the chairman of the United States Civil Service Commission and the director of the Bureau of the Budget, or their alternates. The board from the outset would have an autonomous status somewhat similar to that of the one-time Loyalty Review Board. Nominations for membership in the senior civil service would originate in the departments and would be screened by the board with such advice and assistance as it might require.

The task force on personnel and civil service conceived the primary function of the senior civil service to be management at the highest level immediately beneath the political top command. Its members would consequently occupy such positions as assistant secretary for administration, professional aides to Secretaries and assistant secretaries, general managers and assistant managers of the great commissions, bureau chiefs, assistant bureau chiefs, some division chiefs, heads of regional or district offices, and heads of budget, personnel, and other organic staff offices. Bureau chiefs now often combine political and executive functions. The task force recommended a progressive separation of the two and the rigid protection of bureau chiefs from political connections and duties.

The senior civil service would also include the deputy heads of staff offices concerned with questions of substantive policy. The head of such an office is properly a member of the political top command, where policy issues are necessarily determined. The deputy head has the task of collecting and organizing data bearing on emergent policy issues, of interpreting such data, and of giving advice as to the consequences of any proposed line of action. His advice is professional, equivalent to that of a lawyer or an engineer; political evaluation falls outside his province.

Some members of the proposed senior civil service would, therefore, be primarily concerned with management at its highest levels; others would be concerned with the preparatory study and analysis of substantive policies, the preliminary draft of policy papers, and professional advice to the policy makers. These are, of course, well-established functions in the federal government.

## Status

The task force recommended that the members of the senior civil service have a personal-rank status instead of the customary job status under the Classification Act. Tenure is consequently to resemble that of a general or flag rank officer in the Armed Forces. To quote the task force report,

> Congress should authorize and the President should establish a Senior Civil Service consisting of experienced civil servants who have so well demonstrated their administrative competence, integrity, and qualities of leadership that their rank, basic salary, and status should be vested in them as individual civil servants. This would differ from the traditional practice of attaching rank and salary to the job. In a sense they would be "commissioned officers" of high rank. . . . (p. 51)

A number of corollaries flow from this concept.

1. Pay would not be dependent on the particular assignment of a member of the corps. Presumably each member would be occupied with high-level work, but whether it was equivalent to GS-16 or GS-17 would become irrelevant.

2. Removal from the senior civil service would be only under exceptional circumstances after a hearing before a senior civil service board. This rule, however, would not imply any right to a particular assignment in any agency, nor would it suspend the normal provisions for removal for cause. Departments would remain free to assign and reassign their senior personnel, to lay off redundant officers, and even to refuse further employment. In the last case, failing employment in another agency, the individual might be ruled ineligible by the senior civil service board for further membership in this group. All members would be subject to periodic review and to a "selection-out" process that would restore an unsatisfactory senior executive to the normal classification status, subject to normal agency standards for demotion or removal.

3. Members of the senior civil service could be shifted with relative freedom from one assignment to another; they are by definition suited for varied executive tasks; they could be asked to serve at headquarters, in the field, or overseas.

4. An additional corollary related to the foregoing would be an obligation to serve where needed most. This corresponds to the armed forces tradition, but without the connotation of a customary four-year tour of duty in a given assignment. Members of the senior civil service would presumably be particularly useful as "trouble-shooters," taking over difficult posts where incompetence had resulted in temporary breakdowns. They would be equally valuable for long-term duty as division or bureau chiefs.

5. Political neutrality would be essential. "Senior civil servants as a group should be fully prepared to serve faithfully each administration that takes office.

This means that they must avoid such emotional attachments to the policies of any administration that they cannot accept change." (p. 52) The task force was emphatic on this aspect of their proposal: A senior civil servant should make no public or private statements to the press except of a purely factual nature; he should make no public speeches of a political character and should not contribute to campaign funds; he should avoid testimony before congressional committees except to provide factual material and technical advice, while resolutely and firmly declining to give his personal views.

6. Salaries should be improved. The task force recommended a salary range from the present GS-15 ($10,800 to $11,800) rising to that of undersecretary (at present $17,500).

The senior civil service, in short, is a natural outgrowth of recent trends and of long discussion. It is a plan to make the most effective use of the best executive talent in the whole federal service. It is designed to command the respect of both political parties and in turn, to serve each of them, with equal loyalty and devotion. It is intended to ensure a steady supply of tested high-quality professional administrative personnel to work with and under the direction of the top political command. It provides a corps of men and women who can be assigned flexibly to different posts as needs may dictate. It might easily have a substantial influence in raising the prestige and drawing power of the federal service.

## Schedule C and the Senior Civil Service

Schedule C was originated in 1953 to permit employment outside the civil service system of persons occupying positions of a policy determining or confidential character. Something over 1,000 such positions have been authorized by the United States Civil Service Commission, ranging from bureau chiefs to personal chauffeurs of department heads; they include a number of division heads. Where to draw the line between the political top command and the permanent career service is a perennial problem for which Schedule C gave a merely provisional answer. The task force on personnel and civil service sought to lay down the principles on which a relatively definitive solution might be discovered.

Three criteria were developed by the task force and accepted by the Hoover Commission[6] to identify positions properly belonging in the political category. (1) *Responsibility and authority.* The possession of direct statutory authority normally puts an official in the political executive class. (2) *Policy control.* If an official is authorized to make final decisions as to objectives or to state the principles to control action toward objectives, he is engaged in work of a political executive. (3) *Public political activity.* An official whose duties require him to act publicly in advocating new policies and in justifying or defending the governing policies is also properly a political executive. These propositions form a more precise and sophisticated formula than the vague criterion hitherto employed--policy-determining positions.

Applying these tests, the task force concluded that the line between the political executive and the career executive should be drawn between the departmental and the bureau levels of management. Political responsibility and authority can focus only at one level, properly the departmental or agency level. If such authority were fixed at the bureau level, it would give the President about 350 political line subordinates and would tend to reduce the departmental executives to figureheads. The first Hoover Commission protested effectively against such a situation. The departmental level is the level of control, the policy level, and the political level.[7]

At the bureau level, management requirements and functions are heavily technical and administrative in character. The main outlines of bureau programs are defined and made mandatory by law, appropriations, and departmental policy; the task of the bureau is to maintain operations, often extensive, within these limits. Most of these programs are nonpartisan in nature and beyond the range of partisan dispute. The special interests concerned with each of them are normally bipartisan in character. The prime prerequisite for bureau chiefs is therefore managerial skill, not policy involvement.

The task force recognized that, for historical reasons, some bureau chiefs are nevertheless involved in policy and that a considerable number are selected for political reasons. The task force recommended that over a period of years the political activities of bureau chiefs be reallocated to their political superiors (assistant secretaries) and that, conversely, the day-by-day management operations be delegated to the bureau chiefs.

The task force was led by these considerations to propose a new solution of the problem envisaged by Schedule C. Six types of positions were identified as belonging properly in the political executive group: heads and deputy heads of departments and agencies; assistant secretaries and assistant heads of agencies; departmental solicitory or general counsels; heads of departmental staff offices concerned with policy; heads of departmental information offices; and political aides and assistants to political executives. The task force estimated that there were in 1954 about 750 such positions. It suggested that more might be needed.

To the permanent career service were assigned the assistant secretaries for administration and equivalent positions, an office recommended by the first Hoover Commission; the bureau level executives as a group; the division chiefs; the heads of the auxiliary services; deputy heads and other members of substantive staff offices; heads of the regional or district field offices; and professional (career) aides and assistants. The task force estimated about 4,000 persons in these types of positions. Most of the proposed senior civil service would be drawn from among this body of executives, but the two categories are not identical.

The Hoover Commission accepted this line of reasoning. The precise language of its recommendation follows.

> We recommend that the President designate the positions which should be in the noncareer category and that he use the following criteria to determine positions which should be in this category:

(a) All positions filled by Presidential appointment, with or without confirmation by the Senate;

(b) All positions having vested in them statutory authority or executive delegations of authority requiring the incumbents to make final decisions in the establishment of governing policies, programs, objectives, and in the enunciation of principles which will control the action of subordinates in the implementation of the foregoing;

(c) All positions, the duties of which require the incumbents to act publicly in advocating new policies and in justifying or defending the governing policies or the basic principles or philosophy which controls their department or agency policies. Such duties would include direct participation with, or representation of noncareer executives in public debate, evaluative discussions, and justifications of departmental policies, programs, or activities.

(d) Most positions of a personal and confidential nature, such as personal aides, confidential secretaries, and personal chauffeurs. (pp. 31-32)

Untangling political and management functions in the borderland zone between the top command and the career service will not be the work of a day or a year. Some bureau and division chiefs have long played on both sides of the street and will be reluctant to forego activities that may seem vital to the success of their units. Perhaps no administration will be willing to release its political strings on some bureau or division chiefs. The Hoover Commission does not ask release of political control, but merely a reallocation of its site in the administrative structure. Logic is on the side of the Hoover Commission, and the dual interests of political control and administrative management would be well served by the progressive application of the new standards.

## Two Corollaries

The task force on personnel and civil service drew two corollaries from the foregoing analysis: (1) that attention was needed to build up a more effective political top command; (2) that executive training programs on a much larger scale and at a higher level were urgently required.

A unique contribution of the task force was its recognition that a senior civil service would need to be matched by an able political top command, and that systematic efforts would be required to build the latter as well as the former. "The political executives who are the immediate subordinates of the President, and their political associates in the top command of the departments and agencies, are the key groups in making representative government work within the executive branch," the task force declared. "They are the necessary expendables...." (p. 39) The combination of abilities required is relatively rare—both high-level executive ability and well-developed qualities of political leadership.

These capacities have nowhere been systematically developed in American life.

Where, then, do the political executives come from? Partly they come from the patronage system, rarely are they people with congressional experience, occasionally they have been state or big city executives, most commonly they are from private life—the realm of business, the professions, education, and quasi-public organizations. The task force urged that serious attention be given to the problem of recruiting and training younger persons for these positions, while recognizing the difficulties in taking an able man out of his business firm or profession for a couple of years, or even for six months.

A senior civil service can be maintained only by having available able and well-trained replacements. This need points directly to better executive training programs than are now generally available. The task force laid heavy emphasis upon in-service training at all levels.

> ...What is called executive development is really a harvesting of one important product—administrative ability—out of a total training program designed to promote the development of persons in many ways and in all ranks. In other words it should be the function of the executive development program to develop administrative ability which is over and above professional, vocational or technical proficiency—the capacity to understand and direct the work of others, to accept responsibility, to exercise good judgment in making difficult decisions, and to give confidence to others in trying circumstances. (p. 67)

The task force recommended an executive development program in each department and agency, and an executive development panel in each major bureau; but it added that each agency had a responsibility for finding talent for the government as a whole.

These are perhaps the two principal corollaries of the basic recommendation for a senior civil service. There were others, notably better pay scales, simplification of the classification system, and the coordination of the several merit systems now in force in the federal government.

## Prospects

The Hoover Commission accepted the senior civil service concept substantially as it was developed by the task force on personnel and civil service. At this writing the plan is under study by the President's Advisory Committee on Government Organization, the Bureau of the Budget, and the various departments and agencies, as well as by other interested groups. The outcome of such study is unpredictable.

One fundamental condition will have to be met if the senior civil service becomes a viable reality. It will have to command the confidence of the leaders of the two major political parties. The confidence of one will not be enough. On this matter, also, one cannot speak with assurance, but there is reason for optimism.

The political top command of any administration is now aware of the necessity for the highest quality of management, divorced from partisanship. Both parties have had experiences that would discourage them from leaning heavily on patronage sources to meet their needs. No political executive is saddled with any member of the senior civil service; members are transferable at will so that if any doubt of loyalty or competence should arise, it can be readily resolved. Franklin D. Roosevelt declared in 1937 that he needed help; the political high command in 1955 needs the kind of help that a nonpartisan, tested, flexible, and loyal administrative corps can provide.

The decision to proceed with a senior civil service will be taken by the highest levels of the political command and by Congress. It is not within the competence of the present career service. On the other hand, there should be a degree of support for the program in the present permanent executive corps and their views will properly be weighed in the ultimate decision. They should advise without reference to their own personal participation in such a corps. They are called on to consider an institutional arrangement designed for important public purposes, not to decide whether they as individuals would be willing to enter such a corps. In any event, no career man would be drafted into the senior civil service against his will or preference. The ultimate decision, it may be repeated, will be taken not by the career service but by the President and his advisers, and by Congress.

The decision is important. Two decades of drift and patchwork amidst foreign and domestic crises leave the United States government today with not much more than what barely sufficed in the 1930's so far as the administrative corps is concerned. In the competition for executive talent government is outclassed by private enterprise and does not even take advantage of its own assets to build strength into high-level career echelons. The American people may be gratified with the quality of talent that serves them even under present conditons, but it cannot be content with the system that prevails for maintaining a high quality professional service. The time is overdue for new ideas and institutions.

Over a quarter century ago Graham Wallas wrote, "... Governments have come to be engaged not merely in preventing wrong things from being done, but in bringing it about that the right things shall be done.... A negative Government requires a constant supply of invention and suggestion...."[8] This country is unlikely to have any other than a positive government for the foreseeable future. Its success depends not only on the wisdom of its political leaders but also on the integrity and skill of its career executives.

It depends also on the Fates.

## Footnotes

1. *Better Government Personnel; Report of the Commission of Inquiry on Public Service Personnel* (McGraw-Hill Book Co., 1935), p. 3.
2. University of Chicago Press, 1935.
3. The President's Committee on Administrative Management, *Report of the*

*Committee with Studies of Administrative Management in the Federal Government* (U.S. Government Printing Office, 1937), p. 121.
4. *Ibid.,* p. 122.
5. Commission on Organization of the Executive Branch of the Government, Task Force on Personnel and Civil Service, *Report on Personnel and Civil Service* (U.S. Government Printing Office, 1955), 252 pp.
6. Commission on Organization of the Executive Branch of the Government, *Personnel and Civil Service, A Report to the Congress* (U.S. Government Printing Office, 1955), p. 31.
7. *Cf.* Herbert Emmerich and G. Lysle Belsley, "The Federal Career Service—What Next?" 14 *Public Administration Review* 1-12(1954).
8. Graham Wallas, "Government," 6 *Public Administration* 3 (1928).

MARSHALL E. DIMOCK

## Executive Development After Ten Years

PROFESSOR DIMOCK of New York University stressed needs for executive development and training for policy decisions in this article. He departed sharply from earlier orientations to administrative management roles and from training for "team membership" which were becoming popular by the late 1950s. He said that the biggest problems of executives "are more often concerned with policy and survival issues."

The model which Dimock found closest to meeting executive development needs was the Administrative Staff College at Henley. In this article he summarized the syndicate or learning group approach to policy studies then in use at the British Staff College.

An important focus in Dimock's view was training and development to avoid creation of the organization man—"the spineless conformist who is the opposite of the enterprising executive." He urged recognition of needs for individuals who function as outstanding executives in their own right, with understanding of complex dimensions of policy issues.

EXECUTIVE development programs,[1] that is, attempts to sharpen administrative skills of employees who are thought by management to possess leadership potential, have leaped into prominence in many countries since the end of World War II. Distinguishing such programs from regular academic study, customarily the employer selects participants and pays all or most of their expenses. Distinguishing them from other in-service training which usually concentrates on specialist techniques, emphasis here is on leadership. While in all cases the objective is the same, the motivating needs depend on the stage of a country's industrial and governmental development. In the United States and Great Britain, for example, the need for executive development is induced by a combination of overspecialization and bureaucratic procedures—significantly related to large size—which threaten to drain institutions of their initiative and vitality. In underdeveloped countries, the motivating factors are the need to develop administrative skills that can facilitate industrialization, to secure a better balance between the respective roles of business and government in the economy, and to overcome certain traditional cultural factors that limit administrative effectiveness.

A year ago, an executive of a large corporation in New York showed me a list of forty executive development programs for American businessmen; eighteen of these programs were considered "major" by this particular corporation. Most of them were identified with universities. My informant expressed the opinion that since the war, executive development programs had expanded by something like 400 percent, with the end not yet in sight. When a movement grows so fast, one wonders whether it is not merely a passing fashion, whether many of the programs freshly launched will not prove short-lived, and whether there is not the danger of overselling the idea. The answer, I suppose, is that since the need for executive development is great, the demand for training will continue, and that if present formulas and procedures are found wanting, they will be improved. Since many of these formulas and procedures have in fact been found wanting, the present paper is an attempt to discover the reasons for the deficiencies and to suggest the means of overcoming them.

## Differing Program Levels

Executive development programs are commonly offered at three levels, each with its own goals and methods. Courses at the primary level are designed for relatively inexperienced men and women needing orientation and initial stimulation in the area of administration. Such programs are usually conducted by the employing institution itself, in connection with the process of induction and probation. They constitute a kind of apprenticeship for executives.

Courses at the intermediate stage are for men and women of from ten to fifteen years of experience who are in the ranks of middle to top management. Such programs are the most numerous, both in business and in governments around the world. They attempt to give specialists the viewpoint and the élan that will equip them to become rounded executives; these courses are what has made executive development training so widely known, and it is here that most criticisms are centered.

Courses at the third level—still, for the most part, in the experimental stage—offer training for top management, for people who have top power if not top age. Since this type of program is much less common that the other two, there is less debate about it except for a growing realization that some such training is needed. The approach here must depend upon the aims and success of executive development at lower levels. If executive development does not require continuous attention throughout one's whole career, it would seem better to concentrate our resources at the lower, formative stages than to try to change the set patterns of men in their fifties and sixties. On the other hand, if executive development is a career-long need and the policy responsibilities of the executive increase with rank, then surely, training also must be a continuing process extending through all three levels of the executive's career.

Although the goals and methods at each of these three levels of training may be different, they have at least two objectives in common: first, to prod and mature the individual's philosophy of administration, and second, to prepare him to undertake policy planning and decision-making as his job increasingly requires it. At the intermediate level especially, this means opening up some wide and difficult areas of public policy with which the enrolee must tussle.[2]

## The Need for Executive Training

The higher an executive is promoted, the more must he deal with policy decisions of the most complicated and demanding kind. Will a proposed action, for example, advance the enterprise toward its destination? Will it strengthen the institution and help to guarantee its future vitality and security? Will it enhance the institution's reputation? These are not merely intellectual decisions; they involve questions of judgment and good taste. Indeed, a decision made solely on intellectual grounds is likely to be inadequate; as Chester Barnard has explained,[3] the higher one goes in administration, the greater is the importance of values and judgments growing out of the intuitive and the nonlogical.

The relevance of this line of reasoning to an assessment of executive development programs now appears. We must train men and women to become better operators; but we must also train them to become good judges of policies and of enduring values, a combination that includes both character and the wisdom of philosophers. But if we are to develop sophistication in the matter of policies and values, we cannot very well train people up to the age of forty or so in nonpolicy and nonphilosophical subjects and then expect them suddenly—like a shrub—to blossom forth in the larger area simply by pouring a little fertilizer around the roots.

Or, to change the analogy, we cannot expect a narrow specialist suddenly to take on the glow of executive inspiration, like a sinner responding to a revivalist, simply because we have exposed him for a week, or six weeks, or even twelve weeks, to the magic of an executive development program. Unfortunately, in our enthusiasm for a new method, we have been guilty of entertaining such absurd notions.

We Americans can take some pride in the efficient way we have learned to teach business and public administration over the past twenty-five to thirty years. Relying on the contributions to the administrative process of scientific management, the human relations approach, and more recently on those of psychology and sociology, we have created a respectable body of knowledge concerning institutional organization and functioning and have learned how to communicate this knowledge to others. But the executive's biggest problems are not always administrative in the conventional sense; they are more often concerned with policy and survival issues: pressure groups, institutional size, competition, labor relations, administrative ethics, and so on. Men are not being trained in our universities or in the early stages of their business life to tackle such issues any better than their seniors do.

Executive development courses are a possible answer. In attempting to sharpen the goals of such courses, therefore, I suggest that we begin to emphasize training for policy decisions and that we stop talking about training men to become members of a "team" and begin to think about producing men who are outstanding individuals in their own right. A dozen experts meeting around a table and trying to substitute their combined knowledge of a problem for the knowledge and power to integrate that should be in the head of the top man, will invariably impede administrative decision, slow the pace of execution, and make the process bureaucratic in the objectionable sense.

### Criticisms of Training Courses

What are the causes of dissatisfaction with training programs in the United States? A group of executives in large corporations gave the following replies to this question:

The first criticism was that these programs do not meet the need we have been discussing—preparation for policy-making; that they concentrate instead on administrative techniques and process. Nor is concentration on decision-making as a process sufficient; a better understanding of the elements of desirable policy seems necessary. Second, training methods as well as content tend to follow set formulas which gradually acquire rigidity, slowing the search for what these people feel they really need. The conventional classroom methods, for example, have little appeal for persons who have reached middle years and teaching gadgetry often is mistaken for something that grows up inside a man and gives him impetus to go on educating himself. A short course with its play-acting and prestige may be mistaken for destination rather than departure; or men may get so used to role-playing that they sometimes forget what it's like to be themselves. Finally, there is too much emphasis on the group and too little on the individual, the whole man and not merely the mechanistic man in his limited work role.

On the basis of first-hand experience with executive development programs in some other countries, plus observation of those in which I have participated in the United States, I believe that the questions raised by these business executives are similar to those bothering public administrators.

### Possible Improvements

If these criticisms of training courses are valid, then several major guidelines emerge.

We should spend less time on the *processes* of decision-making and more on *what* is being decided and *why*. I have listened to discussions in executive development programs where it was apparently assumed that if the processes of decision-making could be perfected, the results would be as reliable as the calculations of an adding machine. Fortunately, most practical executives are too skeptical to believe such hocus-pocus, but it must be admitted that a glib talker, equipped with just the right "scientific" lingo, can cast a spell. Instead, we must also teach the wisdom and moral philosophy inhering in the decisions themselves, or at least we must somehow produce individuals who are capable of such decisions.

Training at the top level should be more emphasized than at present, partly because the need for training is continuous and partly because of its tonic effect on the intermediate and primary levels of training. The harder policy decisions become, the greater is the need for peers to come together in a common program and to share the stimulation of joint endeavor. Moreover, when senior executives become favorably inclined toward executive development courses, through direct contact with them, junior executives are more likely to be encouraged to participate in the same type of work.

If top executive training is to catch on, however, both the method and the content will have to be improved over much that is offered at present. There is a greater need for faculty members who understand the field of public policy, which is a combination of disciplines and includes also a measure of practical experience, and less need for men who are narrowly trained as economists or administrative technicians.

Today, many employers in large-scale industry and in government agencies are trying to decide whether to launch executive development programs of their own, as some have, or whether to support and improve those operated by independent institutions. The conception of broad policy-centered training helps to decide this. It seems clear that they should decide in favor of the independent institution. The educational role of the employer is on-the-job training for people needing special skills, which is a large assignment, and the matter should stop there. Administrative agencies have no business organizing advanced executive development programs of their own. They do not have the personnel to teach such courses unless their top executives can spare the time to act as teachers, and of course they cannot. Moreover, the employer, try as he may, will find company policy and method being confused with objective standards in both of these areas, which further increases the process of bureaucratization. Moreover, the independent executive development programs permit officials to get away from their own outfits for a spell and to secure a fresh point of view by associating with men of differing outlooks and experience. And finally, if an employing institution runs its own program, it is hard to resist the temptation to indoctrinate, and if carried too far, the result is more or less open revolt against it.

How long should the course be? If we need executives who are humane and gifted and hence capable of growing in grace, how much time must be devoted to that end? I do not, of course, assume that executive development programs or any formal educational scheme, unaided, can do the whole job. But a substantial program of this kind can doubtless accomplish more than a "quickie" course can hope for. It is argued that a good deal can be accomplished even in a long weekend if the personalities are stimulating and the locus is remote and congenial. At the other extreme it is contended that twelve full weeks, under ideal circumstances and with no interruptions from outside, is hardly enough if results of lasting and measurable importance are to be achieved. The answer, I suppose, comes down to what it is hoped to accomplish. If the objective is to impart specific knowledge and ideas, then a few hours might suffice; but if the aim is to change a man's outlook, his motivation, and even his personality, then twelve weeks is a short time no matter how favorable the circumstances.

A few summers ago I attended an international conference at Geneva where the subject was methods of evaluation in technical assistance programs. The sociologists, and especially the social anthropologists, talked a good deal about changing what goes on in a man's mind, and I must confess that I had some difficulty in understanding what they were driving at. Later, but not at the same conference, I began to see the point, and I think now that it offers the answer to the question of duration.

Put it this way: as a result of stimulus-and-response experienced in the course of several weeks in a training program, does the ethos, or outlook, of a man perceptibly change so that his boss and his associates notice it? Is he himself aware of what has happened, and is his family aware of it? I must confess that when I put these thoughts into print they sound a little like the come-on of a Madison Avenue man. Nevertheless, when with my own eyes I have seen this metamorphosis during an executive development program, I cannot help but believe in it.

Actually, there is no mystery about what happens. At a certain point in this particular type of program a man tumbles to the fact that administration is a philosophy, a way of life, something that is not only challenging in his job but that could even unify his personality and interests in a way he had never suspected. In terms of money and status he has no more ambition or motivation than he had before, but in terms of his attitude toward his job and his fellows he has considerably more of both. I believe that this shifting of point of view occurs when a man sees that administrative techniques and policy decisions are a single element rather than separate ones, when he sees that job and personality fulfillment must go together. I have seen this transformation occur in most members of a group of sixty or so men after nine or ten weeks—not before that—and hence I conclude that we are vainly hoping for miracles if we plan and conduct courses ranging, say, up to six weeks.[4] And I must add that even a twelve week course must be of the highest quality or little observable effect is produced.

A short course can succeed in communicating information, in broadening a man's outlook, and in setting him to thinking, and these are all worthy objectives, but developing top executive material takes longer. Once a man is touched to the quick by the offerings of a first rate course, however, he is set for a long time and does not need the same shots in the arm and frequent returns to school that his less fortunate colleagues do.

## Content and Method

Now, how is the objective of producing executive leadership translated into method? Is there, moreover, a right method of training executives in business and a different one best designed for executives in government, or is there a common method suitable for both groups? Even with two separate methods, it is necessary in each to duplicate much of the content and procedure of the other in order to make either program successful, because both business and government operate within the same culture patterns and belief-systems, both are trying to produce effective leadership, both are interrelated at many points, both are concerned with public policy, both deal with the same elements of administration, and both tend increasingly to fall into a common pattern.

Is it possible in a training program to deal with policy problems as effectively as with administrative techniques? I think there is already enough evidence to show that it can be done. The business school courses on policy-making that make use of case materials, the arts and sciences courses on business and government, the skillful admixture of policy and administrative techniques in the curriculum of the Administrative Staff College at Henley-on-Thames, England, all convince me that it can be done. And it will be done when we begin to understand that a proper administrative technique is only half the solution, and that under modern conditions it is not even the more important half.

It must be recognized at the outset, I believe, that no one method by itself will do all that needs to be done. My observations and those of others I have talked with indicate that lectures should be kept to a minimum; cases should be used sparingly and only when they are related to the main subject under investigation; general discussions and debates should be scheduled only after the subject has been thoroughly explored because then (hopefully) most enrollees will have developed enough humility, in the face of the complexity of the problem and its solution, to be disinclined to talk merely for effect.

The curriculum of an executive development course should be arranged to produce a unified, fully integrated result, which is enthusiasm for the process-policy activity known as administration, in a way that will enable a man to form his own philosophy and provide his own on-going stimulus to improvement. Concretely, a man must learn all about the administrative process and all about the main issues of policy that he will have to decide when he reaches the top ranks of management; he must learn to relate these two bodies of knowledge and to realize that they grow out of a single administrative situation.

In all of the executive development experiments I have observed, this feat of integration is more successfully performed at the Administrative Staff College at Henley than at any other place.[5]

There, the course leads up to the question, "What is needed in order to strengthen a vital national economy?" The matter is approached through the questions, "What can be done to promote foreign trade on which the future of Britain depends? What can be done to maintain administrative vitality in business and in government so that the nation will maintain a leading position in the world? What do these two issues mean to me? What do I need to do?" Except for the matter of foreign trade which is of special importance to Great Britain, I submit that all of these questions are universally involved in most administrative decisions, including those that seem at first glance to turn primarily on a matter of procedure or technique.

Where policy is concerned, furthermore, there is an internal and an external aspect of almost every question. In the handling of people, for example, personnel management is largely internal and industrial relations is largely external; in finance, budgeting is largely internal and taxes are largely external; and it is the same with administrative decentralization and laws governing the location of industry; with internal operating rules and regulations, and the regulation of public utilities by a legislature. This means searching for the principles of political economy on which the future of the national economy and the vitality of its institutions both public and private, seem to depend. Appealing to the intelligent patriotism and to the self-interest of executives as this unified approach does, there is no problem of securing sustained interest and stimulating independent thinking.

Course administrators achieve this objective by carefully thinking through the kind of impact they want to make on enrollees, the number of subjects needed, their interrelationships, the sequence of topics, the variety of possible methods, the materials to be made available, and the time schedule. All of this is worked out in detail, nothing is left to chance.

When enrollees are selected for the course, each man is chosen to fit into a team called a syndicate, the ten members of which are about equally divided between the private and the public sectors of the economy and, in addition, represent a cross section of administrative skills. As the course begins, the enrollees themselves take over, the course directors stay very much in the background, exerting their influence largely through personal social contacts.

Each syndicate member must act as chairman or as secretary of a particular project during the twelve weeks that the course lasts. The projects are arranged under a few major headings so that a week or more can be spent on a single major area, such as personnel, finance, decentralization, business and government relationships. Each project is the subject of a "brief" prepared by the College which states the problem and describes the report which the syndicate is expected to present to be discussed by all the syndicates meeting together.

To help secure integration and show interrelationships among the subject-matter of the different projects, two or three issues may be worked on at different times of the same day. The number of projects is not too large, and hence there is time for reading and reflection, an opportunity notably absent from most of the short programs I have observed. Integration and broadening take place also as industrial and government officials begin to realize that their responsibilities are not dissimilar, that accountants and salesmen are both essential, that an economy, like a management team, must be rounded. The men learn that external policies are the stuff of influence and survival, and that the higher you go in administration the more of high policy there is. But at Henley these lessons appear from the context; they are never taught or drilled into the enrollees. Men, in syndicates and in the evening forums where reports are discussed, are cast in the role of a board of directors or a management committee considering a decision which is likely to have lasting consequences.

In this group method, how do you resolve the age-old conflict between the individual and the group? How do you guard against the appearance of the "organization man," the spineless conformist who is the opposite of the enterprising executive? You do this by combining the best of two methods. Within the group there soon comes to be a division of labor, but at the same time the members all work together on analyses, reading assignments, reports, and so on. They produce a report attempting to solve the problem in question and containing statements of principle covering both administration and policy, and they defend this report together against the attacks of other syndicates as an executive would justify himself when he appears before his policy board or legislative committee.

But enrollees learn also that it is *individuals* who provide leadership and initiative; and that the group is only as strong as the quality of its members. Within the group and among the whole membership of the program, a man speaks for himself and his traits of independence and leadership, if he has them, soon appear in group discussion. He does not hesitate to disagree with the majority so long as he thinks he has the better case. Emphasis is on originality and dissent, initiative and enterprise; conformity as conformity is held in low esteem.

What the administrator should know about the national economy, the enrollees learn for themselves by group discussion, independent reading, and mature reflection. This core of knowledge includes legislative-executive relations, pressure groups and the public interest, resource management, national production, foreign trade, money management, labor relations, monopoly policy, technological and economic change, bureaucracy and enterprise, and decentralization policy. In Great Britain the focus will be foreign trade; in the United States, it is more likely to be the domestic economy. At the Administrative Staff College each subject is stated as a current issue of policy and decision and not as a matter for general philosophical discussion. The philosophy is there, but it derives from the issue; although it is a major goal of the course, it is indirectly achieved and hence indoctrination is avoided.

I have gone into some detail on the subject of content and method, relying mainly on the Administrative Staff College for illustration, because I wanted to make certain points clear. First, the problems dealt with by the enrollees seem different from those with which they are familiar in their normal administrative life because they are shown in a larger setting and as related to other large issues, and external influences are shown to be pertinent. The enrollees soon recognize that their experience, as related to the solution of these large issues is limited; they need lift their sights and identify relationships never noticed but always there.

Second, the majority of administrative decisions are seen as having some impact on public policy, as offering some kind of contribution to national economic strength. As a by-product, a better understanding is brought about between business and government as the men in each area learn to appreciate the distinctive and necessary role of the other.

And third, by the time the twelve weeks of the course are up, it is clear to all that every aspect of administration is related to and tested by the touchstone of policy objective.

## The Future

What of executive development in the decade that lies ahead? My guess is that there will be fewer programs, with refresher courses as needed, but better ones; that significant new advances will occur in the training of top executives and that this will have a beneficial effect on departmentation and training in the universities; that an increasing number of programs will be set up to train top men in both industry and in government; that public policy will come to be more emphasized than administrative techniques; that the administrators of executive development programs will spend most of their time on planning and evaluation and that the actual conduct of the program will be handled primarily by the members themselves on the ground that self-learning provides a continuing motivation and momentum.

And last, I believe that when it is widely appreciated that there is no magic that will produce a qualified executive, especially if he has had the wrong start, then management both in business and in government will increasingly look for workable methods of limiting the size of institutions, decentralizing operations, and favoring the active, independent executive in the interests of an enterprising program.

## Footnotes

1. Although I am stressing courses, it should be understood that they are only part of a larger strategy of executive development that includes the whole shaping of a man's career both by promotion and changes of work as well as by internal and external programs of instruction.
2. The objectives I envision for executive development—including coming to grips with overspecialization and loss of institutional vitality—cannot be achieved simply through this process. Social explorations are needed into the proper balance between business and government, optimum size of institutions, undue concentrations of power, and the feasibility of financial and intercorporate decentralization through deliberate limitations on size and the strengthening of competition. We may have to learn more about the relations between bureaucracy and enterprise before executive development courses can wholly escape superficiality.

3. Chester A. Barnard, "Mind in Everyday Affairs," *The Functions of the Executive* (Harvard University Press, 1938), appendix.
4. I do not mean to be dogmatic about this. The point at which "illumination" occurs may vary with the number and level of knowledge of the individuals in the course; thus, in a small group of sophisticated enrollees, the point at which policy integration reaches its climax may occur earlier than with a larger group of less experienced people.
5. I described the program at Henley in "The Administrative Staff College: Executive Development in Government and Industry," 50 *The American Political Science Review* 166-76 (March, 1956).

PAUL P. VAN RIPER

## The Senior Civil Service
## And the Career System

THIS ARTICLE by Professor Van Riper, then at Cornell University and later at Texas A & M University, picked up where Leonard White's 1955 analysis of the Senior Civil Service left off. Political controversies which engulfed the Second Hoover Commission's SCS proposals were detailed in this article along with the Eisenhower administration's later efforts to deal with those issues and form a career executive service.

Seven "basic considerations" of relevance to creation of a federal executive service were discussed by Van Riper, with the focus on career service concepts. The perspectives of this article were dominant among career civil service opponents of SCS provisions in the 1950s, and they remained powerful at the creation in 1978 of the Senior Executive Service.

EARLY in 1955, former President Herbert Hoover was asked to name the most important of the Second Hoover Commission's 314 recommendations. Mr. Hoover is reported to have replied without hesitation: "I would pick the recommendation for the setting up of a senior civil service. . . . That is why our Report on Personnel and Civil Service is the nearest to my heart."[1] President Eisenhower has characterized the recommendation for a Senior Civil Service as "one of the most far-reaching and imaginative proposals made by the Commission."[2]

An offspring of the career system concept, the idea of a Senior Civil Service has a long and honorable lineage. However, the proposal has generated a great deal of controversy in both official and unofficial circles since 1955. By early 1956 the U.S. Civil Service Commission had designed an "interim plan" for agency consideration. But there was disagreement as to whether a start should be made through the necessarily limited scope of an executive order, as the interim plan envisioned, or through a direct legislative attack on the problem. It also became clear that the proposal, then as now, was receiving its main support from top level political executives in the White House. Many career civil servants have viewed the SCS idea with little enthusiasm.

The Cabinet discussed the matter on April 6, 1956, and the sub-Cabinet on

May 4, 1956. The interim plan was then apparently shelved, but no final decision was made. By this time a number of well-known personnel analysts and political scientists—Leonard D. White, Herman M. Somers, and Everett Reimer, for example—had expressed their views, pro and con.[3] The Executive Development Conference of the Society for Personnel Administration debated the issue in 1955;[4] and the American Political Science Association picked it up again in September, 1956.[5] There was agreement on the need for some sort of prescription for the top levels of the federal service. Great concern was expressed over its morale and prestige, the inadequacy of total available talent, and the flexibility with which it could be used. However, there were extreme differences of opinion as to what ought to be done.

On December 5, 1956, a meeting of persons representing a number of points of view was held under White House auspices. Again, there was acceptance of objectives but reservations on many specifics. Meanwhile, public employee union opposition was mounting. In August, 1957, the President designated a five-member Career Executive Committee, chaired by Arthur S. Flemming, to study the problem.[6] In October, Paul T. David of The Brookings Institution and Ross Pollock of the Civil Service Commission examined the SCS in their *Executives for Government.*[7] The President's committee reported in December, 1957 and recommended the establishment of a Career Executive Service for top "career employees who are competent to serve in staff or line positions requiring administrative and managerial capacity."[8] To develop such a service, a Career Executive Board was created on March 4, 1958, by Executive Order 10758. At last there was action.

Because of the vagueness of the order and the fact that it is a step toward the never-repudiated Senior Civil Service concept of the Second Hoover Commission, let us take another look at both proposals with a view to two things: (1) analyzing the difficulties in implementing such programs, and (2) suggesting some guideposts for an approach to the overall career system concept which underlies both.

### The Career Executive Order

Apparently the decision to scrap the Senior Civil Service label stemmed from the meeting called by the White House in December, 1956. Meyer Kestnbaum, special adviser to the President on reforms proposed by the Hoover Commission, reported: "One of the fortunate things which came out of the discussion was, we found, that the connotation of the title 'Senior Civil Service' placed the wrong emphasis on the kind of a program that it was agreed is really needed. This then led to the development of the term 'Career Executive Program' which is a more accurate description of what is contemplated."[9]

The order provides for a part-time, bipartisan board of five members appointed by the President to serve in an advisory capacity to the Civil Service Commission. Three of the members are to come from private life, one from the Civil Service Commission, and the fifth from some other executive agency. No more than three members may be from the same political party. The President designated Arthur S. Flemming as the first chairman and appointed as other members James P. Mitchell, Secretary of Labor, Frederick J. Lawton, U.S. Civil Service Commissioner, Charles B. Stauffacher, formerly of the Bureau of the Budget and now Vice President of Continental Can Company, and James H. Taylor, Manager of Personnel Administration of Procter and Gamble Company.

The Board is to (1) develop a Career Executive Service, (2) establish "a supplementary roster of career executive eligibles," (3) develop methods for regular appraisal of career executive performance, (4) assist the Civil Service Commission and the agencies in the development of effective training programs for career executives, (5) recommend to the Commission "changes in position classification practices to permit greater flexibility in assignment of career executives," and (6) make such other recommendations "as will strengthen the career executive program."

The Career Executive Service (CES) is presently confined to grades GS-16 and above (and their equivalents) in the competitive civil service. Grades below this level may be included by the Civil Service Commission upon recommendation of the Board. Particular positions must be designated for inclusion "by the heads of the executive agencies concerned with the approval of the Career Executive Board" from among those with "significant administrative or managerial characteristics."

For an individual to become a "career executive" he must be (1) nominated by the head of an agency, (2) approved by the Career Executive Board according to standards which it is to devise, and (3) designated by the President. The order apparently precludes direct application by the civil servant himself.

### The Senior Civil Service Proposal

In its prescription for a Senior Civil Service (SCS), the Hoover Commission largely accepted its task force's recommendations.[10] The Commission proper recommended a Senior Civil Service Board almost precisely like that set up in E.O. 10758 and with similar general functions. By this mechanism the Commission desired to "fill a gap in the existing machinery of personnel administration" and to obtain a "fresh approach to the problems of top management." (The task force proposed a board fully independent of the Civil Service Commission to assure its "... opportunity ... to develop appropriate policies and procedures without being restricted by traditional civil service attitudes and conventions.")

In defining the grades and positions which the board might consider, the two proposals again are similar, except that the SCS envisioned the immediate inclusion of grade GS-15 as well as GS-16 through 18. In numbers, the Hoover Commission suggested an SCS of 1,500 to 3,000 members.[11] The nomination and selection process, too, would be the same as in the Executive order. However, the task force was more precise than E.O. 10758 in suggesting selection criteria: "leadership, judgment, adaptability, skill in working with people, and capacity for continued growth" along with technical competence and a minimum of five years' previous federal service. Except for a suggestion that SCS personnel might be "selected out" if passed over repeatedly for increase in pay, the recommended functions of the SCS board parallel those of the Career Executive Board.

Almost the whole of the CES system set forth in E.O. 10758 is contained in the SCS provisions. The President and his advisers have chosen to implement the SCS proposal first through an Executive order which goes about as far as possible without legislation and thus follows the procedure suggested in the Civil Service Commission's interim plan.

But the Executive order clearly envisions further "steps" which "will strengthen the career executive program." If the remaining recommendations for the SCS were followed, these steps would fall mainly into two categories: (1) those relating to political neutrality and (2) those concerned with flexibility and personal rank. To be fair, it should be noted that the December, 1956 conference participants were inclined against implementing the Hoover Commission report on these two matters, but there is as yet no official statement to this effect.

The Hoover Commission's advocacy of an expanded and sharper concept of political neutrality was designed to fit hand in glove with the Hoover Commission's further blueprint for a strengthened political executive. The Commission has made the most determined effort to date to separate politics and administration in our federal service. In many ways the report on personnel of the Second Hoover Commission is reminiscent of the old separatist doctrines first propounded by Woodrow Wilson and popularized by F. J. Goodnow at the turn of the century. E.O. 10758 contains no reference to any of these matters.

The Executive order does refer in highly general terms to "greater flexibility in the assignment of career executives" and would accomplish this through modifications of our traditional classification plan. But the Hoover Commission underscored "transferability" and stipulated "an obligation upon the part of the senior civil servant to serve where needed most" here or abroad, "subject to a rule of reason." And in one of its most debated recommendations, which some would say is the real essence of the SCS proposal, the Commission advocated personal rank for Senior Civil Servants to facilitate this "flexibility." To make the personal rank (and the possibility of rotation) more attractive, three things, none of which are in E.O. 10758, were proposed: (1) to increase pay in terms of rank rather than position, (2) to provide retirement equities equal to those of the Foreign Service, and (3) to permit members of the SCS who might be "temporarily unassigned" to be kept on at full or half pay for up to six months. Rank-in-the-man would be a major departure from our traditional civil service system which, as the Hoover Commission notes, "emphasizes positions, not people." On the other hand, personal rank is taken for granted in all military services and in most foreign civil service systems as well as in our own Foreign Service.

Finally, the SCS concept is intended to provide a capstone to the Hoover Commission's further suggestions for "Training and Managerial Development at Lower Levels." Thus, while the SCS alone should not be confused with proposals for a full-scale career system, it does have—when considered in tandem with the political executive, political neutrality, and lower-level development recommendations, major implications for the entire federal service and even the nation at large. Though something of a pale copy so far, so does E.O. 10758.

## Pros and Cons

Let us summarize the major arguments deriving from the SCS proposal, many of which are directly relevant to the Executive order and all or most of which are relevant to the direction the order takes.[12]

### Need for a Special Board

There has been little support for the task force recommendation of a supervisory board almost completely divorced from the Civil Service Commission. This partly results from the considerable revitalization of the Commission in recent years so that restriction "by traditional civil service attitudes..." seems less likely. Moreover, the general tendency during the past decade has been to consolidate rather than fragment the federal organizational structure. But most antagonists, except for the public employee unions, accept the utility—if not absolute need—of a special unit for the pin-pointed consideration of top level personnel problems. There is some precedent for this in the creation during World War II of a special Committee on Administrative Personnel, headed by Emery Olson. New proposals, it is argued, often need a more flexible base than traditional organization provides.

But the unions are fearful of the entry of partisan politics through such a board. Actually, they suspect the whole plan—even that laid out in E.O. 10758— of partisan implications, according to recent testimony before Congress. Part of this fear probably stems from distrust of the motives of the present administration, dating back to some of the manipulations of 1953-54. The mass of public employees have much more confidence in our historic Civil Service Commission than in any new group, especially one which might be more closely tied to the White House. Moreover, like most unions, those of civil servants tend to prefer one "bargaining agent" rather than several. Having now—after a long struggle— a centralized personnel agency to their liking, they are loath to fragment its powers in any way. The veterans' organizations and Congress, too, often think along similar lines.

A number of problems stem from the relationship of the board to the executive agencies. Most of these are typical of any "dual-jurisdiction" over personnel matters, and are dealt with under the topics below.

### The Selection Process

There is little quarrel over whether a top career service should stop at the

GS-16 level or go down one step to GS-15. And there seems to be general approval of the E.O. 10758 provision for the development of a roster of eligibles from among even lower grades, something the Hoover Commission was vague about. But the initial selection process has been strongly attacked.

The first problem is a very practical administrative one, which is thoroughly explored only by David and Pollock in their analysis of the SCS plan.[13] To maintain high standards, which everyone agrees is essential, the plan recommends the positive selection of outstanding personnel as opposed to any "blanketing-in" of incumbents. But, even if personal rank were granted, this procedure creates difficulties in the relationship of positions to persons. The fact that both the SCS and CES plans contemplate the special designation of positions as well as individuals makes the problem even more perplexing.

Even without personal rank, there would be a dual personnel system—one for those selected and one for those who are not. All this poses a frustrating dilemma. If one accepts the recommendation against blanketing-in, the implementation is difficult. If incumbents are blanketed-in, the plans lose their basic rationale, which is to upgrade the service.

Nomination of careerists by the heads of agencies—who are political executives—also worries many persons. It is agreed that line agencies must be consulted about implementation of the plan. This has always been done. But both the SCS and CES plans would give department heads what amounts to a veto over nominations. In addition, there is some fear, especially on the part of the unions, that partisanship and ideology might enter into the nomination process.[14]

Just as fundamental is whether the selection process violates competitive principles. Interestingly, the unions are the only groups which have taken much interest in this issue, but it is one on which they feel strongly. The Hoover Commission and E.O. 10758 would not bar all competition, for, presumably, some of those nominated would not be selected. But the requirement of five years prior federal service (this is explicit only in the SCS plan) regardless of other qualifications would strike a heavy blow at lateral entry, a fundamental aspect of any fully competitive system. Moreover, the nomination process also militates against free competition. Not only is there no allowance for the nomination of persons not now in the federal service (regardless of prior years of experience), but also none for applications by present public employees.

Some also emphasize the difficulties inherent in the generalist approach of the SCS proposal. They see the specialist placed at a disadvantage by a pool of rotatable generalists (termed "whirling dervishes" by those more ardently in opposition). Moreover, they doubt the relevance of the generalist approach in many top jobs. Our federal service has been plagued by over-specialization and over-departmentalization, encouraged in part by our classification system. But the SCS concept may go too far in the other direction.

Finally, there is implicit in the SCS selection system a "dilemma of supply and demand." Everett Reimer has stated the problem well: ". . . the demand for its members can be stimulated only by so restricting the supply as to make it impossible to meet the demand."[15] The executive order's provision for a roster of eligibles to fill CES positions would help. But neither plan takes into account the requirements of some new emergency, civil or military. There is no provision for an executive reserve or for any tie-in with the sort of civilian reserve for which plans were laid in 1956 by the Office of Defense Mobilization.

### Selection Out and Location of Responsibility

To compensate for the additional hazard to senior civil servants of the selection out process and required transfer, the Hoover Commission recommended additional pay and perquisites. These are not part of the Executive order and there is some fear that the former may be introduced without the latter.

In carrying out this and other personnel procedures, there is also the question of the power of an SCS or CES board vis-à-vis the line agencies. We have always faced a question of "dual jurisdiction" between the line and the Civil Service Commission. But the SCS plan would add another dimension at a time when there is a generally approved trend, which many feel has not gone far enough, toward delegating personnel responsibility to departments.

### Political Neutrality

The political neutrality provisions of the SCS need only a little more amplification. There are two points most at issue. The Hoover Commission would require a Senior Civil Servant to make no statements to the press on other than factual matters and to avoid testimony before congressional committees on political questions. All this would be to preserve a very sharp line between the political executives, who would handle all policy matters and all but technical advice before Congress, and the career service as a whole (not just SCS personnel). In turn, careerists would be much more protected against political pressure than now. The neatness of this theory of political separatism is agreeable enough, but its reality and workability are questioned. Much high level administration, runs the counterargument, must inevitably involve a great deal of politics and political policy-making. Moreover, can anyone expect congressmen to abide by such distinctions with respect to testimony if some issue of real importance is before them on which a career civil servant might have relevant information?

The other recommendation that has received sharp criticism states that career administrators should "in their approach to their duties" be as "free from emotional attachment to particular policies as possible." To this Herman M. Somers replies, "To identify 'good management' in the civil service with indifference to the objects of management and unconcern with the social consequences of policies is to make of public administration a barren, if not nihilistic, affair which seems unlikely to attract the kind of imaginative competence which the Hoover Commision Report hopes for."[16] Others point out that our Hatch Act and related political neutrality rules are already the most stringent in the world and suggest

## Personal Rank

The arguments for "rank-in-the-man" as opposed to "rank-in-the-job" stress the need for status and flexibility. It is conceded that personal rank would provide a titular status which would have real meaning with an accompanying increase in pay and perquisites. But it is in the flexibility argument that the proponents of personal rank find their most cogent support. It has long been recognized that our service is too parochial and that too many executives have spent most of their careers in only one agency. The concept of personal rank can be supported not only for its prestige but also for its recognition of the relationship of individuality to effective administration, particularly at the higher levels. Even under present classification procedures, many positions are made what they are by their holders, and job descriptions are often thinly veiled biographies of incumbents.

The principal argument against personal rank has also been underplayed. There is little reference to the difficulties experienced with the Foreign Service, which the Wriston Committee *Report*, for example, made abundantly clear.[17] Nor is there, except by Everett Reimer, much argument based on military experience with personal rank. Yet the Hoover Commission's other report which deals with the relationship of military (rank-in-the-man) to civilian (rank-in-the-job) employees in the Department of Defense is replete with problems of civil-military tension, dual staffing of positions as a result of a dual personnel system, the ill effects of the so-called Manchu law governing rotation of the military, and the like.[18]

## The Ends-Means Problem

Even if these proposals could overcome the dearth of top-level administrative talent and the inflexibility in its use, would the total result be satisfactory? Considered in the light of the whole Hoover Commission report on personnel and civil service, either the SCS or the CES proposal can easily be envisioned as a part of a new career system emphasizing the planning of careers and promotion from within, with diminished lateral entry and turnover. The issue here is no longer procedures and organization but social values. Even if we could, *ought* we move toward a closed and more tightly managed career system? This is mainly a matter of political and personal preferences, one's view of the proper role of career civil servants in American politics and the reciprocal relationship of federal personnel administration to American democracy and American life.

### Standards of Judgment

In such an argument very little, pro or con, is provable in a scientific sense.

Nevertheless, there are some fundamental standards of judgment to assist in cutting through the controversy. I suggest seven basic considerations to assist in assessing not only the SCS and CES proposals, but also the career system thinking which underlies them.

## 1. The Need for a Representative Bureaucracy

Above all, we should be concerned with the maintenance in this country of a "representative bureaucracy." This does not mean that business and government should be conducted along identical lines, though we usually think of business as typical of American society. It does suggest the desirability of a bureaucracy which (1) consists of a reasonable cross section of the body politic in terms of social groupings, educational insitutions, and geography, and (2) is in general tune with the ethos and attitudes of the society. Both of these characterize the American federal service more completely than most civil bureaucracies. In fact, during all three periods in our history when the federal service has been in serious political trouble, the principal charges—by Jackson in 1829, at the passage of the Civil Service act in 1883, and by the Republicans in 1953—revolved around its representative character.

In a pluralistic democracy such as ours, emphasizing both liberty and equality, we must at all costs maintain a civil (and military) establishment which is as close to our grass roots as possible. The representative character of the bureaucracy is just as important as that of Congress. The alternative, as Somers has suggested, is at the least an explosion of administrative and political irritation, resentment and personal grievance.[19]

## 2. The Wisdom of Free Occupational Choice

Related to the concept of a democratically oriented bureaucracy is that of freedom of occupational choice. This freedom can be supported solely on ideological grounds as a logical corollary to freedom in general. However, it also can be supported on the practical grounds that employees are much more content and productive when they have a good deal to say about their own future. This is the essence of the vast new literature on human relations. But nowhere does the SCS (or CES) plan provide career civil servants with any clear opportunity to express their interests with respect to their own future. Apparently the Hoover Commission did not contemplate asking civil servants whether they wanted such a plan, expected to place some individuals within the SCS and leave others out whether they liked it or not, and planned to move them around with limited consultation. The only "opportunity" lay in the recommendations for increased pay and allowances which—especially in the CES plan—may or may not come about. It is no wonder that the most negative reactions to the SCS concept have come from the career civil servants whom the Hoover Commission apparently thought it was helping.

## 3. Avoiding Over-Institutionalization

This is in many ways the negative verision of the second consideration. We can manage too much. It is simply not possible to anticiapte beyond modest limits the future occupational requirements of an organization as complex as the federal service, or to second-guess all the vagaries of human behavior with respect to occupational preference in a social milieu which emphasizes choice and mobility.

This third consideration also suggests that we look twice at two other aspects of the SCS and CES plans. First, while for ten years everyone has been prescribing more decentralization for the federal personnel system, both plans represent a move in the other direction. Second, the plans will inevitably involve a dual personnel system where there had been a unified one. All of this implies more structure, more procedure, more restrictions on departmental personnel administration, more regulations, and more complexity. Instead, our goal ought to be a personnel system which is as simple and decentralized as possible.

## 4. Attacking the Executive Shortage at the Proper Point

The shortage of executives has been a national rather than merely a federal problem. If the situation continues to ease a bit, as it has during 1958, the need to create an SCS as a solution for federal executive shortages will be much less pressing. In any case we may ask whether the answer to a nationwide executive shortage does not lie more in increasing the total supply of available talent than in increasing the competition for that which exists. It is probable that, despite President Hoover's deep concern over the SCS, the most important recommendations of the Second Hoover Commission have to do with executive development in the middle and lower echelons. It could be argued that, if this were well done, there would be little need for any SCS or CES at all.

## 5. Placing Politics in Its Proper Role

There is both a proper and an improper role for politics with respect to the federal career service. Let us distinguish them.

There is the eligibility process by which individuals might get on the SCS or CES rolls. It has long been a fundamental principle of career personnel management in the government that there should be no chance for the play of improper motives in the procedure by which eligibility for placement on a civil service register is determined. This is another basic tenet of the Pendleton Act. Yet, as suggested above, bringing department heads into the nomination process—the first determination of eligibility—implies assumptions about political executive behavior quite different from those of the Pendleton Act. At the same time the Hoover Commission has advocated a much tighter conception of political neutrality. In these respects the SCS proposal in particular seems to be working at cross-purposes. Department heads have always been brought into the appointment process—to positions, that is. But to bring them into the eligibility process, in other than a consultative role concerning the process as a whole, is both unnecessary and questionable.

## 6. Clarifying Traditional Analogies

While the Hoover Commission has not itself argued for a more closed career system by analogy to American business and the British civil service, many Americans have. Can we clarify the facts on which these analogies rest?

It is widely assumed that the closed career system is becoming more popular in American business. However, Warner and Abegglen's recent analysis of social mobility among American business leaders and William H. Whyte, Jr.'s study, *The Organization Man*, suggest that mobility of all types is on the increase rather than the decrease.[20] Thus, while it may be argued that business emphasizes promotion from within more than the federal service (though even this is questionable), any move toward a more rigidly controlled and closed type of career system in private enterprise apparently has stopped. The trend may now in fact be against the concept represented by the SCS. Certainly we are hearing much criticism within business circles of the so-called "crown prince" approach to executive development.

In considering going in the direction of the British closed and tightly managed career system, with an administrative class recruited directly out of the universities at its apex, we should note four facts: (1) that the British system was designed for an aristocratically inclined, unitary government, quite different from our own; (2) that the prestige of the British public service, as revealed in the most recent Gallup poll on the subject, is something less in the minds of the British than is the prestige of our own service in the minds of Americans;[21] (3) that the British have been increasing lateral entry at many levels during the past twenty years and are grouping specialists less rigidly; and (4) that even the creation of an administrative class, with far more prestige and power than proposed for the SCS, is now failing to serve as an adequate lodestar in attracting intelligent young people into the British service.

## 7. The Limitations of Administrative Reform

We must remember that we in America often assume that administrative and procedural reorganization along with increased pay will remedy almost any symptom of organizational sickness. The SCS and CES plans are prescriptions of this order. They are based on the ideas that prestige is primarily determined by differentials in rank, pay, organizational status, and tenure; and that prestige, interpreted in these terms, is the main motivating force which brings intelligent and capable men onto an occupational ladder.

But prestige and personal motivations are also vitally affected by power and authority, recognition of the importance of function, and opportunities for individual creativeness and contribution to an organizational whole. A most confused administrative system coupled with chaotic and patronage-ridden personnel management did not prevent the civil service of the New Deal period from attaining the highest degree of public employee morale in our history. And no amount of career system renovation is likely to compensate fully for the fact that our federal service for a decade has lacked not only firm policy guidance but also the support of large segments of both the executive and legislative branches—not to mention the general public. Indeed, the service itself has been a main object of political attack during recent years.

## What Can Be Done?

What can and should be done with the SCS-CES proposal in light of these considerations?

Any SCS or CES must, above all, be presented as an *opportunity* for *all* those who are interested and who think they can qualify. It must really be an opportunity and must be made as attractive as possible. Only if the rewards are high can the sacrifices involved in compulsory assignment and rotation and the potential hazards accompanying selection and selection out be compensated sufficiently for civil servants to look upon membership as more than a dubious honor.

The provision of the executive order for a Career Executive Board closely tied in with the Civil Service Commission seems like a worthwhile experiment, but its advisory jurisdiction should be expanded to the whole realm of executive development at all levels. Let us treat this problem as a whole. Line executives must be consulted on the details of the program but should play no part in the eligibility process other than through normal performance rating. They should not nominate candidates.

The relationship of positions to persons can be more easily resolved if we forget personal rank. It becomes almost no problem at all if we forget nominations and automatic consideration of everyone in top jobs, simply open up a new CES examination for specially designated positions, and permit all those who consider themselves eligible to apply. The CES positions should then be filled as they become vacant, through appointment by department heads from the special CES registers. This may slow the development of a CES, but it cannot be created at once anyway. This process—which is the traditional and well-understood one—will leave the initiative with the individual civil servant. Even if additional pay and perquisites were not forthcoming, this opportunity probably would be of interest to many civil servants. The rewards would not be great but neither would the potential sacrifice. Incumbents of CES positions who do not try to enter the CES should be left alone. Those who try and fail should face no punishment.

I would recommend some degree of specialization within the Career Executive category, as suggested in the Civil Service Commission's interim plan, with several CES registers rather than one but with continually broadening classification standards. Moreover, every effort should be made to establish a CES Reserve and to tie in the CES program with any other executive reserve programs in the federal government. It seems feasible, also, to develop a selection-out procedure for those attaining CES status.

Finally, should Congtess provide special pay and perquisites, as recommended by the Hoover Commission, presidential appointment and more directive assignment and rotation policies are in order, but not before then.

There is much in E.O. 10758 that is worthwhile. Let us keep the Career Executive Service idea and the Career Executive Board. But to turn the proposal in the proper direction, let us balance the hazards for civil servants against the rewards, simplify personnel procedure and structure, put partisanship in its place, and actively seek the cooperation of Congress.

## Footnotes

1. Neil MacNeil and Harold W. Metz, *The Hoover Report: 1953-55* (The Macmillan Co., 1956), p. 29.
2. Philip Young, "A Forward Look in Personnel Administration," an address before the 1956 annual conference of the Society for Personnel Administration, Washington, May 16, 1956.
3. Leonard D. White, "The Senior Civil Service," 15 *Public Administration Review* 237 (Autumn, 1955); Leonard D. White, "The Case for the Senior Civil Service," 19 *Personnel Administration* 4 (January-February, 1956); Herman M. Somers, "Some Reservations about the Senior Civil Service," 19 *Personnel Administration* 10 (January-February, 1956); and Everett Reimer, "The Case Against the Senior Civil Service," 19 *Personnel Administration* 31 (March-April, 1956).
4. See the Society's publication, *Toward Better Career Leadership: Summary Proceedings, Third Annual Conference on Executive Development* (The Society, 1955).
5. Portions of this article stem from the writer's "Dialectics of the Senior Civil Service," a panel discussion paper presented at this meeting of the ASPA; and, with the kind permission of the publishers, from my *History of the United States Civil Service* (Row, Peterson and Co., 1958).
6. Other members were Frederick J. Lawton, Carter L. Burgess, Lt. Gen. Willard S. Paul, USA (ret.), and Robert Ramspeck.
7. The Brookings Institution, 1957.
8. From the *Report of the Career Executive Committee*, December 1957, p. 1.
9. Meyer Kestnbaum, "Career Administrators in Government Service," 74 *Good Government* 30 (May-June 1957).
10. U.S. Commission on Organization of the Executive Branch of the Government (hereafter termed the "Second Hoover Commission"), *Personnel and Civil Service: A Report to the Congress* (U.S. Government Printing Office, 1955), pp. 37-44; and *Task Force Report on Personnel and Civil Service* (U.S. Government Printing Office, 1955), pp. 49-59. (The Commission's report on *Research*

*and Development in the Government* and its subcommittee report on *Special Personnel Problems in the Department of Defense* briefly endorse, but do not comment on the SCS proposal.)

11. The Hoover Commission estimated that there were in 1955 about 3,000 top management career positions. There were then about 5,000 GS-15 through 19 positions; now there are over 6,000.
12. The summary is distilled from published discussions of the SCS, recent testimony before Congress on the CES order, and points emphasized during conversations with a number of federal personnel men and career civil servants over the past few years. I wish to recognize the assistance of Thomas H. Patten, Jr., in developing this section of the discussion.
13. *Op. cit.,* pp. 76-82.
14. This also is the basis of a main criticism by Hoover Commissioner Chet Holifield, a congressman, in his dissent to the Commission's report on personnel and civil service, *op. cit.,* pp. 94-95.
15. *Op. cit.,* p. 33.
16. *Op. cit.,* p. 11.
17. U.S. Department of State, Secretary of State's Public Committee on Personnel (the Wriston Committee), *Toward a Stronger Foreign Service* (U.S. Government Printing Office, 1954). See especially chs. 3 through 7.
18. Second Hoover Commission, subcommittee report on *Special Personnel Problems in the Department of Defense, op. cit.,* especially ch. 8.
19. *Op. cit.,* pp. 16-17.
20. W. Lloyd Warner and James C. Abegglen, *Big Business Leaders in America* (Harper and Bros., 1955), chs. 9, 10, and 11; and Whyte (Simon and Schuster, 1956), ch. 21.
21. In 1947, the American Institute of Public Opinion asked this question in both the United States and England: "Assuming that the pay is the same, would you prefer to work for the United States (the word 'British' was substituted for this in Great Britain) government or for a private firm?" The final tabulation was as follows:

|  | *Government* | *Private firm* | *No opinion* |
|---|---|---|---|
| United States | 41% | 40% | 19% |
| Great Britain | 37% | 45% | 18% |

From "The Quarter's Polls," 11 *Public Opinion Quarterly* 651 (Winter, 1947-48).

DOROTHEE STRAUSS PEALY

# The Need for Elected Leadership

THIS ARTICLE was own of three in a symposium edited by Charles R. Adrian of the University of Michigan. In the first article, Professor Adrian reported on a study of decision making in three council-manager cities. Conclusions were that council members played relatively modest roles in policy innovation and leadership and that the city managers, other administrators, and interest group leaders played stronger roles. In the article below, Dorothee Strauss Pealy, then a postdoctoral fellow at Michigan, warned against intrusion of city managers into policy realms appropriate to elected officials. She suggested that capacities for stronger elected leadership be fostered, mainly through changed political mechanisms. A different view of the manager as a politician was taken in the third symposium article, included as the next piece in this collection.

THE PASSAGE of fifty years has in no way altered early claims of the fundamental soundness of council-manager government, and the plan has great achievements to its credit. With increaseing frequency, however, many have become aware of a restiveness about this form of government. In Michigan, this is manifested in the types of questions asked by citizens, charter commissions, and members of civic organizations where the plan is being considered. In addition, there is emerging an aggressive verbal exchange among local officials, other than city managers, as to their own role in municipal affairs. For example, on May 6, 1958, the newly elected mayor of Grand Rapids, Michigan stated:

> While, as I said before, I do not challenge the merits of commission-manager form of government, there has been a tendency in the past for managers to encroach on the prerogatives of the Commission. The commission-manager or council-manager form of government is essentially a paradox and contradiction. The elective body, chosen by the people to express their will, under this form of government, delegates part of this authority to a single individual who is not responsible to the electorate....

It is human nature to aggrandize power and authority, and the manager, if the commissioners are slovenly, negligent or indifferent in their attitudes, has a tendency to usurp powers that belong to the grass-roots commissioners, even to the extent of advising on policy which is strictly within the province of the elected officials. This should not be tolerated.[1]

These sentiments are not unique. Far from a strong current yet, the restiveness nevertheless heralds the growth of what I see as a fundamental problem: weak policy-making and leadership by the elected officials in council-manager cities and the complementary entry of the manager into policy areas that should be reserved for those elected. Managers, in fact, have found it necessary to espouse their obligation to become "community" leaders.[2] To a great extent the reasons lie in the original goal of the council-manager plan—efficient, economical municipal management *with as little resort to "politics" as possible.* The manager plan suffers from an "efficient management first, politics second" aura.

Here and there in the professional manager literature others have sounded this warning. Kathryn Stone told the International City Managers' Association in 1957:

> ...I think city manager government has always suffered from overselling the idea that the council could act like a corporation board of directors—that councilmen really did not have much to do.
>
> This de-emphasis of the council's role has produced situations which do not redound to the benefit of council-manager government. While it stems from the people and the councilmen themselves, you managers are often involved in it too and sometimes augment it, perhaps without intending to do so.[3]

Although the pattern for the operation of the manager plan was firmly established before the expert in public administration became an accepted idea in governmental circles generally, the manager movement benefited from this later emphasis on expertise, reinforcing the already apolitical bias of the council-manager plan. Advocates of council-manager government envisioned the operation of this form as providing a separation of policy and administration, and the plan reached maturity in an era when this separation was accepted as more valid than is the case today. While the basis of the council-manager plan appeared to be sound and continued growth attested to its success, no change in approach followed this recognition that the simple separation of administration and politics, fundamental to council-manager theory, was not really simple at all. One result has been drift without theoretical conception. Managers have recognized the practical difficulties of operating in a leadership void—born of the fragmented leadership inherent in the political institutions of most manager cities—and have assumed leadership themselves without sufficiently thoughtful questioning of its appropriateness. But to say that a hard-and-fast separation of policy and administration is not possible or desirable is not to say that there is no difference in the role of administrators and elected officials. Perhaps, on the contrary, the uncertainty of the dividing line calls for more active attention to the question. But city managers seem to have become less concerned about identifying and sticking to their policy role.

Indeed, many managers have conceded that they have limited the council's scope of decision-making when they felt prompt action, not expected from the council, was required. A manager's intrusion in policy matters because "the job has to be done, I can't wait for the council to get around to it" is not sound theory or practice. But it is evident in conversations of managers that they too often have slipped into the attitude that the most important goal is to get the managerial job done. To this end, managers frequently feel that the best council is one that asks the least number of questions and leaves the manager alone.

Some citizens, particularly spokesmen for labor, are concerned about this. So long as councils and mayors in council-manager cities fail, or appear to fail, to lead in initiating, formulating, and deciding on policy, citizens will feel that policy has been largely determined by experts in management and acquiesced to by overawed, often badly informed, councilmen.[4]

## Possible Solutions

The weakness I sense in the manager plan—the growing intrusion of managers into the political realm and their rationalization of this as necessary—stems to a great extent, I think, from inadequate leadership outside the manager's office. This weakness in political leadership, in turn, stems both from the attitudes of some managers and from some of the political machinery found in most manager cities: nonpartisan elections, elections-at-large, and the absence of a meaningful office of mayor.[5]

With their weakness in policy initiation, councils often must accept one of a limited number of policy alternatives or adopt no policy at all. The alternatives placed before the council by the manager are those that appear to him most desirable and feasible from his particular vantage point. While these may represent the best managerial judgment, they cannot always be assumed to be the only alternatives. While managerial considerations are important, political considerations cannot be ignored. Questions of timing; social, political, and economic priority; local custom; and even prejudice can and should at times hold precedence over managerial rationale. These are considerations only elected officials can reflect. City managers by training, experience, and professional orientation cannot let their judgments be swayed by such considerations. If they do, they are building necessarily into their recommendations value judgments of a nonmanagerial nature of whose inclusion the council may be unaware.

It is not only for this reason that managers should become more sensitive about their intrusion into policy matters. Where imaginative and colorful leadership of public opinion is required, the job should be left to elected officials. Otherwise, the manager's "above issues" managerial competence is impaired. Senator Joseph S.

Clark, former Mayor of Philadephia, stated the case for elected policy leadership forcefully when he wrote:

> No appointed official—city manager, managing director, or chief administrator—can possibly get to keep the prestige of an elected mayor. Top leadership in American politics is never hired; it is always elected. . . .
> For the essence of leadership is to lead, not to follow. . . . Deciding how far ahead you should be at any one moment is a matter of intuition, not something you can settle according to the formal rules of administration. . . . every successful political executive knows that what *is* possible depends largely on the quality of his own leadership.[6]

The time has come when managers should concern themselves less with their managerial effectiveness and their need to get the job done and more with the values inherent in effective representative government. To this task, they can bring their intimate experience of the subject matter of policy, their concern about good government, and their knowledge of administrative management. The manager's attitude as well as the governmental structure are involved; both should concern him.

Although the council-manager plan makes much of the primacy of the council in municipal affairs, it leaves the council in a poor structural and psychological position to exercise this primacy. Purified by nonpartisan elections, hampered by the absence of a meaningful leader such as a mayor, and confronted by the expert manager and its own lack of expertise, the council usually is in no position to be the primary organ of government.

Whether policy leadership should come from the council or the mayor in council-manager government is arguable, but we should work for structural changes and civic climates conducive to producing leadership by elected officials responsible directly to the people. I suggest four changes that might help:

1. *That councils be better staffed to ask managers the right questions.* Is it too much, in the light of perplexing city problems, to hope that councils might be educated and staffed on matters of policy in the same way that some of our state legislatures are? Can university public administration centers, bureaus of municipal research, or taxpayers associations provide assistance?

2. *That the office of mayor be reconstituted so that its holder is in a better position to exercise more leadership.*

3. *That the manager be taken out of the public limelight;* this, I think, can be done without sacrificing his administrative effectiveness.

4. *That partisan elections (preferably local parties) operate in municipalities* to encourage formulation of a coherent municipal policy where now only the manager's program exists.

## Footnotes

1. *Grand Rapids Herald,* May 6, 1958, p. 22.

2. See A. C. Harrell, "The City Manager as a Community Leader," 30 *Public Management* 290-294 (September, 1948).
3. Kathryn H. Stone, "A Citizen Views the City Manager," 40 *Public Management* 5 (January, 1958); see also Arthur W. Bromage, "Role of the Councilman in a Council-Manager City," *ibid.*, p. 7-10.
4. This point was stated forcefully by Carl R. Westman, executive director of the Metropolitan Research Bureau of Detroit, a UAW-CIO affiliated organization, in his comments about the council-manager plan on a panel at the Annual Meeting of the Midwest Conference of Political Scientists in Ann Arbor, Michigan, April, 1958.
5. Replies to questionnaires sent to all Michigan managers in 1957 by the Institute of Public Administration of the University of Michigan showed that the state's manager cities have retained a striking devotion to these features. Moreover, managers, by and large, seem completely satisfied with the way the plan operates in their communities. In addition, most managers indicated that they have been able to keep councils and mayors out of the managerial arena.
6. Joseph S. Clark, "Notes on Political Leadership," 216 *Harper's Magazine* 29 (June, 1958).

KARL A. BOSWORTH

# The Manager *Is* a Politician

THIS ARTICLE by Karl Bosworth of the University of Connecticut was the third in the symposium edited by Charles Adrian. Based on analysis of reports and publications of the International City Management Association, he described managers as "officers of general administrative direction *and* political leadership." Implications for democracy of political involvements of professional managers were analyzed, revealing the long background of conscious experience in ICMA with these fundamental issues.

The contrast of perceptions of roles of city managers in this article with those of the preceding ones (except Dimock's on training), which focused on federal executives, is striking. The article shows the importance of the ICMA in development of professional standards and ethics for such open managerial leadership at the nexus of politics and administration.

UPPER governmental bureaucrats everywhere live under the imperative of thinking of the continued justification of the activities of their bureaucracies. What are the possible ways of modifying programs and methods? How appealing to whom are the alternatives? What are the dangers to be avoided? Are the achievements impressive? Is there a firm and possibly growing body of public awareness, satisfaction, and support? These and similar considerations haunt the thoughts of the prudent governmental officer. What he does with these thoughts may depend upon the form of government and political system within which the officer works.

Council-manager government, by placing the manager directly in public view, accentuates public interest in how this kind of bureaucrat operates as a political leader. Not only is he inevitably in public view, but the range of his operations is broad, and the fate of his community may be determined in part by the public goals his thoughts lead him to set for his government. Recent awareness of the broad roles in policy leadership admitted by some city managers has raised the question as to whether council-manager government is developing now as an acceptable political system. In other words, given this bent, is it still a popular government or is there a danger that an undemocratic political system is being contrived?

It is the view here that the relatively recent willingness of city managers to admit generally that they are community leaders does not reflect a marked change in their role. City managers, abetted particularly by the International City Managers' Association, have been concerned about the image of themselves presented to the public. The role of the manager has been, after all, in the process of being structured; and the fortunes of the managers and the Association depended upon public acceptance of a described role.

The description of the role as it affects policy leadership has varied from time to time and place to place. Looking at three "styles" of city managers as these roles have been described will, I think, point up the relatively minor nature of the recent changes. One should not think of these "styles" as a historical series. Although some case might be made for a historical trend, the emphasis here is on the presence of policy initiating elements in all the styles of manager that have been described.[1]

## The Administrator Manager

One stylized view of the city manager has so sought to emphasize his role in internal administration as to leave no room for policy initiative. In this view, he just carries out administrative duties such as hiring, setting up the tasks, reviewing the work, and looking for ways of getting more production from the same input or the same production from less input. Of course he also makes up the budget, and therein, if nowhere else, he is in politics.

A manager could, and a few have tried to, provide a council with budget estimates in which there was no firm proposal but rather a pricing of amounts of programs with supplementary programs priced in a fashion so that the council could buy as much or as little as it chooses. But the firm, balanced budget is the rule, and in such a proposal the manager says to the tax-saver that the city "needs" stated amounts for various programs and to the spender that the city "can get by" on the stated totals. The saver must find some program from which he can make deductions, if he would tinker with the proposal, while the spender has either to do the same or to propose the raising of taxes. Even if a manager has had budgetary guidance from the council, he cannot ordinarily escape some public responsibility for his proposed budget: "He didn't include anything new for us," or "They got nearly everything they wanted." Whether such statements emanate from employees or from others interested in programs, they are the essence of politics.

Let us not depreciate the manager's role as an internal administrator, for that is one of the plan's principal justifications. However, even in this role the administrator-manager is likely to set goals whose achievement may impress people with the desirability of the plan and the ability of the manager; good politics, in other words. Short run goals may include the rewriting of some of the city's contracts for services or insurance with a view toward savings or improved service or coverage. These can be matters of policy as well as administration, and if one of the changes proves to be controversial, this is politics. A longer run goal may be the transformation of a mediocre department into a technically proficient one—a change, if accomplished, resulting in changes in the quality of the services and almost unavoidably in the quantity and kinds of service. The effective city policy has changed whether the change has been noticed or not.

It is difficult not to imagine our administrator hearing of state legislation which compels or allows the city council to make some new decision and transmitting this information to the council, along with administrative advice and the news about other cities initiating a service locally unknown; but these items may, if desired, be saved for the next "style" of city manager.

### The Policy Researcher and Manager

The manager may have learned that all policy issues have their administrative aspects, and that he, as administrative expert, should advise the council on the ramifications of their proposals, including the budgetary consequences. It is likely, further, that in comparison with council members, the manager is highly informed about municipal affairs and about sources of municipal information and how to mine these sources. The council will insist that the manager enlighten their deliberations.

In this role, the manager who is also a policy researcher will contrive to know about what is coming up in a council meeting from sources other than his desk so that he can be somewhat prepared with relevant information. He will further seek to school the council to refer to him for study and report nearly all issues which anyone wants seriously to consider. Councilmen, impressed with the manager's expertise and concerned with their own responsibilities, fall readily into the pattern of asking his assistance.

It should be noted that these policy proposals may come from anywhere: councilmen, other individuals and organizations in the community, or the manager. It has long been accepted that managers should bring overt policy ideas to the council. This was implicit in the manager's presumed expertise in municipal affairs. He had had more opportunity than the council to learn about alternative and supplementary municipal services or regulations, and he could be expected to give attention to the channels of current municipal information.

The standard role of managers, in fact, goes well beyond the passive or reactive patterns suggested above. The manager has been expected, like any good mayor, to study the problems, programs, and facilities of *his* city and to make proposals to the council on these matters. Any perusal of the several editions of *The Technique of Municipal Administration,* including chapters devoted to administrative research, planning, and particularly programming, shows that the International City Managers' Association has been hoping for a strong measure of city-statesmanship in its managers. The current word is that it is one of the responsibilities of the manager to see that issues of the maintenance, discontinuance, and initiation of program elements be systematically reviewed by the legislative body.[2] It is, of course, official dogma that the manager be in a position to participate in long-term planning as well as the planning of programs for current operations.

The researcher-manager acknowledges all the while that he is the council's man. He works for the council. He studies the proposals they refer to him and reports to the council. He initiates policy studies for presentation to the council. He advises the council; warns it and even argues with its members. Others may read or listen, but the role is structured in relation to the representative body. He is aware of the community, but he works for the council. They hired him; he works for them; they are responsible for the decisions.

Although our manager is the council's man, he gives attention to public relations. He seeks to have the city avoid offending the public unnecessarily. He wants all elements of the administration to present an appearance of courtesy, consideration, and effective operation. He seeks through news channels and reports to get city accomplishments told to the public. Many managers also seek ways to get some communication from the public. Systems for handling complaints aid the manager in gauging public expectations as well as in reviewing operations. And managers everywhere explain to publics the council-manager form of government, an inevitably self-referring form of communication.

It may be important to note two models of this researcher-manager style, differentiated by their policy presentations. One seeks to emphasize factual materials, stating alternative policies and predicting the consequences of following each. He seeks to avoid making recommendations. The other model, perhaps at the council's insistence, or perhaps by personal inclination, presents his policy proposals as recommendations, with reasoned factual support but a minimum of "confusing alternatives." This could be an important enough difference to merit thinking of the recommender as a separate style of manager. However, the manager with facts and alternatives does not make recommendations—as in his budget. And he will surely weigh the values of his council and community in considering alternatives to present to the council. Interest in economy of time and of effort in explanation will lead even the cautious manager to prejudge a great many policy issues for council.

## The Community Leader and Manager

Throughout the history of the movement, some city managers have ventured into overt community leadership in the settlement of public problems. Through the same period, some students and proponents of the plan have feared that the role of active policy leadership would bring discredit to the form of government. Although the argument has never terminated, the common doctrine has described the manager in clear and continuous subordination to council, expressing his activist political inclinations upon and through council. A minor variation would include the mayor as an alternate in the immediate role.

In the last ten years, however, there have been numbers of instances in which managers have admitted or proclaimed the broader role for themselves, and there is now a common doctrine of valid, if limited, manager initiative in policy formation. Different ones would draw the limitations variously, so the picture of this manager is less precise.

Even the latest edition of *The Technique of Municipal Administration* states that "The city manager is free to act as a community leader in the great majority of municipal policies which do not involve political controversies."[3] The 1958 edition also gives what may be the key to the newly described role:

"A manager can often serve effectively as a community leader without heading a committee or taking direct leadership in civic programs. By searching out and discovering the many real leaders existing in the community, interesting them in new improvements for the community, and keeping them supplied with new ideas and encouraging them to work together, he can achieve far more than by direct leadership of his own."[4]

Managers are thus expected to study the informal power structures of their communities and to use the persons in these channels of influence in so far as they will cooperate to achieve the managers' goals. This may be simply a more candid expression of what experienced managers have commonly done or it may emerge from a more sophisticated perception of the distribution of influence. In any case, relevant power may rest elsewhere than in the council and the managers are seeking to use it.

What are other characteristics of this style of manager? He accepts without question the role of city emissary to state and federal government organs, including legislative committees, to state and national professional and civic associations, and to other municipal governments. To some he will express the city's point of view and with others he may negotiate for his city.

He will pay particular attention to all organized groups in his community, partially as a means of making the acquaintance of the natural leaders of these groups. "It is the manager's job to provide facts, offer counsel, encourage and tactfully to guide community groups in the planning of worthwhile improvements."[5] The telephone numbers of the executive directors of associations presuming to speak for the interests of commerce, health, welfare, education, industry, religion, labor, good government, and real estate, among others, ought to be readily at hand. These executives may include most of his cohorts outside his administrative team, for they and the manager may have adjacent goals as well as similar methods of operation.

He may seek to participate in the meetings of boards and commissions of his own government and, whenever possible, the meetings of boards of special districts covering his city. "Personal contacts by the manager with various county officials open the door for unannounced leadership."[6]

When he has acquired acceptance in the community power structure, his opportunities for influence will broaden and he is likely to be consulted by groups making plans for any segment of the community. "In this concept a manager can and should deal with political parties on much the same basis as other interest groups. By avoiding any sign of preference or of dealing in personalities, a constructive influence can be had."[7]

What are the limits to this role? In one sense, the question is unanswerable, for managerial leadership "is a function of the instant, the setting, and the personalities."[8] In another sense, the community-leading manager is limited by his sense of appropriate behavior for his role as servant of the public. In yet another sense, although conscious of his power, the manager must remember that this power is a result of the tolerance for him of the present city council and any council membership which may soon be elected. Any Tuesday night could be the last, particularly the meeting following election of a new council. No one suggests that managers should depart from their traditional watchful obliviousness to these elections, although a few will admit that they seek to develop possible candidates for the council among board and commission membership.

## Are There Serious Risks?

The city managers in any of these styles are not simply master mechanics of bureaucratic routine. Even our administrator-manager had better be able to sense the public pulse at budget time. And he may have more difficulty predicting public satisfaction with his planned administrative achievements than does the community leader who feels free to try his ideas on his local acquaintances. City managers, whichever role they wish to follow, must seek to be among the best politicians in town, for their work deals with the satisfaction of the wants of people who have the privilege of discussing and voting about this work.

There are risks to popular government in council-manager cities. A manager could convince his council and significant elements in the community that only by his nonpartisan, objective mind can the city problems of first, second, and third importance be identified and only through his skilled, impartial analysis can the correct solutions be found. The special risk here is that the values the manager uses in making these decisions will reflect those of some limited group within the city rather than values representative of his city.

There are risks that a city's effective policies may be determined increasingly through processes of negotiation between the city and other governments, and with banks, utilities, development and other corporations, professional and business groups, and unions. If the manager is an uninstructed ambassador in these negotiations, his negotiating premises partially may foreclose later consideration by his governing body of alternative policies to those on which negotiation has been concluded.

These are real risks, but the risks of concentrated political leadership are not limited to council-manager cities. We are thus thrown back to the question of whether the values of managers will represent those of their communities and whether the local political and representative system will enforce some correspondence between popular wishes and governmental performance.

With regard to the political systems in council-manager cities, it may well be time to give thought to both informal and formal arrangements. If only stooges for some manager-supporting power combine are elected to the council, or if the system has made the ardent practice of political leadership unprofitable for all save the manager, or if the political system is incapable of expressing either discontent or contentment, or if a competing point of view to the government position cannot gain intelligent expression, it is time to be inventive. Perhaps there is need for a tax benefits association, with research staff, publicists, and publications, as well as a taxpayers' association. Perhaps it needs to be recognized that local parties are not going to develop and that charter groups are commonly going to confuse the public about the manager plan by asking the voter for support of the plan or the manager rather than support of a program of current policies.[9] Perhaps thought needs to be given to findings suggesting that the nonpartisan election does not readily permit the registration of protest and perhaps permits no clear indication of assent.[10] Perhaps it can be remembered that our national political parties are federations of state and local parties, that political parties have demonstrated a capacity to express ideals with some contrast, and that not only "nice people" but most of the talented ones who are aspirants for elective office are now accustomed to working in parties. Although we have had enough of faith in gimmicks, perhaps it is time to think of some system which will assure the representation of both parties on the council—where this is feasible—rather than no parties. If we want a political system which will diffuse the public attention now placed on the manager as political leader, perhaps we should ask the parties for assistance in providing public discussion from some variety of points of view. In any case, care needs to be given to the selection of a governing body. It may decide to govern; or in the absence of a manager it may have to govern for a time.

Governments depend greatly upon the values held by their important bureaucrats, and democratic governments depend on the capcity of these bureaucrats to sense the values of the communities the governments serve. There appears to be a basis for some belief that government employment, including the manager profession, attracts individuals whose values seem realizable in service to the public, in contrast to more dramatic or more pecuniarily promising roles. Helping to achieve public goals, to "do some good," is appealing. A stronger than usual ethical sense may be present.[11] The training of these people is likely to be highly inculcating and reinforcing of values of personal integrity, fair play, just dealing, and appreciation for the rights and views of others.

The leadership of the International City Managers' Association has used its literature and conferences to seek to maintain in managers values consistent with their roles in democratic government. The injunctions to walk uprightly before men, compassionately before the weak, and humbly before the council stand out in the tracts.[12] The personal moral tragedies among managers must be relatively few, judging from the small publicity of such events.

The problems with regard to the values of managers are in part concerned with their own values and in part concerned with those of the community. A risk that as the manager becmes an upper-income citizen, that he may learn to think like those with whom he lunches, or to think that no good idea could come from a source that has seemed not to appreciate him. These risks are probably no greater, however, in the administrative leader manager than in the other styles, for the leader in his varied community contacts must sometimes listen. The manager's staff and department heads may also be correctives for his preferences.

City manager dogma used to include the notion that the plan of government was appropriate only for those cities that wanted this form of government—cities whose people were willing to sacrifice some of the fun of political controversy and patronage for the benefits of a skilled management. Without exploring in detail the boundaries set by such criteria, it may be possible to suggest that cities in which there are very strong and deep disagreements over values test, perhaps beyond reasonable expectation, the possibility of any career general executive representing in his decisions the preferences of the community. Similarly, in communities where the relevant local government values shift, as a result of population mobility or new problems, or where the electoral system results in frequent changes in the value components of the community being represented, the capacity of any manager to sense and move with the changing dominant values of his community may be tested beyond his or the council's endurance. Can a particular manager shift back and forth in his preference system as the majority on the council shifts from labor to conservative inclinations? Probably in situations such as these one should not expect the manager to stand exposed and alone.

These calculations undoubtedly leave most of the suburbs, many independent cities, and some central cities appropriate grounds for the manager plan. And where managers are used, let us think of them as officers of general administrative direction *and* political leadership, for that is what they are.

### Footnotes

1. For a historical view noting relevant changes in the managers' "Code of Ethics," see Hugo Wall, "Changing Concepts of Managerial Leadership," 36 *Public Management* 50-53 (March, 1954). Compare Douglas G. Weiford, "Changing Role of the City Manager," 36 *Public Management* 170-72 (August, 1954). For a view of kinds of city managers in terms of occupational sociology see George K. Floro, "Types of City Managers," 36 *Public Management* 221-25 (October, 1954). Any attempt to think about the roles of managers must depend heavily upon the work of Harold A. Stone, Don K. Price, and Kathryn H. Stone (and others) done in the late 'thirties and, especially, their book, *City Manager Government in the United States* (Public Administration Service, 1940). They seemed to weigh more heavily than one would today the formal responsibility of the council, and they seemed to have had a clearer distinction between policy and administration than can be mustered today, but one cannot much project their insights.

2. Institute for Training in Municipal Administration, (4th ed., International City Managers' Association, 1958), p. 109.
3. *Ibid.*, p. 31. In a book of biblical character coming from many hands one should not expect all statements to agree with that quoted.
4. *Ibid.*, p. 32.
5. "Leadership Functions of the Manager," 37 *Public Management* 53 (March, 1955). This is a report prepared by a group of managers for discussion at the 40th Annual Conference of ICMA held December 5-8, 1954.
6. *Ibid.*, p. 52
7. *Ibid.*, p. 54.
8. *Ibid.*, p. 53.
9. The Stone, Price, Stone findings on this point sound quite contemporary. *Op. cit.*, chap. 12.
10. Charles R. Adrian, "Some General Characteristics of Non-partisan Elections," 46 *American Political Science Review* 766-76 (September, 1952).
11. A professor may be indulged in some judgments about his students. Consideration is being given to methods for studying the values of administrators of various sorts.
12. "Relations of the Manager with the Public," 37 *Public Management* 77-83 (April, 1955), esp., p. 79.

EARL H. DeLONG

# Who Are the Career Executives?

SHORT EXCERPTS from a longer article by Earl DeLong are included here because they capture much of the intensity of career federal executive opposition to senior executive service proposals in the 1950s. A more detailed and systematic critique of basic considerations relevant to creation of a federal executive service, by Paul P. Van Riper, appears elsewhere in this volume.

DeLong had entered federal service at the beginning of World War II after teaching political science at Northwestern University for eight years. He worked on recruitment and placement of executives for the Civil Service Commission during the war and was then employed in the Office of the Secretary of Defense and the Veterans Administration before going to the Central Intelligence Agency for nine years. At the CIA he worked on development of a career service.

Program expertise was stressed by DeLong as essential to federal executive service. He argued that most top career civil servants must not be thought of as members of a corps of "interchangeable management technicians." During the 20 years after this article was published the perspectives presented remained strong among career federal employees, particularly those associated with defense activities. This argument for specialists was accommodated in large part in the Civil Service Reform Act of 1978, although the SES provisions of Title IV of that Act provided also for some movement toward meeting needs for generalists.

WHEN THE current session of Congress is hesitating over the appropriation of even $10,000 for the Career Executive Program, it is one of the signs that a worthy purpose is still in substantial trouble. In this observer's view, some of the trouble, at least, has come from failure to start from the fundamental questions: Which ones are the senior career executive positions in the federal government, and what do the people in them do?

The objectives of action cannot be just the abstract purpose of finding abler people to put somewhere in government, and the process of finding them cannot be just a parochial personnel exercise which is insulated from the more general problems of management. If a senior career executive program is to be worth special attention, the personnel policies and procedures which constitute it have to be designed by working backward from the basic managerial needs and their climate.

We can assume that the aim of such a program is the improvement of offiicals in the level between the top political executive layer and the permanent working bureaucracy. Whether all or just some of such officials should be included is a part of the problem. The solution to the problem seems to pivot on these questions: Does the function of the officials at this in-between level most resemble that of their political superiors or that of their bureaucratic subordinates? Or is that function such a mixture of characteristics from both above and below as to be distinguishable from both in the manner of its performance, in the climate required for its performance, and in the specifications for the kind of person to perform it?

In most of the federal government, the bulk of the personnel, including senior personnel, can be left in one place indefinitely and will increase in value with longer time. The organizational units of the federal government, throughout which the members of an executive corps would be deployed, are not similar organizations with constant repetition from one to another of the same position structures and functions. Except for a small number of positions, such as chiefs of administration, the senior bureaucrats of the federal government are program specialists, and their value depends heavily on their specialization. The men who marry general bureaucratic expertise with functional specialization are the greatest strength of the career executive level. They should be the major membership of the career executive service because it is most important that they meet the general quality standards we have discussed. Any career service system which leaves out these men and which limits itself to special recognition for a small number who can repeat their functions from agency to agency is missing the major issue and would be unjustly discriminatory against an indispensable body of career officers.

To repeat: the federal government's personnel requirement at the senior bureaucratic level is double: (1) high competence in the performance of the characteristic general function of the senior career executive; and also (2) thorough competence in the program activity in which the general function is to be performed.

These comments do not mean that we should go overboard on the matter of specialization. We have tended to draw specialty lines too tightly, and we have given insufficient credit to the ability of the good general executive to move to a new subject and learn it rapidly enough to do a good job. Nevertheless, while we should be more flexible in these respects than we have been, we cannot ignore the importance of subject matter competence. Good executive performance still requires its possession or its rapid acquisition.

The man who has the versatility should be discovered, kept in mind, and made available to other locations where he may be needed more than where he is. If it is to the government's advantage to move him around with inconvenience to him, we can properly give him extra recognition for the inconvenience, but the difference between his recognition and his stationary colleague's should not be so great as the difference between membership and nonmembership in the Career Executive Service. It is the use of the versatility for the advantage of the government that deserves extra pay, not just its possession. There will be much less need and use of it than many think. A system which fully combs the prospects within and without the federal government will find enough versatility to meet the need.

The U.S. government does not have a clear need for a cadre of generalist administrators waiting in a pool to be assigned by a central authority to agency heads—who have few, if any, generalist jobs to use them in. If there is need for a group of senior officers available for emergency need, the need can be met by the device of the reserve list of men who can be borrowed from where they are.

The U.S. government does not have need for a system which gives special rewards and recognition to just a part of its senior career executives, just because they happened to choose administrative functions instead of line specialties and, therefore, can be used in more places. Such a system would be a discriminatory kick in the teeth to the men who carry the bulk of the load of making the federal government work.

The U.S. government does imperatively need:

1. High standards of general and special executive capability for the overwhelming majority of its senior career positions and much improved methods for finding the men or women who meet the standards.

2. A central register of these people and of positions where their services are most needed, with a staff which works aggressively and continuously to match places with people.

3. A method of recognition for its senior civilian career personnel which distinguishes them from the general body of civil servants in much the way the military officer's first star makes him a man apart from the rest of the military personnel structure.

If these things are just more civil service, they would at least be much better civil service. These are the things which would meet the substantial and critical requirements of federal senior personnel administration, and their contribution would deserve the distinguishing title of "Career Executive Program."

JOHN B. BLANDFORD

# Executive Leaders —
# Career and Political

EXCERPTS from a review of Marver H. Bernstein's book, *The Job of the Federal Executive,* are included here both to focus attention on issues raised by the book and the reviewer and to highlight a series of important publications which started with this volume in 1958.

Bernstein's book grew out of roundtable discussions held in 1957 at The Brookings Institution. The discussions probed political and career executive role differences, the federal environment, and problems of obtaining and developing effective executives for federal service. The reviewer, John Blandford, then U.N. Advisor to the President of Argentina, skillfully summarized and critiqued the book. He suggested discarding the policy-making distinction between political and career executives and allowing career executives to accept non-civil service posts, an approach which was adopted in 1978 as a feature of the Senior Executive Service.

The Brookings Institution produced several later publications of importance in federal executive developments. In January, 1964, two volumes were issued: *The Image of the Federal Service* and a *Source Book of a Study of Occupational Values and the Image of the Federal Service* (Franklin P. Kilpatrick, Milton C. Cummings, Jr., and M. Kent Jennings). In November of 1964, Brookings published David T. Stanley's, *The Higher Civil Service,* and a biographical profile of federal political executives, *Men Who Govern,* was published in 1967 (David T. Stanley, Dean E. Mann, and Jameson W. Doig). A related book in the same time frame, *Men Near The Top,* by John J. Corson and R. Shale Paul, was issued in 1966 by the Committee for Economic Development and published by the Johns Hopkins Press. That volume focused on federal career executives.

ONCE UPON a time a score and more of veterans gathered round an oaken table and reminisced about their many missions for the public weal. Guided by mellow scholarship, molded by faithful scribe, emerged a tale of challenge suggestive of Greek choral drama or Arthurian round-table ballad.

Polex and Carex are to be off to the wars as commanders-in-leadership. Polex, a bit perplexed and hesitant, carries the banner. He will make the strategic plans, the speeches, and the treaties. Carex, confident but watchful of his colleague, mobilizes. He will determine tactics, be responsible for logistics and direct operations.

And off they go. Polex and Carex press their multiple mission of public weal on many fronts. They achieve a measure of success. But they are harassed by their mission-makers and bankers, misunderstood by the peoples whom they seek to help, infiltrated and divided by tensions and plots within their own ranks. To top it all, the reality of field operations plays havoc with the preconceived pattern of their respective responsibilities.

They return—Carex striding and intact, ready for more missions—Polex scarred and supported by Carex, ready for demobilization. Polex departs, but with an inner glow of pride in his adventure. Carex stays on meditating on future missions and speculating as to his next Polex.

He who will read the detailed story of this crusade will be well rewarded.

### The Round Table and the Knights

The Brookings Institution acted with good timing and right priority in turning its institutional spotlight on the area of leadership in the national government. Its Round Table on the Federal Executive produced a rich record of realism. Professor Marver H. Bernstein of Princeton University has skillfully shaped a readable and significant report: *The Job of the Federal Executive.*

The central purpose of the study was to explore and chart the roles, the relationships, and the environments of political executives and the high level career executives in the executive branch of the national government. The principal explorers and guides were seasoned practitioners, both political and career. Their performance was impressive and their product frank and revealing.

Always hovered over the scene a problem as old as political parties and governmental reform and as new as big government and the cold war—the problem of reconciling political and administrative considerations in the upper reaches of government operations. This problem was highlighted in the transition from Truman to Eisenhower in 1953. Later a Hoover Commission task force ventured a solution. It proposed a precise boundary line between policy and administration. It would push back the career territory and purge it of policy. Political executives and career executives should not trespass. This solution has not been accepted.

### The Method of Inquiry

Twenty-four distinguished persons—principally senior federal executives—met bi-weekly, eight times, around a table in The Brookings Institution and shared generously their individual executive experiences. They were chairmanned by Professor Wallace S. Sayre of Columbia University. Bernstein prepared the agenda and summarized each previous discussion. The verbatim transcript served as the basis for this report.

The product speaks well for the process. The round-table arrangement stimulated frank and penetrating observations. Sayre's chairmanship and Bernstein's secretarial and reportorial contribution gave cohesion and balance. The participants agreed that the round table was a productive method of developing and distributing information, probably more productive, they felt, than interviews with executives "by a student or researcher."

Probably as a result of the method of inquiry, there was an inevitable emphasis on problems and difficulties rather than achievements. The round table participants did not attempt to present a full portrait of the executive nor a balance sheet of his successes and failures. Rather there was concentration on *modus operandi* and the immediate environment.

### The Target

Brookings has opened the door to an important field of inquiry in the area of executive leadership. Within this area are multiple missions of surprising variety and range. Moreover many executive "jobs" change in content and performance as personalities and relationships change. Craftsmanship prevails rather than line production. Fluidity and flexibility challenge conformity. It is the province of the individualist rather than the organization man.

Brookings has set a happy precedent in the shift of inquiry from the personnel positions and procedures to personal performance and problems—from the sructure and processes of government to the behaviorism of executive leadership.

### As Executives See Their Jobs

Some quotations from the round-table testimony will outline the story and perhaps whet the appetite for its revelation and realism.

The political executive when he comes to Washington notes that he "gains power in magnitude of operations and loses in having to share with others the power of decision." He is "shocked to discover that almost all important questions of policy impinge on some other agency." He "does not have the same measuring sticks to help him manage his affairs that the business executive has." Often he does not "talk the language of the career employee," does not know the program of the department and of other agencies and it takes him "a long time to find out." Whereas in business he is "told in advance exactly what the aims and purposes are of the organization," in government he has to find out for himself his role and the aims of the department.

The political executive has a broad mission, including "the task of harmonizing the programs of his agency with the political point of view and the aspirations of his party." But at least one career executive testifies that he "has more political sensitivity than the political appointee who directs him. A political appointee does not necessarily have political acuteness." Furthermore, the political executive discovers that he has a "relatively small area where he can really make policy, compared to the roles of Congress on one side and the career executives on the other." He finds it difficult to "grasp the public interest character of problems and issues." There is concern about the conflict of interest between private interest and public responsibility. He may even wonder "whether it is a good thing to associate himself with a government that many of his associates regard as a great spending machine that is eating away the vitals of our liberties."

And yet we know there are offsetting moments of triumph and satisfaction. At least one alumnus looked backward with satisfaction at the period when he "was wielding a small brush," but "painting on a very large canvas."

The career executive has problems too. A large one looms as he confronts a new political executive. One career man admitted that "a sort of conditioned reflex" leads him to begin to cover up. "To put it plainly the staff is scared." He may even offer to resign. But ordinarily the career executive conscientiously approaches the task of orientation of his political associate. Also his job is to explore their prospective and respective roles and "to find out where certain types of decisions are going to be made."

Partly because of this periodic adjustment to transient political executives but basically because of the range of government and the many forms of citizen intervention, the job of the career executive is one of great variety. "It varies from one Secretary to another." And "there is more difference among career jobs than there is between my career job and that of my immediate political boss."

The round-table career executives tended to focus on the subject of political neutrality. One contended that "the career executive must have policy commitments and these commitments must be of the stature to hold men of dedication and capacity." Apparently this type of incentive is ever present because "all of us career executives have testified on the Hill and will continue to do so." In further support a career commentator advises "that overworked and relatively inexperienced non-career executives have tended increasingly to rely upon career administrators to carry part of the load." And still another explains "with all deference to the political executive, who comes and goes, he does not have the same familiarity with program as his career staff."

However, on sober second thought the career executive contends that he gets involved "in political matters not to provide political leadership in resolving political issues but rather to help to clarify the political issues for resolution by political executives." And, he adds, "the able career man can be useful in standing between the political executive and Congress, just as the able political executive can protect his career men from political attack."

Of course the major contribution of the career executive is continuity of governmental effort and of know-how in governmental relationships and processes. So he carries on probably with much feeling of adequacy and achievement until the time of retirement. And yet the round table record includes a few negative footnotes. "Perhaps the one thing that keeps many of our fine people in the service is the lack of confidence in themselves to cut loose from the government and make their way in a competitive environment." Again, "many people in the federal government are just not exposed to opportunities to get out." "They are often in jobs that have no counterparts in private life."

Despite different origins and preparations, once the introductory period has passed the political executive and the career executive ordinarily move along in programs and projects through much the same environment. Whatever the distinction, their setting has the common landmarks of budget bureau relationships (in terms of honesty or "pockets of fat") and civil service regulations (with long-sought loopholes). They stand shoulder to shoulder in the interagency rivalries and may even agree that "frequent explosions inside an administration can be very healthy. They are an essential ingredient of opinion making in a democracy." Furthermore according to the record, "the executive branch alone cannot define who is a career man and who is political." Congress has its own opinion.

Certainly they both have experiences on the congressional front. Sometimes the relationship is awkward, sometimes reversed, sometimes effective through well rehearsed lateral passes. They both are concerned with the detour of petitioners through congressional halls on the way to the agency. They both are wary of congressional intervention, but either may in a weak moment acquiesce in a congressional veto to the damage of President and executive branch.

### Where Do We Go from Here?

But new and specific proposals to strengthen executive leadership are not to be ventured lightly. There are deep-rooted vested interests. There must be time to evaluate the impact. There is a Congress to consult. While awaiting further studies and recommendations perhaps we should seek agreement upon priorities.

## Agree Upon More Realistic Relationships Between Political and Career Executives

I suggest that we discard the yardstick of "policy-making" for distinguishing the roles of political and career executives. There should not be this limitation upon the use of top career executives' experience. It should be possible to use his talents fully either in his civil service post or on a career assignment outside the civil service, even in a non-civil service executive post, without losing his career status. Given good sportsmanship by party politicians and cooperation of political executives, the career executive should be able confidently to carry program conception and program presentation well up to the point of significant public controversy and then yield to the political executive. On the other hand the political executive may well bring fresh stimulus to administrative improvement.

The career executive has know-how of the processes of the public service and sensitivity to the public interest. The political executive normally should come from outside the civil service with special insight on national resources and needs and with fresh zeal and purpose for a new stage of national development. This team must be harnessed—these contributions meshed.

### Create a Positive Role for the Political Executive

The political executive has a mission of great stature, of representation and leadership for evolving national policy and program. This includes a major responsibility for relationships within the executive branch and with the Congress and the public—in other words, for making our system work.

The adequate political executive should enter upon his mission with confidence and enthusiasm, with full orientation and in a positive relationship with the career executive. The top priority task of strengthening executive leadership is here.

There are about 1,100 political executive positions in the federal government. Perhaps a first step is to try to cut down the task of recruitment to a size that is more manageable.

Perhaps the next step is to complete the portraiture of the political executive so we can better know where to look, how to appeal, and what to teach.

Then might follow an attempt to put together an educational project that would be both promotional and preparatory. Basically the curriculum should convey information on the role and environment of the political executive that will appeal to a select representation of individuals, institutions, and corporations as *useful* insight into national government affairs at the top level. Beyond that it is hoped that it would, here and there, stimulate readiness to respond when the call comes. It should be possible to make participation seem not only useful but also a form of public recognition and public service.

The partisan political aspects of the role of political executive seem to be so subordinate and of such low priority that they can be omitted from orientation through this channel.

### Toward a Greater National Purpose

Sputnik and Quiznik are driving complacency and cheapness out of the temple of national life. The demand for more purposefulness, more progress, and more quality will impact heavily on the nucleus of executive leadership in the national government. The political and career executive must sharpen their traditional tools of program projection and management improvement. Then they must reach for something more—greater science orientation, more enlightened individualism in public administration, new stimuli and motivations for continuous growth and development, and a working environment charged with urgency.

*PAR*, Volume 20 (Winter, 1960)

W. LLOYD WARNER, PAUL P. VAN RIPER,
NORMAN H. MARTIN, and ORVIS F. COLLINS

# A New Look At the Career Civil Service Executive

THIS ARTICLE reported research on backgrounds of federal career employees at the GS-14 level and above. It compared them with other categories of federal executive-level employees and with private business executives. This research was characteristic of much of the 1960s surge in interest in U.S. federal government executives. As noted in the article, this research was later published in a book, *The American Federal Executive.*

RECENT American politics has been described as in stalemate, with neither major party able to govern decisively. Under such circumstances the role of the career civil servant assumes greater proportions and responsibility, particularly at the upper levels. Much of the continuity and reservoir of expertise in the American national government depends upon him.

There has been much speculation about higher civil servants in recent years: about what they are like, where they come from, and how they got where they are. For the first time concrete information on the socio-economic backgrounds, education, and career routes of large numbers of these men and women is available.

This is a report on a sample of 7,640 career civil servants in high administrative posts located in both Washington, D.C., and the field. The analysis derives from a much larger study devoted to the backgrounds and characteristics of federal executives in general, civil and military, involving data on nearly 13,000 persons as of 1959.[1]

## Who Was Studied

The sample includes nearly 140 women.[2] Both men and women come from General Schedule (GS) grades 14 (and the equivalent in other pay systems) or higher. Two-fifths of these executives come from the GS-14 level, nearly one-half from GS-15, and the rest from grades 16, 17, and 18 (6.6, 3.0, and 0.7 percent respectively). The group is divided almost 50-50 between Washington and the field, with, of course, the field service disproportionately heavy in GS-14's and 15's and the departmental service in "supergrades."

Some 61 executive departments and agencies are represented in reasonable proportions, excluding, however, all legislative and judicial agencies such as the General Accounting Office and the Library of Congress, as well as the District of Columbia government. Excluded also are all members of the U.S. Foreign Service, Foreign Service Reserve, and Foreign Service Staff; the uniformed personnel of the U.S. Public Health Service, the Coast and Geodetic Survey, and the Coast Guard; plus any persons occupying positions under *Schedules A, B,* and *C.* Of course, all persons occupying political posts and the uniformed military are by definition omitted.[3]

There is no need to go into research methods in detail here. The data were obtained by questionnaires filled in by the executives themselves. Our original mailing list was derived from all personnel at the GS-14 (and equivalent) level or higher as shown in the 1958 edition of the *Official Register of the United States,* which lists "persons occupying administrative and supervisory positions" in the federal government. This list was supplemented by the personnel directors of the agencies for which the *Register* was determined to be incomplete. Almost precisely 70 percent of these persons responded. There is no evidence that non-respondents differed significantly from respondents.

We estimate that our final sample of respondents—those discussed here—includes about 20 percent of the career civil servants at the GS-14 level or equivalent and approximately 50 percent of those from GS-15 up through 18, exclusive of the agencies and services deliberately omitted as noted above. Moreover, while our sample may not be entirely limited to persons in "administrative and supervisory positions" at these levels, due to some uncertainty as to the application of *Register* definitions by some agencies, those described below certainly exclude most persons occupying scientific, technical, or professional positions involving little executive, administrative, or supervisory activity. The final group is almost equally divided between those describing their present position as *line* and those terming it *staff.*

## The Career Executive in Profile

It is hazardous to describe a *typical* executive of any kind. But we can say that, on the average, the career civil service executive was 49.6 years old in early 1959. He entered upon his career in government service via a competitive examination or, less frequently, a temporary appointment at age 27, taking 17.4 years to achieve the position he held when studied by this research. He had been in this position almost exactly five years. He is four years younger than the big business executive.[4]

Like most of us, he is at least second or third generation American. He was probably born in one of the states comprising "The North" during the Civil War. His place of birth was either a small town, rural setting, or a very large city. But he has long since moved away from home, the career civil service executive being characterized—as are all federal executives—by a high rate of geographical mobility, far exceeding that of businessmen.

His father was not in the public service; except in the military there is little or no family tradition of career public service. More likely, his father was in the middle ranges of private enterprise—that is, somewhere between the big businessman and the unskilled worker or farm laborer. There was little financial assistance for the son at the time he went into the public service.

But the son—the present career civil service executive—was able to obtain a first rate education. He probably graduated from one of the large, well-known universities with, most likely, a degree in the applied fields of engineering and administration or in the physical or biological sciences. Along the way he picked up some graduate work, perhaps even a master's or law degree; about one in ten attained the doctorate. Although not quite as highly educated as other categories of federal executives (political, foreign service, and military) in terms of proportions graduating from college, the career executive has still graduated from college in significantly higher proportions than men at the helm of big business.

He can also be described as a man of very considerable organizational experience. The odds are better than even that he has seen service in the armed forces. In at least one out of three cases he has been a member of an employee association or union. In addition, he has probably had some experience in private enterprise before entering the public service.

Even with the career executive, lateral entry into the public service has been more the rule than exception. Compared to big businessmen, who typically spend most of their careers in one or two business firms, all civilian federal executives, including those in the career service, have, on the average, served in four to five separate firms and/or government agencies. Career routes through these organizations and into present positions are complex, but one fact can be emphasized. Much higher proportions of career civil service (and political) executives than businessmen enter the professions early in life and, through them, complete much of their rise to executive status.

Finally, while the career civil service executive must be partisanly neutral, we can say that he is clearly politically interested. Despite his frequent residence in the capital, which has made voting more difficult, he (and all other civilian federal executives) has voted in the four Presidential elections between 1944 and 1956 in significantly greater proportions than the electorate as a whole.

In summary, the above analysis indicates that career civil service executives differ from big business leaders in at least three matters of major importance: (1) education, (2) interorganizational mobility, and (3) career routes. There are, in addition, some differences in (4) socio-economic origin, not stressed thus far. Let us examine each of these more precisely, with some attention to other types of federal executives (political, foreign service, and military) as well as big businessmen by way of comparison.

## Education a Basic Requirement for Career Executives

What do we mean when we conclude that career civil service executives (indeed, all federal executives) are more highly educated than the leaders of business? Primarily, we are commenting on the *level* of educational attainment. We have at best only indirect evidence of the *quality* of that education for either group. Nor do we have any concrete evidence or conclusions as to the precise relevance of a particular type of education for particular positions in either government or business.

Nevertheless, rightly or wrongly, it is clear that formal education is increasingly the key to occupational mobility in American life. Certainly college training is a basic step in the careers of an overwhelming proportion of all federal executives, regardless of occupational and geographical origins. And it is becoming increasingly important that part of that training be at the graduate level.

For the several executive groups the basic information is shown in Table 1. Contrary to most hypotheses, in terms of graduation from college the career federal executive lags behind his other federal cohorts. Even the uniformed military has percentages of educational attainment almost precisely equal to those of the foreign service as shown in Table 1. But career executives do considerably exceed business executives in level of education, even correcting for the general rise in educational levels throughout the country between 1952 and 1959. A *Fortune*

Table 1

Educational Levels of Federal Executives in 1959 as Compared to Business Executives and the Adult Male Population

| Education | Career Civil Service Executives | Foreign Service Executives | Political Executives | Business Executives in 1952 | U.S. Adult Males 30 & Over, in 1957 |
|---|---|---|---|---|---|
| Less than high school | 0%* | 0%* | 0%* | 4% | 46% |
| Some high school | 2% | 0%* | 1% | 9% | 17% |
| High school graduation | 5% | 2% | 2% | 11% | 21% |
| Some college | 15% | 10% | 7% | 19% | 7% |
| College graduation | 78% | 88% | 90% | 57% | 9% |

*Less than one-half of one percent.

survey of nearly 1,700 top businessmen in 1959 showed a rise in college graduates among them, but to only 67 percent.[5] At the postgraduate level there is a slight shift in rank order, with career executives moving ahead of the military in percentage with some graduate work, but still behind the other civilian federal executives. There are no satisfactory data on postgraduate work among business leaders.

Compared to other civilian federal executives, the careerists also differ in undergraduate areas of specialization. A third were trained in engineering, nearly a quarter in the physical and biological sciences, followed by about 16 percent in the applied areas of business administration, education, and public administration, 16 percent in the behavioral sciences, 9 percent in the humanities, and the rest scattered among pre-medicine, pre-law, and military science. At the graduate level the proportion with work in the behavioral sciences increases somewhat, but that in the physical and biological sciences increases even more, with the humanities declining. Law also becomes of some importance at this level. By comparison 62 percent of the foreign service men and 45 percent of the political executives were trained in either the behavioral sciences or the humanities (in about equal proportions in both cases) at the undergraduate level.

All federal executives, including the military, show considerable postgraduate work at the master's level. Almost one-third of the foreign service officers report the master's degree, slightly less than one-fourth of the career civil servants and the military, and about one in five of the political executives. Almost 40 percent, however, of the political executives hold law degrees compared to one quarter that number among career executives and still fewer among the foreign service and the military. Our data support the traditional view that legal training is important for public service, especially at the political levels.

The overwhelming importance of higher education and advanced degrees in the careers of federal executives suggests attention to the insitutions which produced them. There are over 2,000 institutions of higher learning in the United States, but thirty of them produced 40 percent of all the civilian federal executives' undergraduate degrees, and thirty granted three-fourths of all the Ph.D.'s.

These thirty institutions producing the largest number of four year degrees reported by career civil service executives compared to all civilian federal executives are shown in Table 2. Benjamin Franklin, Georgetown, and George Washington are, of course, in the capital district. Otherwise the representation is nationwide. For the most part the thirty comprise well known and top ranking institutions, both public and private. Slightly fewer career civil servants attended private institutions than was true for other civilian executives. Of the fifteen institutions among the top thirty for all three groups of civilian federal executives, eight are state and seven are private. The former are California (Berk.), Illinois, Michigan, Minnesota, Missouri, Ohio State, Washington (Seattle), and Wisconsin; the latter are Cornell, Georgetown, George Washington, Harvard, M.I.T., Pennsylvania, and Stanford.

The top institutions at the master's level closely resemble those shown in

## Table 2

### The Thirty Institutions Producing the Largest Number of Four Year Degrees as Reported by Career Compared to All Civilian Executives

| All Civilian Federal Executives | %* | Career Civil Service Executives | %* |
|---|---|---|---|
| George Washington | 3 | George Washington | 3 |
| City Col. of N.Y. | 6 | City Col. of N.Y. | 6 |
| California (Berk.) | 8 | California (Berk.) | 8 |
| Harvard | 10 | Ohio State | 10 |
| Minnesota | 12 | Minnesota | 12 |
| Illinois | 14 | Illinois | 14 |
| Michigan | 15 | Washington (Seattle) | 16 |
| Wisconsin | 17 | Wisconsin | 17 |
| Ohio State | 19 | Mass. Inst. of Tech. | 19 |
| Washington (Seattle) | 20 | Michigan | 21 |
| Mass. Inst. of Tech. | 22 | New York | 22 |
| Princeton | 23 | Cornell | 24 |
| Yale | 25 | Benjamin Franklin | 25 |
| New York | 26 | Purdue | 26 |
| Cornell | 28 | Missouri | 27 |
| Benjamin Franklin | 29 | Nebraska | 29 |
| Pennsylvania | 30 | Pennsylvania State | 30 |
| Missouri | 31 | Colorado | 31 |
| Purdue | 32 | Pennsylvania | 32 |
| Georgetown | 33 | Iowa State | 33 |
| Nebraska | 34 | Harvard | 34 |
| Chicago | 35 | Kansas State | 35 |
| Stanford | 36 | Maryland | 35 |
| Pennsylvania State | 37 | Tennessee | 36 |
| Colorado | 38 | Cincinnati | 37 |
| Iowa | 39 | Syracuse | 38 |
| Iowa State | 39 | Stanford | 38 |
| Columbia | 40 | Alabama Polytech. | 39 |
| Kansas | 41 | Georgetown | 40 |
| Syracuse | 42 | Oregon State | 41 |

*Percentages of total accumulated through the rankings.

Table 2. But at the doctoral level the picture changes considerably. For federal executives receiving the doctorate, the top ten institutions in rank order are Harvard, Chicago, Wisconsin, Columbia, Johns Hopkins, Cornell, California (Berk.), Minnesota, Yale, and New York. These institutions produce 47 percent of the Ph.D.'s. The next twenty produce another 33 percent.

## Agency Hopping Is Typical

It has sometimes been assumed that federal executives spend too much of their careers in one governmental agency. In fact, however, it is quite clear that federal executives of all types (except the military) have had, in comparison to business leaders, fairly wide organizational experience. Our data have not been fully analyzed as to the meaning of the very considerable inter-organizational mobility of federal civilian executives, including careerists; but the basic facts are portrayed in Table 3.

Table 3

Total Number of Organizations Associated with During Executive's Career: Three Groups of Executives Compared

| Number of Organizations* | All Civilian Federal Executives, 1959 | Career Civil Service Executives, 1959 | Business Executives, 1952 |
|---|---|---|---|
| 1............ | 13% | 13% | 25% |
| 2............ | 14% | 15% | 23% |
| 3............ | 17% | 17% | 22% |
| 4............ | 15% | 15% | 13% |
| 5............ | 12% | 12% | 7% |
| 6............ | 10% | 9% | 5% |
| 7 or more .... | 19% | 19% | 5% |
| Total ..... | 100% | 100% | 100% |

*For business executives this refers to "firms." For government executives it means "government departments, independent public agencies, business firms or other private organizations" with the Departments of the Army, Navy, and Air Force being considered separate agencies along with the Office of the Secretary of Defense. Because of different definitions there may be some understatement of the organizational experience of business leaders.

In inter-organizational movement career executives closely match federal civilian executives as a whole. Typically, these men have moved into and out of four organizations, twice the movement of business executives. We have no way of knowing whether this relative movement is increasing or decreasing, nor have we yet analyzed in detail how much of the organizational experience of government executives is in private enterprise. We do know, however, that the latter is considerable.

One may ask whether such movement is characteristic of governmental executives *after* they have reached the executive level. The answer is "yes," for both careerists and federal civilian executives as a whole. *As an executive,* two-thirds of the careerists have been associated with two or more organizations compared to one for the business executive. That is, the proportions shown in Table 3 hold at this level too.

Indeed, inter-organizational mobility (and lateral entry) appears to have an accelerating effect on the careers of federal civilian executives, even when this experience has been in seven or more organization. In general, this is not true of business.

### The Path to the Top

Any portrayal of the career routes of over 7,500 persons must be oversimplified. Nevertheless, there are patterns which can be outlined fairly precisely for career civil servants. This has been done in Table 4.

From these data we see the immense importance of the professions as avenues of opportunity for careerists. What is true of these men is even more true of political executives, but somewhat less true of those in the foreign service.

Comparing civilian federal executives as a whole to business executives, we can summarize three basic differences. First, much higher proportions of civilian federal executives than of business leaders are professionally trained. Second, much higher proportions of business leaders rise through laborer and white-collar occupations. Third, much higher proportions of business leaders reach minor and major executive status during the first fifteen years of their careers.

Government at the higher levels is a world dominated by professionally trained men who have gone through a long period of specialization. In this it is in strong contrast with the world of business, dominated by men who move up into their high positions through the white-collar route of clerical work and sales. These are not black and white differences but they are significant and may be of fundamental importance. One question occurs immediately: how much of the conflict arising between men in government and men in business is rooted in these quite different career experiences and the resulting cleavages in perspectives, rather than from—on a rational level—differences in interests and policies?

Table 4

Career Sequence of Career Civil Service Executives, 1959, Compared to Business Executives (in parentheses), 1952

| Occupational Categories | First Occupation | | Five Years Later | | Ten Years Later | | Fifteen Years Later | |
|---|---|---|---|---|---|---|---|---|
| Laborer | 16% | (14) | 7% | ( 3) | 4% | ( 1) | 3% | ( 0) |
| White collar worker | 27% | (44) | 20% | (29) | 9% | (11) | 4% | ( 4) |
| Minor executive | 4% | ( 9) | 15% | (35) | 29% | (43) | 27% | (25) |
| Major executive | 0%* | ( 1) | 1% | ( 6) | 6% | (26) | 20% | (57) |
| All professions | 43% | (21) | 45% | (21) | 44% | (14) | 40% | (10) |
| Uniformed service | 5% | ( 2) | 7% | ( 2) | 5% | ( 1) | 3% | ( 1) |
| Business owner | 1% | ( 1) | 2% | ( 2) | 1% | ( 3) | 1% | ( 3) |
| Other occupation | 4% | ( 5)† | 3% | ( 2) | 2% | ( 1) | 2% | ( 0) |
| Total | 100% | | 100% | | 100% | | 100% | |
| The Professions in detail: | | | | | | | | |
| Engineer | 17% | | 20% | | 19% | | 18% | |
| Lawyer | 2% | | 3% | | 3% | | 3% | |
| Medical doctor | 2% | | 2% | | 2% | | 2% | |
| Professor | 3% | | 3% | | 3% | | 1% | |
| Public school teacher | 6% | | 2% | | 1% | | 0%* | |
| Scientist | 6% | | 7% | | 8% | | 8% | |
| Accountant | 1% | | 2% | | 2% | | 2% | |
| Management analyst | 1% | | 2% | | 2% | | 2% | |
| Other profession | 5% | | 4% | | 4% | | 4% | |

*Less than one-half of one percent.
†One percent of this figure represents "government service"; this percent remains through "ten years later" but has disappeared by "fifteen years later." This plus "uniformed service" provide a rough index of "reverse lateral entry."

## The Question of Representative Bureaucracy

The concept of representative bureaucracy has been important to our research because it is concerned with the institutional consequences of the mobility process, particularly as applied to government. It stems primarily from a growing concern among political scientists in theories of responsibility: how vast civil and military bureaucracies can be kept responsive and responsible to the general public and its elected representatives.

The idea that the social composition and outlook of a civil or military bureaucracy has an important bearing upon its actions is by no means new; nor do present advocates of this approach propose a civil or military establishment which in social origins, skills, and abilities would copy the total society. But they do imply that, to achieve democratic ideals, recruitment and promotion of personnel should be from all social, racial, and religious groups on the basis of ability.

The federal structure provides an especially significant field of inquiry into the problem of representative bureaucracy since, in both the civilian and (to a lesser degree) military establishments, statutes and regulations attempt to keep them free of the typical barriers to occupational mobility. It is not possible here to present all the evidence stemming from our research on this matter; but it is feasible to conclude this discussion with consideration of one fundamental question especially significant in assessing bureaucratic representation.

*Do federal executives, particularly those in the career civil service, come from all occupational levels in American society?* Do their fathers occupy only the elite positions in business, government, and the professions; or do the sons of laborers and white-collar workers, of farmers and small businessmen, move into the higher levels of the federal service? In these matters how do government executives compare to business executives?

We do not have accurate and precise information about previous generations of federal executives; but for the present generation (1959) of *civilian* executives, with comparisons to business executives (1952), the basic data are shown in Table 5.

Based on these and other data, we can say that big business and government executives, insofar as their social and economic characteristics are concerned, are more alike than not, yet differences are present and significant. In terms of Table 5, it is clear that both derive more often and significantly from the higher occupations, but the range of occupations of their fathers runs from the top to the lowest levels.

The fathers of civilian federal executives were well distributed among the several categories present in the work force of the country at the time present federal executives became self-supporting. In socio-economic origin civilian federal executives are somewhat more representative of the population at large than are business executives. Of all the executive elites studied in this research, those in the career civil service are, in this respect, the most representative.

In still broader perspective, the research on executives in big business and

Table 5

Occupational Distributions of Business Executives' (1952) Fathers and of the U.S. Adult Male Population in 1920 Compared to Those of Certain Federal Executives' (1959) Fathers and of the U.S. Adult Male Population in 1930

| Occupation | U.S. Adult Male Population 1920 | Fathers of Business Executives | Fathers of All Civilian Federal Executives | Fathers of Career Civil Service Executives | U.S. Adult Male Population 1930 |
|---|---|---|---|---|---|
| Unskilled or semi-skilled laborer | 31% | 5% | 4% | 4% | 33% |
| Skilled laborer | 16% | 10% | 17% | 19% | 15% |
| Owner of small business | 5% | 18% | 14% | 15% | 7% |
| Clerk or salesman | 10% | 8% | 9% | 10% | 12% |
| Foreman | 2% | 3% | 5% | 5% | 2% |
| Minor or major executive; owner of large business | 4% | 31% | 17% | 15% | 3% |
| Professional man | 4% | 14% | 19% | 16% | 4% |
| Farm laborer | 7% | 0% | 0%* | 0%* | 6% |
| Farm tenant or owner | 20% | 9% | 14% | 15% | 16% |
| Other occupations | 1% | 2% | 1% | 1% | 2% |
| Total | 100% | 100% | 100% | 100% | 100% |
| No. of cases | | 7,500 | 10,419 | 7,353 | |

*Less than one-half of one percent.

government indicates that opportunity for the person born into low socio-economic position to rise to the top during one lifetime is not decreasing. Pessimism about decreased flexibility and mobility in American society is not warranted.

### Footnotes

1. This larger study, involving data on 10,851 civilian and 2,078 military executives in the federal government will be published this winter by the Yale University Press under the title of *The American Federal Executive*. A subsidiary volume concerned entirely with the uniformed military is in process.
2. For a special report on women executives in the federal government see: W. Lloyd Warner, et al., "Women Executives in the Federal Government," 23 *Public Personnel Review* 227-234 (October 1962).
3. In this research "political executives" are those whose positions are not under complete merit system regulations; positions in *Schedules A, B,* and *C* are included here. The political executive category goes up through Cabinet level. "Military executives" are the uniformed only, from full colonel and naval captain up through all ranks of general and flag officers in the Army, Navy, Air Force, and Marine Corps. The "foreign service" category includes persons in the U.S. Foreign Service, Foreign Service Reserve, and Foreign Service Staff wherever they may be assigned and whatever their position.
4. Data concerning business executives in this article, with the single execption of the item cited in note 5, derive from W. Lloyd Warner and James C. Abegglen, *Occupational Mobility in American Business and Industry* (University of Minnesota Press, 1955).
5. "1,700 Top Executives," 60 *Fortune* 139 (November 1959).

JOHN J. CORSON

# Equipping Men For Career Growth In the Public Service

THE CHART in the following article, adapted from Henri Fayol, conveys much of John Corson's thesis: that different "understandings" are required by career public servants at progressive levels of responsibility which they may achieve and that pre-entry education and in-career training must take that into account. Corson based his conclusions on more than 25 years of observation, research, and practice. When this article was published, he was a professor of public and international affairs at Princeton University and a director of McKinsey & Company, Inc. He had just completed service in 1962 as chairman of the Municipal Manpower Commission, and he had served as a member of President Kennedy's Advisory Panel on Federal Pay Systems. He had also served earlier as ASPA national president. Three years later, his book with Shale Paul, *Men Near the Top*, was issued by the Committee for Economic Development

This *PAR* article was published shortly after the National Institute for Public Affairs had proposed creation of a Federal Staff College. Discussions in that direction continued, building on such ideas as those of John Corson in this article and of Marshall Dimock in the 1958 article earlier in this collection. The Federal Executive Institute was created in 1968 as a result of these efforts, as noted in two later articles in this collection.

IT IS ASSUREDLY a propitious time to take stock of the variety of efforts being made, in and out of government, to develop men and women for top jobs in the public service. The persistent growth in government—federal, state and local—recent pay raises in the federal and some state and local governments that may make them more effective in competition for talent, more frequent assignment of mature staff members to universities for advanced training either in short courses or for year-long programs, the launching of the Princeton program of education for public affairs, the National Institute of Public Affairs proposals for a "Federal Staff College" and a "National Foreign Service Academy," and the competitive offering by universities of training—pre-entry and post-entry—

for the public service, all makes 1963 a propitious time for stock taking.

The need is for joint re-evaluation—by governmental executives and training officials, on the one hand, and by university deans and faculties, on the other. The need is for reconsideration of what a public official does and, hence, of the relevance of the intellectual menu offered as in-service training and in the universities as pre-entry and post-entry training.

This paper seeks to stimulate such re-evaluation. It is addressed to those in government and in the universities who should give their attention to the task: the public officials, who have a prime stake in the development of their staffs, and the university deans and faculty members, who train men and women for the profession.

## An Historically Grounded Idea

A starting point for such a re-evaluation can be found in an essay that Henri Fayol wrote in 1916. It was entitled, "The Relative Importance of the Various Abilities Which Constitute the Value of Personnel of Concerns."[1] That early essay contributed two interrelated and generally accepted ideas that deserve attention. The first was that performance in any position requires a combination of abilities. The second was that "as one goes up the scalar chain" the mix of abilities required varies markedly.

To paraphrase the table by which Fayol portrayed the "relative importance of requisite abilities" Chart 1 reflects what over twenty-five years observation in and about the public service seems to show as to the growth of the civil servant and the understandings he requires. Chart 1 is suggestive; no claim is made that the curved lines depict the exact points in the career of each civil servant when each "understanding" must be acquired, nor does the diagram indicate by the breadth of each shaded area the proportionate importance of each understanding at each "level" of employment.

## The Vertical Dimension

The columns at the left of this diagram offer an analysis of the professional life span of a public servant expressed in terms common to the federal civil service. This analysis suggests, first, the nature of the understandings that the beginner in the profession may be expected to bring with him to "apprentice-like" starting jobs, which will likely consume the first years of this employment. Here he will likely spend his time on quite narrow assignments, either as an aide to a "line" operator or in a staff unit as a budgeteer, management analyst, specialized statistician, or economic analyst. Only a few—a very few—fortunate ones will be assigned to posts affording them anything like a panoramic view. After three to seven years the typical career civil servant reaches the first professional level. Here he is called upon to direct the work of others, to "represent" his unit in negotiations with other organizational units, and to "speak for" his staff to those

## Chart 1
### REQUISITE UNDERSTANDINGS OF THE PUBLIC SERVANT

| CLASS OF EMPLOYEE | | OF THE SUBSTANTIVE FIELD IN WHICH HE WORKS | OF WAYS AND MEANS OF DIRECTING THE WORK OF OTHERS | OF THE FUNCTIONS OF OTHER UNITS WITHIN THE ORGANIZATION AND OF RELATED GOVERNMENT ENTITIES | OF THE SOCIETY, ECONOMY AND THE CITIZENS HE SERVES | OF WAYS AND MEANS OF PROJECTING THE POLICIES AND PROGRAMS THROUGHOUT AN ENTERPRISE AND SEEING TO IT THAT THEY ARE CARRIED OUT |
|---|---|---|---|---|---|---|
| TOP PROFESSIONAL LEVEL | BUREAU DIRECTOR, COMMISSIONER OR ADMINISTRATOR | | | | | |
| SECOND PROFESSIONAL LEVEL | DIVISION CHIEF OR REGIONAL DIRECTOR | | | | | |
| FIRST PROFESSIONAL LEVEL | SECTION OR BRANCH CHIEF | | | | | |
| | FIRST LINE SUPERVISOR OR UNIT CHIEF | | | | | |
| APPRENTICE-SHIP | BEGINNING PROFESSIONAL, TECHNICAL OR ADMINISTRATIVE EMPLOYEE | | | | | |

*As adapted from Henri Fayol's Table II—Relative Importance of Personnel in Industrial Concerns, *ibid.*, p. 10.

who will prescribe its work, determine its budget, and evaluate its performance. These tasks necessitate acquaintanceship with areas of understanding which were of minor or of no significance during his apprenticeship.

The average man or woman who makes a career of the public service attains the second professional level after eight to twelve years of public service. In a job at this level—e.g., the assistant chief of a division in the Department of Agriculture or the principal adviser to an administrator within the Department of Defense—perhaps a third to two-thirds of his time and attention must be devoted to an addditional range of activities requiring understandings which the individual might not have retained, or which would have been obsoleted, had he focused his energies on mastering them before entering the government.

Visualize next the responsibilities of the Director of the Federal Bureau of Prisons, of the Chief Forester of the United States, of the Director of the Bureau of Mines, or of the Director of the Air Traffic Service in the FAA. At this topmost career level of professional work in the federal service,[2] the individual needs a vast comprehension of the substantive field in which he is looked to as a leader (or he does not get there!) *and* a deep understanding of the processes by which he must mobilize and motivate many human beings working together, even when scattered over a nation. Consider, for example, the role of Walt Disney in Walt Disney Productions, as pictured by *Newsweek*, December 31, 1962. He is "hailed as the father of a new art form," yet he is the "total boss" of an enterprise employing thousands and grossing in 1962 more than $70 million.

### The Horizontal Dimension

Early Wynn the veteran big league pitcher, recently commented that: "More baseball people should be in baseball [in administrative positions]. You don't take a guy out of a trucking concern and make a baseball man out of him any more than you can take a guy out of baseball and put him in the trucking business." Unknowingly, perhaps, the fabulous right-hander parroted the words of many a public and business executive. Yet training for the public service, in and out of government, during recent decades has tended to focus on training in administrative technique, assuming that administrators are interchangeable from one substantive field to another.[3]

If more precise data were available as to the positions occupied by top-level civil servants in the federal government and in the best of the state and city governments, the unreality of this assumption would be apparent. The unreality is also suggested by the single fact that more than 30 percent of the incumbents in positions classified at grade 16 and above in the federal civil service are required to have training in one or another science or in engineering. Finally, it is confirmed by an analysis of all requests from federal departments to the U.S. Civil Service Commission between March 1961 and November 1962 for the referral of qualified individuals from those listed in the Executive Roster. Of ninety-two requests (i.e., for placement in positions classified at grades GS-16 to 18 and statutory positions paying more than $18,500), only four were for individuals with general administrative skills and where no subject matter knowledge was required.[4]

Young men and women who enter the public service are recruited in major proportions as accountants, biologists, chemists, engineers, lawyers, physicists, statisticians, or specialists in international affairs or in one of a score of other fields.[5] To grow in the public service, an obvious dedication to the objectives of the agency or bureau for which the entrant to the public service works is a decided advantage in gaining the respect of his peers. It is essential for the individual in a line job and equally important for the staff man. No characteristic tends to limit the success of the staff man more than a tendency to concentrate on his specialization—personnel, accounting, or what not—and to lose sight of the objectives of the agency and its operating program.

Both the line and the staff man will normally have to demonstrate not only an increasing understanding of the substantive field in which they work—be it agricultural marketing, airport operations, tax administration or weather forecasting—but an interest which approaches a zeal for the problems of this substantive field. Such understanding can be planted in the individual's mind during his university training, but it will be acquired in large part (and ofttimes in too parochial a form) on the job.

Surely there are men and women who rise in the public service even though they lacked at the outset a firm, beginner's grasp of any substantive field. They do so, in part, by acquiring a familiarity with the techniques of administration; but they do so more often by digging earnestly into a substantive field and acquiring at least a foundation understanding. And they do so by adding to their intellectual arsenals "understandings" suggested by Chart 1 that has been presented and is to be defined more precisely in subsequent paragraphs. The more successful of those who bring to the public service only a beginner's understanding of the skills of administration—of budgeting, of personnel administration, of personnel training, of supervisory techniques of planning and control, or of purchasing—and who confine their growth to these areas end up, in most instances, in staff positions perhaps near but not at the top of the career service. For top managerial jobs in the public service, as in industry, are reserved for those who are so steeped in an understanding of the functions of the enterprise which they serve that they can be counted upon to supply the independent judgment, the intuition, and the innovative capacity that are expected of the manager.

## Capacity for Work Direction

For the apprentice who brought to the public service a firm beginner's grasp of a substantive field (or gained such a grasp during his apprenticeship) there is an important skill he must begin to acquire before he will rise to higher echelons. It is the skill, defined very broadly, of using others in achieving an organizational end—the skill of work direction.

The term "supervision" usually connotes a face-to-face relationship with subordinates for whose work the individual is responsible. Such a relationship obtain at the highest as well as the lowest echelons of organization. In their respective ways both the president and the foreman must plan the work of their subordinates, must interpret and implement policy, must organize their staffs, participate in budgeting, and control expenditure. Over and above these elements, the skill of work direction involves understanding of human relations at two levels—relations with subordinates and relations with equals and superiors. A flawless understanding of the elements of work direction will be of little value to the supervisor who cannot achieve effective relationships with those who work for him, with him, and above him.

How does the beginner learn this skill? He can be introduced to the nature of work direction and to what the psychologists and sociologists have recently learned about it while he is still at a university but much of what he needs to learn, he will learn as golfers learn their skill—by watching and, consciously or unconsciously, mimicking good golfers. And, perhaps like the golfer, he must learn more and more of the subtleties of the skill as he rises.

And how does the career man learn, as he rises from echelon to echelon, to direct effectively the work of professional workers or administrative colleagues? The process is similar in kind, but markedly different in character, from that of supervising clerical or manual workers. The degree of delegation which the supervising vice president grants to his professional or administrative aides is markedly greater and the degree of accountability (in terms of regular periodic reporting) is markedly less than the delegation accorded and the accountability required of clerical or manual workers.

## Understanding of Other Functions

"The memoirs of almost any president of a major corporation," Wight Bakke wrote a decade ago, "will include a description of experiences in getting the sales, production, and comptroller's department together in the solution of a particular company problem."[6] Surely the corporation president's experience is duplicated by every federal bureau director or department head who has frequently had to bring together division and bureau heads who identify themselves largely or exclusively with the programs, manpower needs, or budgets of their respective divisions or bureaus. A public executive spends much of his time countering the "Ptolemaic" outlooks of his staff members, helping them to see that the bureau or department does not revolve around their respective divisions or bureaus.

The man who becomes a first line supervisor learns very quickly the underside of this problem. If his wits are about him, he learns that he must know what each other unit of the enterprise—the personnel office, the budget office, the comptroller's office, the training division, the treasurer and the auditors, and particularly the other substantive (or operating) units—are doing. It is not enough that he knows *what* these units do; it is essential that he knows *why* they think the way they do. The need for such understanding is reflected in the curricula of most of the many university executive development programs. Indeed, analysis of this curricula will reveal that some offer little more than illumination of the several functions of the enterprise.

But, much that the individual rising within an enterprise needs to learn about other functions of the enterprise, he must learn by becoming involved. The city planner, for example, probably an engineer or an architect by training, needs to study urban economics and sociology. But he will never come to know the city for which he plans until he has been "involved" in the economic and social life of the community and until he has come to know the factors that influence businessmen in deciding where to locate branch stores, office buildings, and factories, that influence welfare and police officials in deploying their forces and facilities, and those that plague traffic engineers. He can learn much by reading, but there is much he must learn through his forearms, with his sleeves rolled above his elbows.

### Understanding the Environment

Felix Frankfurter has written of the "great realm" which public officials must understand if they are to ply their trade successfully. At least four factors give rise to an especial need for the individual, as he rises in the federal service, to gain an understanding of this "external realm" within which his agency operates.

The first and obvious factor is the consequence of his decisions upon the lives of many citizens. The second is the isolated work lives that most federal civil servants live. Since the careers of most federal civil servants are lived in a single bureau or department, their experiences are not likely to acquaint them broadly *with the society they serve* and the groups within that society.[7] The third is that the civil servant, "hemmed in" over most of a working lifetime by exposure only to that part of the "external realm" that he serves, acquires a myopic view of the society of which his constituency is only a part. A fourth factor is illustrated by the comment of one observant career civil servant on a related bit of the environment: "This is especially true of Washington, D.C. careers and less true of field careers. Living in Boston, I was a part of the non-government society in a very active sense: we didn't know people socially, or in community activities, who worked for the Federal government. In Washington we know nothing else." It takes an eminently broad-gauged man in the position of Chief Forester of the United States not to become unduly impressed with the special and often conflicting concerns of the lumber manufacturers, the graziers, the recreationists, and others who have daily pressed their views on him over a working lifetime.

What makes up the "external realm" of which public officials must gain an understanding? It can be described only in the broadest terms, for it is the nature of public service that the public official is concerned with the public interest. And his need for understanding is the greater because, in comparison with the executive in private enterprise, he can less often control or even influence the forces which give rise to the problems he must resolve. Consider, for example, the "external realm" with which the Assistant Secretary of State for African Affairs (and his immediate career deputies) are concerned and the forces that give rise to the problems he must resolve.

A few beginners bring to their assignments in government a textbook understanding of governmental structure, of the role of the legislature, of the relationship of government to the individual, of the structure of the society (i.e., the American society) that government serves, and of the impact of government on the economy and on the individual enterprise. This textbook understanding is expanded, tested, and distorted by their experiences (most of them secondary) during the years they work their way up through the apprenticeship and first and second professional levels of the service. Consequently, their need for understanding of the external realm becomes acute (whether they realize it or not) by the time they reach the second professional level.

For many this need is manifested by a deep-felt belief that the legislative branch, the congressional committee, the individual congressman is the natural enemy, or at least opponent, of the executive branch, the department or bureau, and the career executive. It is manifested, too, by a minimum of understanding of the congressman as a voice for his constituents, as a legislative committee member, or as a candidate for election and reelection.

In others the need is manifested by overzealous concern with the interests of particular citizens (e.g., those employees who belong to unions) and by insufficient regard for the appropriate relationship of government and the citizen (be he organized employee, employer, unorganized employee, or taxpayer). Other career executives manifest a view of the relationship between government and society that prevailed before the enactment of the Securities and Exchange Act, the Social Security Act, the National Labor Relations Act, or the development of the Marshall Plan.[8] Still other career executives bring to their tasks in the second professional level or top-management level an understanding of Marshallian or Taussig economics that is of little help in understanding either the current administration of regulatory bodies, enforcement of antitrust laws, or, especially, the impact of defense, housing, and social security expenditures on the economy.

## Understanding the Executive Role

For most career executives who rise to the top of the heap there is a rude awakening. It is the shock that an executive experiences when he first realizes that he bears, and bears alone, the ultimate and whole responsibility for the department, service, or bureau he heads.

"I woke from a sound sleep one night, sitting upright in bed," one career executive has said, "when I realized for the first time that I alone in the bureau, in the department, or in the whole wide world was concerned with carrying out a function that the people of the United States had determined, by democratic processes, should be performed. I could look to my division heads, the departmental staff officers, and even to constituencies for help on individual problems, but I alone, I realized then, was responsible for the *whole* show."

    Chester Barnard, a quarter of a century ago, defined all too simply the tasks expected of the executive in discharging the ultimate responsibility that awakened this restless executive.[9] Perhaps Robert E. McNamara, the fantastically efficient Secretary of Defense, takes too seriously Mr. Kennedy's declaration and example that as President he "would be involved in the fray." For Mr. McNamara insists upon doing more than Mr. Barnard prescribed. As the *Wall Street Journal* pointed out (in one of the most significant comments on public administration in recent months), the Secretary, to the dismay of many of the admirals and generals, insists upon participating in the formulation of decisions.[10] He will not content himself with "blessing" decisions which the staffs propose that he make. He refuses to limit himself to serving as arbiter between the services and between the various specialized staffs (e.g., the line officer and the research scientists) and insists upon the right to consider, personally, all alternatives available.

    Since Mr. Barnard described the executive function in 1938, the dimensions of many public executive positions have changed markedly. The numbers whose work they direct have grown by leaps and bounds. The variety of specialists whose work the executive must interrelate has markedly broadened. The complexity of each field of specialization has greatly increased. The "purposes, objectives, and ends" of the individual enterprise—be it in business or in government—are more often multiple and more often complex.

    The public executive in the 1960's, hence, requires a far broader range of competence than was required in the 1930's. The career executive who rises to the level of bureau or service director, or to the post of commissioner of an "administration" (e.g., the Commissioner, Food and Drug Administration) is expected to "understand" a wide assortment of specialists. This he needs that he may facilitate the communication one with another, appraise the projects for which they expect him to find financial and/or political support, and relate them to the ends for which the agency was created.

    An executive who doesn't gain a working comprehension of the range of specializations over which he presides is not likely to make decisions effectively. He can serve only as a rubber stamp that is used by others to approve *their* decisions. Moreover, he will never gain the respect of the people of his agency when they believe that he doesn't really know what they are talking about. To get and hold his staff's respect the public administrator must possess a substantial comprehension of and belief in the agency's program. A private business executive may "manage men and money" and leave the substance of the business to his colleagues (although few successful private business executives do), but a public administrator cannot.

    He must learn how, on the one hand, to project to thousands of employees he can never face, the plans he makes in simple, intelligible language that attract their cooperation and better their zeal, and, on the other hand, to learn recurrently what and how they are doing. He must learn how to interpret and to "sell" the activity for which he is responsible to numerous constituencies within the body politic, without becoming the "tool" of any constituency. He must acquire a progressively heightened understanding of what is in the mind of his employees, other governmental executives, congressional committee members, and constituency spokesmen with whom he must deal.

He must learn how to be, at one and the same time, a symbol that typifies the program to the public, and the "leader" to his staff, while an active participant in the administrative process who sees to it not only that programs are carried out but that high standards of performance are insisted upon and that real and substantial accomplishment and loyalty—and nothing else—is rewarded.

## Implications for Education for the Profession

For public officials concerned with the development of their staffs and for university deans and faculties who offer training for indivudals entering or in the public service, the foregoing analysis—(1) the life span of the career public executive and (2) the increasing range of understandings that the individual must acquire as he rises in the public service—poses three general conclusions.

### The Base and the Overlay

The first is that the career executive, if he is to succeed, requires an expanding grasp of a substantive field and an "overlay" made up of both an understanding (a) of the role of government in a democratic society and (b) of administrative and executive skills and processes.

To get a running start in the public service, most men and women need both an apprentice's firm grasp of a substantive field (e.g., international affairs) or a skill (e.g., accounting) *and* an acquaintanceship with the environment within which they will work. To be "wanted" in the Langley Laboratory of NASA, they need a firm grounding in one of the sciences or in a field of engineering. And, if they are to understand the objectives of the Laboratory, the institutional framework of agency policy and programs, of civil service rules and processes, of budgets, and of administrative regulations, they need an elementary, but solid, understanding of government and its administration.

What is the relative importance of the "base"—the grounding in a substantive field—and of the "overlay"—the acquaintanceship with government and its administration? In terms of the relative time the beginner should devote during his years in undergraduate and graduate study, I would suggest 80 percent to the "base" and not more than 20 percent to the "overlay."

But by the time the beginner has gotten a good start on his professional career in the administration of public affairs, i.e., within the first six to eight years of his public service, he must acquire a solid understanding of the processes of work direction and a whole-sided view not only of the agency in which he serves, but of the federal government and, at least for many, of its relationships to state and local governments.

### Learning by Doing and by Study

Some career public servants—but not a great many—enjoy the invaluable opportunity of working with and for broad-gauged, effective, and continually growing executives. They will learn of the processes of work direction, consciously or unconsciously, by the example that is set for them. Others will learn through internal training programs that aid them to "pick up" much of what they need to know about work direction and about the functions of other units of the organization and of this country's governmental structure. Few departmental training programs deal effectively with the techniques of work direction at other than the lower echelons. As one observer has declared: "There is too much attention to the theme of 'Don't bawl out the foreman in front of his crew.' This isn't enough in a government peopled increasingly by M.S.'s and Ph.D.'s that too have to be led, if not directed." Few training programs, too, deal with other than descriptive (rather than analytical) consideration of the functions of the several subdivisions of the agency. And few aid the executive after he passes through the first professional level.

For most career men and women there is an urgent need, after six to eight years in the public service, for a rigorous stocktaking of what they have learned as to work direction and as to the function of other units of the agency and of the government. Simultaneously, this is the time for them to begin to underpin their personal philosophy of public service with clear thinking as to the role of government in relation to the individual, the society, and the economy.

Relatively few men have the critical faculties that enable them naturally and unconsciously to examine, as they go along, what they are doing and why they are doing it in the way prescribed for them. Fewer yet can do this while at work without raising questions in the minds of their colleagues as to whether they are as loyal and as dedicated to the enterprise and its goals as they should be.

If they are to be enabled to "dust off" the intellectual inventory they accumulate from experience, to classify this stock-on-hand that it may be readily available to them as a tool, they need an opportunity to step back from the enterprise and consider where they are and what they need to go ahead. They need a chance to examine critically the processes of the agency of which they are a part in a detached setting, unhampered by the parochial constraints that inevitably, and should, obtain within.

### Substituting the New for the Obsolescent

The higher the career executive rises, and the more years that elapse after he commences on his career, the greater is his need for replacing the obsolescent both in his understanding of the substantive field in which he works and in administrative technique. The rapid advance in science and technology makes it essential that the scientific administrator periodically up-date what he knows of the field in which he once may have been a broadly and intensively equipped specialist. Similarly, the continual development of decision making, planning, and control processes and the changes in the makeup of the work force makes necessary the substitution for methods he learned by example of advanced and previously unknown methods.

Consider but two examples: An outstanding physicist working in the space program, fifteen years after he received his Ph.D. and five years after he had been catapulted from the laboratory bench by advancement to an administrative position, seeks an opportunity to "catch up," an opportunity to replenish his understanding of the science. Another career executive, who has presided for more than a decade over an agency with 35,000 employees, is confronted with a succession of proposals for the introduction of new programming, decision making, and control techniques that he feels incapable of evaluating. Should he insist upon maintaining the "tried-and-true" processes with which he is familiar or can he find an opportunity to up-date his understanding in fields in which he feels less confident than he once did?

Both of these men, and many like them, require detachment and stimulation. William James once wrote of the infinite scarcity of individuals with "the capacity for non-habitual perception," i.e., of looking at customary problems in uncustomary ways. Psychologically, as most men grow older, they find it more difficult to adopt new ways and to encourage new ideas. To refresh their spirits, to make more flexible their reasoning processes, as well as to acquaint them with the new that should replace the obsolete in what they earlier learned, they need detachment from the day-to-day environment and the stimulation of new faces and new places. A first-rate university can provide such an environment if it recognizes the individual's own need and resists the temptation to force him into a patterned program reflecting the faculty's conception of a public executive's needs. The proposed "Federal Staff College" must be so structured as to provide the same detachment, stimulation, and individualized opportunity or it will add little of consequence to the development of public executives.

## Conclusion

In the military services the needs of the officer are viewed over his total career. The cadet, the plebe, or the airman are not trained in the techniques they will require if ever they rise to the rank of colonel or captain. A system of schools is designed to enable the officer to acquire, at each successive stage in his career, the additional understandings that he then requires. This system of internal schools is supplemented at a variety of points by the universities to which officers go for detachment, for stimulation, for an opportunity to order and make the most of the experience they have had, and for the acquisition of what is new to replace what they learned long ago and no longer is so, or what they had never learned at all.

It is high time that the civilian career executive's advancement received similar attention. His competence will be enhanced by a similar view of this training, over his whole working career and the public interest served.

## Footnotes

1. Henri Fayol, *General and Industrial Management* (Sir Isaac Pitman & Sons Ltd., 1949), Chapter XI, pp. 7-13.
2. Statistical data developed by the Office of Career Development, U.S. Civil Service Commission, indicate that this level is not reached by most occupants of such positions until after 20 years of service and attainment of age 50-55.
3. See, for confirmation of this contention, the analysis of the need for public service training and the prescription in *Education for Public Administration,* "Graduate Preparation in the Social Sciences at American Universities," by George A. Graham (Public Administration Service, 1941), and in *Educational Preparation for Administrative Careers in Government Service,* Stephen B. Sweeney, ed. (University of Pennsylvania Press, 1958). A contrasting view of the need was presented earlier by O. Glenn Stahl, "Public Service Training in Universities," 31 *American Political Science Review* 870-878 (October 1937).
4. Data derived from a special tabulation and analysis prepared under the direction of J. Kenneth Mulligan, Director, Office of Career Development, U.S. Civil Service Commission, December 1962.
5. An analysis of 1,150 Federal career executives occupying positions classified at GS-16 and higher in 1960 disclosed that 1,052, or 90 percent, had had their major collegiate education in the fields of "business and commerce, economics, law, engineering, physical sciences, geology, mathematics, and agricultural and biological science." Ross Pollock, "Federal Career Development Needs—An Overview," Working Paper No. 1, prepared for the University-Federal Agency Conference on Career Development, Princeton University, November 2-4, 1961.
6. *Bonds of Organization* (Harper and Brothers, 1951), p. 19.
7. Data developed by the Office of Career Development, U.S. Civil Service Commission, show that the federal executive in most instances starts in the service at a beginning job classified at grade GS-6 or lower and spends most of his working life in one agency. See memorandum entitled "Data about Federal Career Executives," an appendix to a proposal of the U.S. Civil Service Commission for the establishment of a staff college, July 1962. See also Don K. Price, "Administrative Leadership," *Daedalus,* American Academy of Arts and Sciences (Fall (1961). There he writes: "If you talk to a college senior about going into the civil service, you cannot tell him that he will get promoted on the basis of his usefulness to the government as a whole ... to

get ahead, he may have to plan his career in terms of the specialized interest of a single bureau."
8. Harold Laski asserted that there is a recurring need for updating the understanding of the civil servant of a democracy as to the relationship of government and the society. "The Education of the Civil Servant," 21 *Public Administration* 13-22 (1943).
9. Chester I. Barnard, "The Executive Functions," *The Functions of the Executive* (Harvard University Press, 1938).
10. "McNamara Centralizes Pentagon Control, Puts Civilians in Command," *Wall Street Journal,* February 19, 1962.

NORTON E. LONG

## Politicians for Hire—
## The Dilemma of Education
## And the Task of Research

IN THIS ARTICLE, Norton Long focused on the central quandary of American public administration, the eroded doctrine of separation of politics and administration and the high ambition of many, driven by necessity, to be successfully involved in policy as administrative generalists. City managers, particularly, were described by Long as managerial mercenaries—politicians for hire. His central concern was the nature of education needed in schools of public administration and planning to equip this growing "governing class" of appointed politicians for their real responsibilities. What education may equip public administration practitioners to govern wisely?

Norton Long was a professor of politics at Brandeis University when he wrote this article. Besides engaging in university teaching and research, he had earlier served as a staff consultant to the Governor of Illinois while at Northwestern University. He was an assistant to the administrator of the Office of Price Administration during World War Two, and he then served as an assistant administrator of the National Housing Administration (1946-48).

SCHOOLS of Public Administration and of Planning are in a quandary. What should be their curriculum? When asked what special expertise there is to be taught they are hard put for an answer. The planner feels most comfortable, most secure that he is really planning, when he is at his drawing board. Yet he knows that physical planning by itself is a woefully limited thing. Public administration is most secure when it deals with personnel and budgeting. These are two distinct career lines for which it feels, with some assurance, it can prepare. But as with planning, what it can do well it feels to be, though undoubtedly useful, merely instrumental and hence of minor interest.

Both public administration and planning are victims of high ambition. They wish to be concerned with policy, and high policy at that. Their adepts are to be generalists, not instrumental hewers of wood and drawers of water for others. However, they are both heirs to a tradition and a mystique that denies them an overt political role. The professions are supposed to produce experts, not politicians for hire. Their power is supposed to be derived from expertise, not politics. Yet as their pretensions to general competence expand, the character of their expertise becomes more and more problematic. What is it that they really know and what courses can teach this general knowledge? The distinction between the expert on things in general and the politician becomes more difficult to draw in theory. In practice it means he has been to school, carries an academic card, and is appointed rather than elected to office. The problem is as old as Plato and his poetic effort to distinguish the philosopher king from the inexpert mere politician. The source of the difference was supposed to derive from the process of selection and education. However, examination of the curricula of the Platonic philosopher king or of the latter day policy generalists in planning and administration lends little confidence to their claim to produce policy experts. Hence the malaise in schools of planning and public administration.

## A Trace of Intellectual Quicksand

The erosion of the dichotomy between politics and administration has undermined the Wilsonian doctrine that provided much of the phisosophical underpinnings for schools of public administration. The attempt of Herbert Simon to revive the doctrine by the logical positivist distinction between propositions of value and propositions of fact, as Dwight Waldo pointed out, was less than a success. Since its moral for planners and public administrationists was to stick to the role of expert advisor rather than that of policy maker it was both distasteful and utopian. In practice the dogma of the separation of policy and administration has been abandoned but the church erected upon it has failed to crumble. The demand for planners and public administrators has increased while the intellectual basis of their profession disintegrated.

Two conclusions might be drawn from this, one that regardless of the theory's inadequacies the human material proves useful and two, that what Simon calls uncertainty absorption is not only met by patent drugs but by patent professions. Doubtless both conclusions have a basis in fact. There is a need for able people in the governmental bureaucracy as well as the legislature. Some of what is learned in graduate school as well as college is of some practical use. Beyond this, even when they know better, politicians and public alike endow their doctors and other experts with a special knowledge that can cure their ills. In many cases the belief reduces anxieties and permits society's own search processes to find or create the remedy. The experts are themselves a social placebo. Their presence, like the doctor's, calms the nerves even when they have little else to offer.

In addition, administration, like much else, is a species of learned behavior in which, as in driving, the side of the road is unimportant if everybody sticks to it. If the schools produce a folklore, it may be highly functional in producing common cooperative action—a set of rules of the game which if widely accepted make determinate an otherwise indeterminate situation. POSDCORB administration has, as not the least of its virtues, the structuring of administrative behavior in a fashion that made that behavior routinely predictable. This is a clear gain for the participants and even to a degree produces conditions conducive to systemically functional outcomes. The undermining of the faith by the logical positivist critique may destroy confidence in working rules while failing to replace one socially necessary structure with another. Here the pragmatic test and the scientific test should coincide. The savages may be right for the wrong reasons, and destroying their customs may disorient without meaningfully reorienting.

## The Inevitability of Administrative Creativity and Power

Weldon's distinction between puzzles, problems and difficulties is highly relevant to an administration largely concerned with solving problems and surmounting difficulties. As Weldon points out, some problems may be treated as a puzzle and solved. He illustrates this with the Keynesian analysis of the business cycle. But, as he points out, other problems do not lend themselves to solutions as puzzles and rather must be treated as difficulties to be surmounted rather than solved. That is, the solution must be created out of the materials at hand and is not built into the logic of an existing puzzle. The administrator's problem thus requires creativity in the same sense as the engineer's or the artist's. As with both of these he cannot excogitate his solution from the truths of science though he will certainly make use of them to the extent that he is conversant with them and to the extent that they have useful application. The creation of solutions to difficulties, race relations for example, is preeminently the task of the politician. Yet it is precisely to policy problems of this magnitude that the administrative generalist or planner would hope to make major contribution. In fact, since the politician is predominantly concerned with assessing the politically possible and maintaining viability, the administrative generalist as idea man develops, hopefully, the range from which the political operator may pick the most promising alternative.

If this is the highest task of the administrative generalist, it is clear that he is in politics. Indeed it has always seemed that plans, if they were to be more than art for art's sake, must be policies, and that policies to become actualized must become politics. But if this is so, perhaps the public administrator and the planner are in reality hired politicians, hired politicians who are interested in a range of policies, would like tenure, and wish to eschew elective and partisan politics, though in a pinch—like school superintendents—are willing to manage public opinion, rally pressure groups and even run a bond campaign.

The democratic dogma has made it difficult to face up to society's need for a governing class and the bureaucracy's place in such a class. The doctrine of self government has almost made it appear that there was not a specialized social role of governing and that there did not therefore need to be a specialized body of governors. Indeed the Jacksonian doctrine escaped the dilemma by maintaining that everybody could play the role and that everybody should for short terms with the turn of the political wheel. The Jeffersonian answer was to so limit the functions of government so that the inevitable establishment would have little power or pickings. These solutions have failed before the development of complex urbanized industrial society. The rustic idyll has remained a haunting dream for utopians of the right and of the suburb. As the scale of the society increases the public sector and the public goods it produces mount. The problem of staffing the management of the public sector also increases and the power of its managers becomes increasingly difficult to overlook. With the fading of the dogma of the separation of politics and administration, the power becomes more visible, the question of its legitimation increasingly unavoidable. Hyneman's return to fundamentalism in which "the will of the people," acting through the legislature, furnishes Simon's value premises, while instrumental bureaucrats confine themselves to fact premises has the appeal of that old time religion but it seems scarcely more than a theological dream.

The managers of the bureaucracy not only have power, they openly express their desire for it. The preparation of policy generalists is scarcely a school for political eunuchs. The facts of our political life are at war with our political theory. The neutral civil service that can be conveniently disposed of as being of the same order as the desks and typewriters, impartially and passively available to all legitimate and political superiors alike, is a figment of the ideal type of British parliamentary government. But the lack of a legitimate theory for the current facts is real enough. The power of the business community is dealt with by denying it in theory. Businessmen are supposed to be the powerless instruments of the public good governed by competition. Where they aren't, they are supposed to be regulated. Labor unions are conveniently ignored as a painful anomaly. The power of public administrators is treated as the power of doctors. Their power is legitimated through a presumed expertise whose exercise is assumed to be for the public good. Built in professional standards are thought to control a power whose naked exercise might be harmful, to be sure in both cases, and far more so in the case of public administrators who exercise a degree of control through the public's formal political representatives. The legitimation by expertise goes so far that in the case of planning commissions and civil service commissions the politicians, the transmission belt of Hyneman's "will of the people," are told to keep hands off. Thus develops a doctrine of the virtual representation of the public through expertise, though the doctrine is seldom more than a nuisance to the holders of major political power when they come in conflict with it.

## Managerial Mercenaries

The city manager is perhaps the most striking case of the public administrator whose role has outrun his profession's self rationalization. The city manager today is an expert politician for hire, rather than a political expert. His professional mortality is more likely to arise from his political failings than any inadequacies in what was once supposed to be his appropriate expertise. As Martindale following Weber has pointed out, the city manager had a forerunner in the medieval Italian podesta who was also a governor for hire. The public's ultimate control here, as with other goods and services, is to switch brands. The education of the city manager presents in acute form the problem of public administration. How do you educate a politician? At least since Plato's *Republic* and through the De Regimine Principum literature there has been controversy over the nature and teaching of the statesman's art—whether it can be taught at all. But the manager as an educated, more or less experienced politician for hire gives us at least the empirical answer—some people given some instruction can get themselves hired and at least in many cases the public appears satisfied.

In a democracy it appears odd to have hired politicians; the normal expectation is that they should be elected. While we praise the amateur and revere him in theory, we at least lately have come to recognize the merits of the elected pro. Present day democracies, despite the happy versatility of the Greek ideal, have come to recognize the inevitability of specialization. The citizen army revived in the 19th century seems well on its way to replacement by mercenaries. Indeed as Fehrenbach has pointed out, if we are to wage frontier wars these latter are indispensable. The *condottieri* and the podesta are phenomena of urban specialization. Yet the one thing seemingly incompatible with democracy is a governing class, even a meritocracy. The Chinese literati belong as servants of an emperor not as the differentiated rulers of a free people. But public managers are in short supply and the modern state, democratic or otherwise, is going to need them in increasing numbers. As Selma Mushkin has pointed out, in the last three years forty percent of the new jobs were in the public sector. The area requiring administrative policy formation by public officials is rapidly expanding. With mechanized and automated industry following agriculture in the decline of its manpower needs the public sector is a likely candidate to carry a sharply increasing role in a full employment society.

## A Political Mirror Image

All this means unless extraordinary measures are taken to restrain the growth of the public sector of our mixed economy that we shall be no longer able to treat the management of the management of our bureaucracy as a minor task. If we cannot in any exclusive way depend on the legislature or the political executive to insure responsible performance, and it is highly doubtful that we can, other means must be sought to keep the growing power of public managers subservient to the purposes of the general public. Problems that beset the socialist camp, problems that we but tasted in World War II experience, seem fated to perplex us. Paradoxically, our experience with the management of the management of large business bureaucracies offers leads that the dogmas of the communists have only recently permitted them to examine. The interest of the Yugoslavs in analogues to the market mechanism as means to control bureaucratic behavior is an indication of a direction our own research may shortly need to explore.

## In Education, the Knell of Scientism—

The problem of the education of public administrators has been clouded by the misconception that only scientific knowledge constituted reliably useful instruction. Since it is generally agreed that politics is not a science there is considerable doubt as to what should be taught to give the administrator politician, the policy generalist, his appropriate expertise. If policy development is the primary task to be performed the subject clearly involves not only scientific questions of technical feasibility, but equally and perhaps more the question of valuation. The administrator must face the serious problems of choice, for there is no scientific escape hatch into value neutrality. The public's interest in the education of the administrator politician is vastly more in his value orientation than in the bits of social science knowledge he may attain. Even such scientific knowledge as the administrator may call from the odd assortment now available depends on his capacity imaginatively to make use of it in the concrete and more or less unique situations that confront him. As Clausewitz remarked, everything depends on the situation.

*Public administrators are a sizeable and increasing part of the governing class of this republic; they are our appointed politicians and the nature of their education is of major import to the future functioning of our institutions.* We can no longer confront the formation of their values with the fiction that they are neutral instruments to be exclusively directed by elected politicians. This is not a case of civilian control of the military, though that problem is far from solved. There seems little room for doubt that the public does not wish, if indeed it could have, a neutral civil service, nor do those aspiring to public management wish to assume a merely instrumental role. Given this as the case, we need a theory that recognizes the policy role of public managers and gives it the legitimacy it now lacks. Such a theory might give us clues as to the kind of education that could build in the value orientation that would restrain and direct the imagination of public managers along lines approved by our political philosophy. The present conflict between theory and practice provokes a dangerous cynicism, a value neutral escapism or a mealy mouthed or unconscious hypocrisy.

The public attractiveness of the city manager as politician for hire lies in his association with a profession possessing built in values that give his performance some degree of predictability. Far more than his expertise, this presumed value orientation appeals to at least those segments of the public for whom it has meaning. The built in self control of professional indoctrination, the institutional control of membership in a profession that constitutes a concerned public, and the experience of career lines that bring together goal achievement and professional performance provide devices for the attainment of important public purposes. They do not replace but they add importantly to the democratic elective model of how to achieve the public interest.

Concern with means to make "the public interest" a meaningful conception for public decision making expresses the felt need for a value orientation that gets beyond the ejaculatory emptiness of logical positivism. Growing consciousness of the problems of conflict of interest—consciousness that itself speaks for a marked advance in public sensitivity—mark a realization of the primary importance of ethics for the realm of administration. Indeed the cognate problem of corruption goes to the heart of value orientations in public life. The human actions manifested in these problems can be studied and need to be. There is clearly great need for a sociology of corruption. But science can only make partial contribution to the difficulty. For the solution lies in the development of value orientations and roles that themselves have no scientific warrant. Fundamentally we are concerned with operative political philosophy a species of moral architecture in which men can live and move and whose very structure supports and directs the ethical imagination. Research into this is a far cry from the cross sectional sample survey but it can well make use of it. It is no obscurantism to say that scientific enquiry is not a substitute for moral construction. Men need purpose as well as analysis.

### Case, Cross-Cultural, and Other Studies

The complex nature of policy formation with its many facets of values, personalities, pressures, institutions, information, information lack, misinformation and the general deficiency of tested applicable social science makes the vicarious experience of case studies of the greatest value to those who expect to be in the thick of it themselves or those who wish to think realistically about it. Case studies have frequently been attacked as tales with a supposed moral which the authors refuse to draw. If they have a moral it is asserted why not out with it? If not, of what use are they? This is faintly reminiscent of the Mohammedan Emir who asked, concerning the library of Alexandria, whether the books in it taught anything contrary to the Koran. If so, the library was noxious; if not it was superfluous. On either finding burn the library. The Koran of scientism is not quite so demanding. The cases have many morals. As vicarious experience they give the next best thing to first hand. As pieces of administrative ethnography they serve to edit theory. They indicate a multitude of things to which one needs sensitizing. They even in rare instances show how someone has taken the abstractions of social science from the laboratory and made concrete use of them in the real world of multiple unknown and unmeasured variables.

Cross cultural studies of administration have done or perhaps more accurately stated can do as much for the study of administration as they have for social psychology and psychology. Where we are inclined to frame sentences of the character of all men we learn to say some men and under specifiable conditions. Our involvement in the underdeveloped countries has forced an appreciation of the culture bound nature of administration upon us. We learn that it may be easier to transfer a jeep, nylons or Coca Cola than bureaucratic institutions. In learning this abroad we acquire perspectives on our own administrative subcultures.

Administrative history provides wide ranges of experience that underline the variety of ways men have had for doing things. The encounter of Pyrrhus' streamlined Hellenistic monarchy with the seemingly fantastically structured Roman Republic must give the orthodox O and M man qualms as to the universality of his dearest maxims. Nearer at hand in time the English municipality with its clerk and its seemingly cumbrous committees defies the model charter and yet produces its claimed fruits. We are hicks in time and space and prisoners of our own parochialism. Fortunately we can, and are being forced to learn.

There is much obscurantism and patent medicine hucksterism in the modish scientism that offers large promissory notes on an unceratin future. But equally there is a fatalistic defeatism of complacency in those who think science has little or no role in the study of public administration.

Already March and Simon and Blau and Scott have provided useful handbooks of the state of our knowledge about administrative behavior and formal organizations. As the authors are the first to point out, tested knowledge is far less than one would like. But helpful bits and pieces do appear. What seems reasonably clear is that most of the scientific work will be done in the study of comparative administration. Here, as in the more inclusive field of comparative government, is the best chance for the development of generalizing theory. Studies of administrative institutions in particular countries provide the field anthropology for determining the scope and limits of theory. Beyond this students of public administration will find their interest join those of sociologists in the study of formal organizations and social psychologists in that of the group and individual behavior as it relates to organizations. Despite the limited achievements of social science there are now enough and the promise of more to make the student and practitioner of administration aware of the contribution social science can make. An awareness of this, if it is realistic, leads to a realization that science can assist the man of action to solve his problems. Yet there are few problems for which it alone provides solutions.

## Developing Unconventional Wisdom

Public administration is inevitably and deeply involved in the articulation of needs, the statement of problems and the formulation of policy alternatives. In these tasks it is concerned with equipping its practitioners to govern wisely. Wisdom is frequently a matter of scorn for those who contrast it with the certainties of mathematics and the tested propositions of experimental science. Accordingly, its existence is either denied or at least regarded as intuitive knowledge, which may be correct but is impossible to teach. There is certainly abundant reason for skepticism concerning the claims to wisdom of those who resist public verifiability. And yet one does not for this reason reject all psychiatry.

As a clinical and applied science, indeed as an art, public administration has an affinity to the situation of the psychiatrist. Each situation is in some respect unique, and must be dealt with on its own terms. Hopefully, the recurrent elements can be isolated and brought under control, and bit by bit the intuitive yield ever larger areas to the tested uniformities of a publicly verifiable science. But always beyond the elements of the administrative situation that can be clarified by scientific inquiry lie the policy problems that can only be resolved in terms of a consciously held and critically examined political philosophy. Here we are indeed deficient. Though we have paid lip service to the importance of such a philosophy, we have really doubted that reason has a meaningful research role in its development and criticism.

ROGER W. JONES

## Developments in Government Manpower: A Federal Perspective

ROGER JONES was a principal force behind federal executive workforce developments for over two decades, particularly from the period of his service in 1959-61 as Chairman of the U.S. Civil Service Commission. He had entered federal service in 1933 with the Central Statistical Board, and he first went to the U.S. Bureau of the Budget in 1939. He returned there in 1962 after distinguished service in a variety of executive positions and, when this article was published, he was special assistant to the director. He was later assistant director of the Office of Management and Budget, 1969-71, and he remained there as a consultant until retirement in 1975 after 42 years of federal service. His interest in federal executive development continued thereafter in attention to such activities as the Federal Executive Institute.

In this article, Roger Jones took note of several important developments, including the creation in 1967 of the Bureau of Executive Manpower in the U.S. Civil Service Commission (later the OPM Executive Personnel and Management Development Group). This article contained analyses of many issues which are omitted from this version. Throughout, the principal focus was on essential linkages between training and quality career service for democratic government.

ANY EXAMINATION of what has happened in recent years to government manpower has to start with the Government Employees Training Act of 1958. Signed by the President on July 7, 1958, that Act became a benchmark of indisputable validity almost at once. In spirit and philosophy, it has provided a point of departure for significant manpower developments of serveral kinds, and they are not so unrelated as they may seem. Of course, everything did not fall neatly into place upon passage of the Act, but constructive movement cannot be denied.

In less than nine years, the concepts, principles, and stated purposes of the Training Act have pointed a sternly critical finger at deficiencies in: (1) manpower planning; (2) career development, with particular reference to executive training; (3) employee mobility; (4) analysis of losses and turnover; (5) pay and fringe benefits; (6) labor-management relations; (7) use of modern technology in personnel administration; (8) attitudes toward, and knowledge of, contributions which the social sciences can make to personnel administration; (9) cooperation among governments at all levels and academic institutions in defining and filling requirements for new kinds of government personnel; and (10) acceptance of Federal responsibility for trying to alleviate at least part of the crisis in intergovernmental manpower matters. A retrospective look indicates that the Federal government as a whole may have come further than many agencies realize in facing up to manpower problems—but not as far as the agencies can with the right combinations of use of existing authorities.

## Manpower Planning and Career Development

Whatever the judgments of hindsight about timid acceptance of responsibility to make quick and full use of the 1958 Training Act, the Act and its implementing Executive Order (No. 10800, issued January 15, 1959) did have one immediate consequence. Manpower planning and career development became respectable concerns—not simply of personnel officers but at the highest levels of program management and policy formulation. It was a sobering experience to many at the top to discover some of the bleaker aspects of the Federal manpower outlook, of which four deserve mention.

1. The Federal government has to compete in the marketplace to fill its manpower needs. It can no longer spend time in leisurely contemplation of ways to limit eligibility for appointment. Nor can agencies delay appointment decisions for long periods of time. Young people are not flocking to the flag of the career civil service, but they will choose government careers if: recruiting and examining are streamlined and made positive; employment offers are backed up by sensible inducements, including clear statements of duties and firm commitments that demonstrated ability will be accompanied by promotion; and mobility is not frowned upon.

2. Death, eligibility for retirement, and resignations because of attractive outsider offers—all have been taking heavy toll in the "Great Depression" generation of young competence, which entered Federal service between 1933 and 1937.

3. There is insufficient depth in replacement ranks because too little training has been done, and the effect of limited high-quality intake of college graduates during World War II (1941-45) and the Korean War (1950-54) was underestimated.

4. There has been so much pressure *to do*, for so long, that structured, planned career development and management of middle and higher-level personnel in the civilian agencies have been badly neglected.

It is no wonder, then, that the Brookings Institution's announcement in 1958 of a modest conference program for Federal executives met with wide acclaim. The program was expected to perform miracles, and it did, both in setting the stage for use of Training Act authorities and in proving the value of getting Federal executives to rub elbows and ideas in an off-the-job environment. Brookings deserves much credit for stepping up Federal awareness that executives do not just happen and that Federal program managers can profit from knowing more than how to tend their own small garden patches of activity.

The net result of the first three years of ferment about the possibilities of the Training Act was not only to make manpower planning and development respectable enterprises but, equally important, to give impetus, first, to the Civil Service Commission to shake up old ways of doing business and, second, to agency executives to get themselves into the personnel business.

The 1959, 1960, and 1961 annual reports of the Civil Service Commission, muted and low key though they were, contained flashes of small and distant lightning which showed how badly the parched fields of manpower needed the steady downpour to come.

For example, in 1959, special efforts were begun to attract scientists and engineers, to select persons with research skills needed in Federal laboratories, to train Federal employees for space programs, to recruit superior college graduates, and to put merit promotions on a firm basis. In 1960, a greatly increased effort was made in the area of management and executive development programs; in addition, the Commission established an intern program in management applications of computers. In 1961, agencies identified 11,490 positions as targets for exectuive development programs and forecast replacement needs. They also increased executive training available through their own agencies or at outside institutions. The Civil Service Commission began a study to determine successful career development methods and to give them continuing evaluation.

The small specifics of the years 1959-61 have been extended into developments of larger scope. Perhaps as many as twenty departments and agencies have formalized their manpower planning activities and in many cases have reinforced manpower planning with career development programs, either within the agency itself or by collaboration in interagency training programs.

In addition to extending its series of institutes for specialized training, the Civil Service Commission now has two Executive Seminar Centers for short-course, midcareer training, one at the U.S. Merchant Marine Academy at Kings Point, New York, and the second at Berkeley, California. Demand for spaces for the forthcoming year already far outruns the capacity of the two Centers.

Almost ten years of discussion about the need for some kind of high-level civilian staff college have culminated in action. Within the last few weeks the President, acting on a recommendation of his Task Force on Career Advancement, has directed the Chairman of the Civil Service Commission "to establish a center for advanced study for executives in the upper echelons of the Civil Service." The program at the center will emphasize the major problems facing our society and the government's response to them.

Overall, interagency training has grown from opportunities for a few thousand employees in 1959 to 40,000 persons receiving some form of such training in 1964, and 65,000 in 1966. Something over 2,000 interagency courses will be available in this fiscal year of 1967.

Also worthy of note are a number of developments in training activities within specific agencies. The Internal Revenue Service's Executive Selection and Development Program has been so successful that of its 111 graduates, 2 are now regional commissioners, 11 are assistant regional commissioners, 29 are district directors, 37 are assistant district directors, and 1 is service center director.

The Federal Aviation Administration has begun a new long-term training program to develop air controllers. The program of the Foreign Service Institute has been extensively revised. The Department of Defense is in the process of establishing a Career Executive Institute for its civilian personnel. The Post Office Department has requested funds to start a Postal Management Academy. Similarly, the experience gained under the Brookings Conference Programs, the National Institute of Public Affairs Fellowships, and the Princeton Fellows Program is leading to growing use of the Training Act authorities by the agencies at a growing number of colleges and univesities.

The issuance of Executive Order 11348 on April 20, 1967, changes the report of the Presidential Task Force on Career Advancement from a handbook of the desirable to an action program. (The order revokes Executive Order 10800 of January 15, 1959, referred to earlier.) The clear statements of responsibilities vested in the Civil Service Commission and in the agencies and their heads give a clear focus of action for the years ahead.

However, if the Civil Service Commission and the agencies are to avoid a start-and-stop approach to building the fully cooperative structure required by the new Executive order, four undertakings appear to be the most needed next steps:

1. Establishment of an effective and continuing system for *evaluating*: agency manpower and career development programs, agency and interagency training efforts, and the special competence of particular colleges and universities to provide curricula for specific governmental manpower training and education.

2. Early decision to define and delimit the kinds of training which can best be undertaken within the Federal government to meet its own needs and related needs of State and local governments.

3. Determination of academic capability and willingness to undertake short-term, specialized training as opposed to longer-term "horizon-broadening" education.

4. Development of a hard-core catalog of management skills needed by career executives to improve their performance.

While Federal agencies could effectively use some additional money to accelerate the progress of manpower planning and career development systems, it is just as well that they have been cautious about pressing their demands too vigorously. Development of a program and a philosophy which are not flamboyant, and do not require large infusions of new money, requires an orderly buildup. It appears that "lack of money" has been an excuse rather than a reason for the failure of some agencies to move toward more adequate manpower planning and career development programs. More money, however, clearly is needed for outside training in academic institutions. And it should be accompanied by conviction that training is a component of all personal services appropriations.

### Employee Mobility and Analysis of Losses and Turnover

The list of occupations in the Federal government has increased rapidly in the last decade as government programs have been extended into new fields. The need for most effective use both of the specialist and of the more generally trained executive or program manager also has become more pronounced. Figures supplied to the Task Force on Career Development indicate that specialists now make up 27 percent of Federal employment, or some 761,000 persons. The report estimates that there will be need for an additional 225,000 employees in professional, administrative, and technical occupations in the decade immediately ahead, and that the gross turnover figure will be in the neighborhood of 675,000. In other words, 900,000 of a total employment estimated at 985,000 by 1975 will represent either new positions or turnover.

In some rapidly developing specialties, the percentage increase in employment will be very large. For the computer occupations, the Bureau of Labor Statistics forecasts a 74 percent increase between 1965 and 1975; a 44 percent increase for engineers; and a 36 percent increase for chemists.

If the Federal government has to recruit 90,000 professional, administrative, and technical employees annually, it must develop more sophisticated means of analyzing turnover and sharing manpower shortages. The number of shortage occupations in American life shows no sign of decreasing, but government programs requiring shortage skills show every sign of increasing. These trends, when complicated by rapidly changing methods, technology, and content of government programs, point to needs of crisis dimensions for maximum deployment of skills where they are most needed. In other words, employee mobility (once looked upon with some disfavor) has become a requisite characteristic of Federal careers.

To meet these two needs, the Civil Service Commission has taken two important steps: creation of a Bureau of Executive Manpower and central compilation (to complement agency efforts) of an annual Federal Workforce Outlook. This publication analyzes the structure of the workforce and makes employment projections for five years ahead.

The Bureau of Executive Manpower has as its charter the development and administration of the Executive Assignment System. Due to come into full operation later this year, the System is designed to bring modern manpower management techniques to the task of finding and using the best possible talent in key executive posts in the civil service. The major components of the System will be a servicewide talent bank, reinforced by flexible recruitment of quality talent from outside the government. To meet rapidly changing technological and program needs, agencies and the Civil Service Commission will continuously relate executive manpower and organizational structure to mission requirements. A primary goal is the development of a top staff ready for assignment where needed and committed to the concept of response to overall government needs, rather than to entrenchment in a single agency or an individual program.

The new Bureau will do well, indeed, if it can devise a rational and effective system for handling a total universe of 8,750 top-level positions—so-called "supergrades" and their equivalents. Mobility, however, must begin at lower levels. The agencies, themselves, must undertake responsibility for developing the organization and procedures for sharing shortages and making best assignments of shortage skill personnel who are scattered through another 50-55 thousand positions in the next lower grades. They must also be kept fully abreast of what is happening to the incumbents of these positions in their own and related agencies. It is this level of Federal employees on whom heavy leadership responsibilities will soon fall, and they must be ready to move up. The management of this resource will require a more imaginative approach to interagency training than agencies so far have devised.

## Labor-Management Relations

The period 1961-66 ushered in a new era in employee-management cooperation in the Federal government. The report of a special Task Force designated by President Kennedy to advise him on employee-management relations in the Federal service led to the issuance, on January 16, 1962, of Executive Orders 10987 and 10988. These orders provided for:

- A more uniform system of appeals within agencies and extension to non-veteran employees of rights given to veterans.
- Recognition of the rights of employees to join or refrain from joining employee organizations.
- Three forms of recognition for employee organizations—informal, formal, and exclusive.
- Negotiations with organizations granted exclusive recognition of appropriate written agreements on matters of personnel policy and working conditions.
- Adoption of advisory arbitration of grievances.

By the end of calendar year 1966, exclusive representation agreements covered 1,054,000 employees, as compared with 19,000 in 1961. There had been 598 negotiated agreements by the end of 1966, as compared with 26 in 1961. Formal and informal recognition also was extensively used. Relationships between unions and agency management—particularly at the local installation level—showed marked improvement in communication with employees and in practices relating to safety, tours of duty, health and working conditions, and the scheduling of leave and overtime. While there have been some disputes, charges of unfair practice, and other unsatisfactory situations, the labor-management relations program is developing with tolerance, understanding, and resolution to make it a success. The need for revision of Executive Order 10988 is undergoing serious study.

The program has also produced much valuable information which augurs well for better training programs for rank and file employees and for more attention to opportunities to advance, with proper training, from the skilled crafts into the ranks of the technical specialists. The government's need for technicians possessing greater knowledge of professional and scientific methodology is increasing rapidly.

The Task Force on Career Advancement has recommended that the heads of agencies establish systems whereby:

> ... opportunities for upgrading to technician jobs are effectively communicated to employees and to employee organizations; those who express interest are ranked as to their potential for such assignments, and the best of these are trained for technical positions.

Here again, there can be little doubt that agencies will respond affirmatively by using Training Act authorities to unite technicians and professionals in a more effective manpower management system.

## Intergovernmental Personnel Matters

The Federal government must lead the procession in finding effective and constitutional means for abandoning sporadic and less than full use of the combined powers vested in Federal, State, and local governments. Congressional grant of broad authority to deal with the large complexities of our time reflects public concern about the growing interdependence of every segment of our society. It does not mean the dissolution of State and local governments, but opportunity to advance into partnership with the Federal government in solving problems which neither they nor their people can solve for themselves. Clearly the need is for government employees who are trained to be public affairs activists.

The examination which academic institutions are making of their curricula and teaching methods and which government agencies are making of their current and future manapower requirements is as significant a development as any which has taken place in government manpower in the last decade.

Belatedly, but not reluctantly, the Federal government has recognized that it must help to alleviate the manpower crisis facing State and local governments. In response to advice and views obtained from many sources inside and outside the Federal structure, President Johnson has recommended enactment by Congress of two bills designed to assist in upgrading and training State and local governmental personnel. The emphasis of the first bill is of two kinds:

- To improve the capability of administrative, professional, and technical personnel who handle over $17 billion of Federal appropriations for grant-in-aid programs and to promote merit system standards.
- To bring about an effective partnership between the Federal government and State and municipal governments in recruiting, examining, and exchanging personnel between levels of government.

Separate emphasis is given in the second bill to provision of financial assistance to students who plan public service careers and to colleges and universities for improvement of all kinds of public service education.

## Conclusion

America has the right to expect high quality in the men and women who carry on the public's business. And those who choose either careers or limited tours of duty in public service have the right to expect that they will not have to make undue sacrifices for their choice—whether in pay, supplemental benefits, mobility, opportunities to improve their skills, effective use of their talents, or willingness to accept responsibility for their actions.

Although anti-intellectualism has sometimes seemed to dominate the American political scene, there appears to be solid evidence that it does not now control personnel policy. Federal manpower developments in the last nine years point to acceptance of public service as a demanding calling, and public administration as a professional way of life.

JOHN W. MACY, JR.

# Executive Preparation For Continuing Change

THIS ARTICLE was adapted from John Macy's address, as chairman of the U.S. Civil Service Commission, at the dedication of the Federal Executive Institute (FEI) in Charlottesville, Virginia, on October 13, 1968. The FEI came into being as a result of efforts begun much earlier by such career/political executives as Roger Jones and John Macy and by such scholar/practitioners as Marshall Dimock and John Corson, whose articles are included earlier in this collection.

It was no accident that the Institute was located in Charlottesville, near the University of Virginia, and yet not far from the Nation's Capital. John Macy's article conveys much of the reasoning that, from its beginning, connected FEI's functions to the deep currents of America's heritage of constitutional democracy.

IN A LETTER to John Adams, Thomas Jefferson said:

> There is a natural aristocracy among men. The grounds of this are virtue and talents.... There is also an artificial aristocracy, founded on wealth and birth, without either virtue or talents; for with these it would belong to the first class. The natural aristocracy I consider as the most precious gift of nature, for the institution, the trusts, and government of society. And indeed, it would have been inconsistent in creation to have formed man in the social state, and not to have provided virtue and wisdom enough to manage the concerns of the society. May we not even say, that that form of government is the best, which provides the most effectually for a pure selection of these natural aristoi into the office of government?

Today, in our new Executive Assignment System, we have endeavored to design a system "for a pure selection of these natural aristoi"—people of virtue and talent—"into the offices of government."

## A World with Rapid Change

I need not draw the contrasts in change between Jefferson's day and our own. You are all experts on today's supersonic rate of change. You have furthered the collapse of space and time. You seek the measure of revolutionary change in our social and economic environment.

A world without change would be dismal and untenable to the modern mind. A world with rapid change—the kind of world we know today—is certainly exciting, but it is also frightening, especially to those who find themselves outstripped by a psychedelic cyclone of events swirling around them.

I do believe that in many areas of our national endeavors the best that is being done to meet the hard challenge of change is being done by the federal executive and professional—that thin but talented layer that spreads across the top of government.

Through their ideas, professional skills, and experience flow the intellectual resources from which many of the new policies relating to change can be generated. This resource is drawn upon by the Chief Executive and the Congress in their formulation and articulation of ultimate policy direction for our nation.

To these talented men and women, the challenge of change is that of translating new public policies into efficient programs that produce desired results. This is simple, relatively speaking, when the desired result is simple—such as a new highway—but it gets exceedingly complex when the desired result has to be achieved through technology that itself must be advanced inch-by-inch along with program implementation.

More and more, the dynamics of public policy are meshed with technology that only *promises*—rather than guarantees—to deliver the goods. During this decade we have witnessed a new phenomenon in public policy formulation: that of policy anticipating technological breakthroughs that are *expected* but have not *occurred*.

When we made a national commitment to land on the moon by the end of this decade, we did not have a rocket ready and waiting. In fact, we hardly knew what kind of rocket we would need. And certainly we did not know what our flight path to the moon would be. The policy—the commitment—came first, based only on the promise of a technology that could *probably* be made to produce the desired result.

## Policy of Forced Change

When policy precedes enabling technology, the manager has to exhaust all resources to fill in the gap. He has to keep the technological fires lit, so that spin-off sparks can quickly light other fires. He has to choose between imperfect alternatives when no computer and no operations research model can point the way to guaranteed success. In short, it is up to him to *program*—and to overcome—the technological lag. In closing that gap he meets one of his most difficult challenges.

Today's executive is struggling to meet the challenge of improving the quality of life; of assuring equality and justice; of cleaning up our air, rivers, and streams; of rebuilding our urban cores; seeking a cancer cure; controlling our nation's airways; harnessing the atom's energy; eliminating poverty and unemployment; and he is engaged in a host of other pursuits from a base of knowledge that is developing rapidly and imperfectly.

Tomorrow . . . will be even more challenging.

The whole world spins today in a whirlwind of change, but somehow, I believe, the world of tomorrow—five, ten, twenty years from now—will be changed to a degree that we may think impossible today. Let us keep in mind that the year 2000 is only a generation away.

The federal executive—the manager of much of today's change—will not only be the manager of more than his full share tomorrow—he will be the developer of much of it.

### Manager of the Future

But what of the manager himself? The executive? Will *he* be different? Will *he* have to change—or be changed? The answer, of course, is an obvious "yes." Certainly he will be different.

Let me touch on ten ways in which I believe he will be different.

1. He will be more broadly educated. Instead of being well-versed in *one* primary discipline and conversant in one or two secondary ones, he may have to be the master of *two* or *three* primary disciplines and conversant in several others.

Some of today's executives and professionals are already hybridized by program need and individual preparation. *Most* of tomorrow's will be.

In addition to being more broadly educated, tomorrow's executive will be more *continually* educated. The Federal Executive Institute will provide some of this continuing education for those of highest leadership responsibility. But the universities and other centers of knowledge must be our partners in this quest of learning. It may well be, as Warren Bennis says in his new book, *The Temporary Society,* that "a dropout should be redefined to mean anyone who hasn't returned to school."

2. Tomorrow's executive will be far more mobile. Less and less will he rise—a career rung at a time—on the ladder of his own organization. He may spend portions of his career in state and local governments, in universities, foundations, research centers, businesses, and industries. In short, he will be moved by a rising trend, already advancing toward us, known as *executive interchange.* Already we see the joining of forces, the joining of heads and hands, between the federal government and state and local governments—a joining that is not a mere gesture of friendship and good will, but rather mutual cooperation, a sharing of resources, born of necessity.

He has fostered the beginnings of a new era in intergovernmental cooperation— a mutual effort to join forces and share resources in solving our common problems.

Such cooperation is already a fact in some areas, in some programs—and I believe it will expand greatly in the next few years and will be highly causative in increasing the mobility of the federal executive.

3. He may lose much of his current identity as a federal executive. We may well borrow from the title of CPA and designate tomorrow's executive a CPE—Certified Public Executive. Though federally based, he will be trained and conditioned to serve where needed.

4. Tomorrow's executive may be *less* committed to his parent organization and *less* committed to specific programs *and* their own special methodologies. But, he will be *more* committed to a specific public policy, regardless of where he may be working at any given time, in the interests of carrying out that policy.

5. He will *identify more* with his constituency—the people to be served by his programs. In spending part of his career at the local level, he will see that the people as well as program results are highly visible.

Roger Jones, writing recently about the changing role of the federal career executive, said very simply but very pointedly: "The Federal career executive should be just as much a representative of the people as a legislator." Tomorrow, perhaps, he will be.

6. He will have new and sharpened tools with which to work. He will be more facile with systems analysis, program evaluation, manpower planning, operations research techniques, computer programming, cost effectiveness, and PPBS. And, of course, there will be *new* tools as yet unknown to us.

7. He will be more carefully—even scientifically—selected for training, assignment, and reassignment.

The new Executive Assignment System ... has already told us something we never knew before: what kind of executive talent we already have. This is only the beginning of a system that promises to revolutionize executive manpower programs.

This System is our best hope for solving the mushrooming problem of providing capable executives for changing programs in a new era of public management and intergovernmental cooperation.

It will form an operating base on which we can build executive personnel programs. These new programs will have a marked effect on all personnel operations down to the lowest level.

Already we have hitched computers to the star of executive search, selection, education, training, and assignment. This has triggered new program goals in identifying what tomorrow's executive must be and which of today's executives and professionals have the best foundation on which to build through advanced training and education.

8. Tomorrow's top career official will have greatly expanded career opportunities. There will be great demand for leadership in all of our changing institutions, both public and private. Men and women trained in a variety of federal positions of increasing responsibility will be in demand to play leadership roles in many theatres of American life—in business and labor, in education, and in the professions.

Tomorrow's executive will most certainly find abundant opportunities in the public service at the highest levels of government. A principal source of future presidential appointees will be the top career element in the Executive Branch.

9. Tomorrow's executive will have greater recognition and prestige. He will, especially through interchange, become better known and better appreciated throughout the nation.

10. The executive and professional of tomorrow will discover and enjoy many new personal interests and satisfactions. Freed of his old-style commitments and career boundaries—and projected into new arenas of endeavor—he will meet many more interesting and stimulating people. This will do more than enlarge his circle of friends and professional associates. It will enlarge his *thinking* and his own interests and satisfactions in what he and others are doing for the benefit of mankind. He will find new excitements, new challenges, and new rewards.

And with these elements of change must be preserved and nurtured a sense of individual dignity and creativity for each man or woman who accepts public responsibility of such great magnitude.

This is a mission worthy of the Jeffersonian tradition and the challenge of tomorrow's world. May what we start here today match that tradition and challenge in both "the promotion of the general welfare" and "the improvement of the quality of American life."

KEITH F. MULROONEY

## Can City Managers Deal Effectively with Major Social Problems?

THIS WAS the lead piece of a six-article symposium published on "The American City Manager: An Urban Administrator in a Complex and Evolving Situation." Keith Mulrooney, the symposium editor, was then city manager of Claremont, California, and he had served as the president of the Los Angeles ASPA Chapter. He was later city manager of Alexandria, Virginia, and then ASPA executive director.

This article focused on changing urban social problems of the 1960s and 1970s and capacities of council-member governments generally and city managers particularly to handle them. Other articles in the symposium are briefly noted in the last part of this article.

AT 2:10 P.M. ON May 7, 1970 (two months after the burning of the Isla Vista Branch of the Bank of America), I stood feet planted in the open doorway of the Yale Avenue Branch of the Bank of America in Claremont, California, and watched as 1,000 singing college protest marchers with picket signs hoisted aloft, red headbands, and Viet Cong flags rounded the corner of Harrison Avenue, about 15 abreast, proceeded forward down Yale, arms linked, and closed up their ranks about 20 feet away while their leader began an anti-Cambodia, anti-Bank of America speech. I could see our police chief, in plain clothes, gauging the mood of the crowd from across the street. I knew our mayor was somewhere in the tight mass of emotion-charged young people, trying to reduce tensions. About 25 SDS types stood immediately in front of me, urging the marchers to enter the bank. Would the protesters maintain order, or would they enter the bank?

Confronting antiwar demonstrators, holding council meetings in Chicano houses, sitting with hippies in a park discussing last week's narcotics bust, bargaining against a labor pro, or contracting with the Black Students Union to conduct reading improvement programs for low-achieving black school children ... all seem a little far removed from POSDCORB, from budget calendars and techniques of municipal purchasing, or from Public Administration 501. They illustrate new challenges facing the city manager and changes coming over the city manager profession. They also illustrate the need for this symposium and for fresh research about urban administrators. Events in the field have rather seriously outrun the literature. Managers, for their part, may need some new literature, some new models to lean on in this complex and evolving situation. The classical model of the plan may still be alive and well somewhere, but it doesn't provide an adequate theory to cover what is actually happening today in many cities under the plan, either in the operation of the municipal organization or the functioning of the city manager.

## Changes and Challenges

Change abounds. The problems and opportunities of today's city manager are different from those which faced the early managers.[1]

The last *Public Administration Review* symposium on the city manager was published in 1958 and dealt with the questions of leadership and decision making. From 1958 to 1962 the articles on the manager which appeared in *PAR*, for the most part, continued to treat the question of the manager's policy role and his relationship to the city council. Two perhaps prescient exceptions were pieces by John Pfiffner in 1959 and E. L. Sherbenou in 1961. At the close of a book review Pfiffner asked, "What are the value systems of the managers?" Commenting on his own experience in preparing students for city management, Pfiffner closed by saying, "Nevertheless, one is occasionally haunted with the apprehension of having possibly failed in the inculcation of a broad philosophy in which social values will have counterpoised those of the counting house."[2]

Reporting on his study of the relationship of the council-manager plan to social class and participation, Sherbenou said, "This situation as a whole strongly suggests that those citizen groups which have an interest in the council-manager plan especially need to study the problem of communication with those members of the community of lower social rank."[3] After Norton Long's essay on "Politicians for Hire" in June 1965, *PAR* carried no articles directly on the council-manager plan (except some retirement reflections) until this issue. Note that all of the above contributions were essentially pre-Watts and Black Panthers, pre-War on Poverty, pre-SDS and Weatherman II (read pre-campus rioting), pre-drug culture, pre-massive concern for ecosystems and pre-COG's and the large-scale federal movement into urban programs. Due to the lapse of time and the major changes which have dominated American life since the last major treatment of the subject in *PAR*, it is time for a new look at the city manager, his problems and prospects.

Cities and city managers are being questioned and challenged...

—by city managers themselves: In the conclusion to his piece for this symposium, Tom Fletcher speaks of the "danger of the managerial bankruptcy that we are facing."

—by the urban management profession: In its statement, *Managing for Social and Economic Opportunity,* adopted in October 1969, the International City Management Association said,

Local government's efforts to assure justice and provide service equally to all citizens have failed too often to serve adequately those whose needs are greatest. The poor, the old, the handicapped, the subjects of ethnic and racial discrimination have often been overlooked by local government. That society as a whole has failed increases the responsibility of the local government management profession to intensify its efforts now to serve them better.[4]

—by the academic sector: Bollens and Ries have claimed that the overriding trend appears to be toward political structures, characterized by conflict, the least congenial environment for council-manager government.[5]

—by men in high places: John Gardner of the Urban Coalition has said, "The plain fact is that most cities are not organized to cope with their problems. Their haphazard growth has brought such rampant administrative disorder that good government is scarcely possible."[6]

—by federal administrators: Thomas Paine, then Administrator of the National Aeronautics and Space Administration, has claimed, "Few cities today have the managerial structure and resources to take early advantage of technical opportunities, much less foresee new possibilities and deliberately bring about needed technical advances applicable to urban systems."[7]

—and by federal commissions: The National Advisory Commission on Civil Disorders (Kerner Commission) asserts that, "City manager government has eliminated an important political link between city government and low-income residents."[8]

## The Plan Is Growing

If one were to judge solely from the growth of the council-manager plan, one could almost afford to ignore such comments. By September 1970, the plan covered the majority of all United States cities over 10,000 in population; in addition, 106 Canadian municipalities and approximately 1,800 European cities use the plan. There were only 388 managers in the nation in 1930; by January 1, 1970, there were 2,132.[9] In 1970, among the 3,192 United States cities over 5,000 population, 47 percaent had the council-manager plan as compared with only 17 percent under this form in 1940. During the same period, the mayor-council plan declined from 62 percent in the same population bracket to less than 51 percent, with minor forms making up the difference. The council-manager plan is now found in all states but Hawaii and Indiana. California, with 303 out of its 404 cities (75 percent) having the plan, leads in total adoptions.

The growth of the council-manager plan continues to be strong and, despite the Bollens-Ries thesis and some of the traditional doubts about the effectiveness of the plan in central cities and large cities, the trends definitely look favorable for its expansion even there. Press accounts of preliminary 1970 census data show Dallas as the eighth largest city in the country (from 14th in 1960) and that San Diego and San Antonio are now both in the top 15. All three are council-manager cities. Since the plan is now in effect in an absolute majority of all municipalities over 10,000 in the United States, if these cities continue to gain population and if they retain the plan, even if no more cities over 500,000 adopt the plan, it is only a matter of time before the plan becomes the major form in most cities over, say, 250,000, and most central cities, except perhaps the largest two dozen cities in the United States. This is true because big cities grow from smaller cities, and most of the latter (over 10,000) are council-manager cities. In other words, most of the newcomers to the ranks of big cities will be council-manager cities unless the cities without the plan get bigger disproportionately faster than the cities with the plan. In addition, most of the big nonmanager cities now have mayor-appointed administrators; the classical model of the strong-mayor plan therefore is changing too. So the growth of the council-manager plan and the central versus suburban city questions are really not the issues.

## . . . but the Problems Remain

Although the council-manager plan continues its healthy growth rate and outwardly gives all the appearances of remaining a provident and robust development in the history of the governance of cities, the fact remains, not surprisingly, that cities and their city managers still have problems. Simply stated, the challenge to the nation's cities is the challenge to city managers. When invited to edit this symposium, I set out to determine how matters currently stand relative to some of the questions and challenges posed above.

Let's reexamine the Kerner Commission statement more closely. President Johnson appointed the Commission in 1967 after the Watts, Newark, and Detroit riots to determine what happened, why it happened, and what could be done to prevent it from happening again. The Commission said,

> Finally, these developments [reasons for the failure of all levels of government to come to grips with the problems of our cities] have coincided with the demise of the historic urban political machines and the growth of the "city manager" concept of government. While this tendency has produced major benefits in terms of honest and efficient administration, it has eliminated an important political link between city government and low income residents.

The Commission went on to recommend: "Effective communication between ghetto residents and local government" and "Improved ability of local government to respond to the needs and problems of ghetto residents."[10]

Query: *Is there anything inherent in the council-manager plan or in city managers themselves which would make the plan or the manager himself constitutionally unsuited to deal effectively with major social problems?*

Query: *Can the manager communicate with and be truly responsive to the needs of minority groups?*

To find the answers to these questions, I asked several city managers, representatives of urban government associations, consultants, and academicians who have concerned themselves at one time or another with developments in the council-manager field. I received a number of written replies from both groups and, in addition, conducted a discussion session with the manager group.

Here's what they said. To the question about the manager's ability to deal effectively with major social problems, almost all the respondents except John Bollens of UCLA and Frank Sherwood of the Federal Executive Institute seemed to feel there was nothing inherent in the plan or the manager which would make either unsuited to deal effectively with such problems. Bollens did not answer the question directly but referred to his monograph on the city-manager profession quoted above, stating that his replies were contained in that document. Therein, Bollens and Ries describe one category of government which they call "the arbitrator." In this form, they assert, government consumes most of its energies managing the conflict among competing interests. They state that life for the manager is nowhere nearly so hazardous as in the arbitrator city where the manager would have to spend most of his efforts in alliance building and in bargaining among conflicting interests. Bollens and Ries state that the core city in a metropolitan complex is frequently in this category.[11]

Sherwood feels there are constitutional limitations with the plan which severely limit its effectiveness in dealing with social problems. "You just can't have one person pulling all the levers. It's a basic question of organization theory. The classical model of the council-manager plan is a closed-system theory. It is not adaptive. A lot of the issues aren't being addressed." Sherwood goes on to postulate, "The lesson of the Penn Central is going to bring about a lot of changes in organization theory. We can't afford to have the failure of one leader bring down a huge organization. The organization theory for the plan hasn't changed enough; the earlier writings about the concept are anachronistic."

While doubting that there is any inherent difficulty in the council-manager plan regarding the manager's ability to respond to major social problems, Ernest Miller of the University of Washington says, "A little reflection, and the evidence that we do have, seem to me to indicate that the only arena where the manager plan is inappropriate (defective) is where there is a high degree of partisanship or a relatively intense political conflict pattern, where the values and demands of visable and direct *representation* dominate the civic arena." To this extent, Miller appears to line up with Bollens, but the balance of his comments were on the other side of the issue.

On the other hand Charles Adrian at the University of California, Riverside, says, "I would see nothing inherent in the council-manager plan that would make it unsuited to deal with major social problems. What is needed is not a different plan of government, but more representative city councils and managers who have a broader training and understanding of social issues. The former does not seem to be happening very rapidly, but I think the training of managers has changed considerably in the last ten or 15 years." William Cape of the University of Kansas says, "It is significant that in the popular image, the local governments are usually considered incapable of dealing with the major social and economic issues that transcend local governmental boundary lines. The unwillingness, inability, and hands-off attitude of city officials to sponsor many federally aided poverty programs is some indication that the barriers are human ones, not inaction which can be attributed to organizational deterrents."

James Banovetz of Northern Illinois University is very direct in stating, "There is nothing inherent in the council-manager plan which would make a city manager constitutionally unsuited to deal effectively with major social problems. As a matter of fact, we appear to be in the midst of an era of executive government, in which it is the strong executive official who is proving to be most capable of dealing effectively with major public problems. This era of 'executive government' shows no signs of ending, and in fact we may still be in the early stages of this era."

Taking issue with the Kerner report, Edwin O. Stene of the University of Kansas says, "I regard the Kerner Commission statements as a reflection on the experience and traditional outlook of the members themselves. Their references to relative difficulties of council-manager government had no statistical evidence to support them." In support of Stene's charge, it is interesting to note that a study on American civil disorders of 1967 and 1968, published in Urban Data Service, found that there is no relationship between governmental structure and riot occurrence.[12]

Stene continues, "Managers have found it necessary to shift their attention from physical and technical problems to human problems; but they have probably taken up the latter role as well as any other officials. Difficulties that managers may encounter in this area seem to derive from tradition rather than from any constitutional feature inherent with the plan. Politically oriented groups, whether they are minority groups within a city or agencies of national and state governments, tend to think that they must deal with political officials of the city." Stene asserts, "In the face of these problems, city managers appear to have maintained effective roles more consistently than school superintendents."

Lyman Cozad, city manager of Arcadia, California, believes the council-manager plan has good reason to recommend it as a vehicle for dealing with major social problems. He stresses the need for improved communication between the citizen and his local government and cites the City of San Diego where 18 neighborhood groups are actively participating in the specific planning of their neighborhoods. These groups are staffed by the city manager's office and it is the manager who is actively stimulating this approach to problem solving. Miller notes,

"... that over the years the personalities and attitudes of managers, as developed from their family backgrounds, their social classes, their education and training (including the dominant philosophy about the nature of the plan), are probably major factors in explaining a disposition to be more comfortable in handling physical rather than social problems." Randy Harrison of the staff of the League of California Cities and a leader of the New Public Administration Group feels that the managers can perform in the social sector but need to change. He says, "Managers and administrators can be relevant to today's social problems; however, the existing technocratic rationality which produces organization and institutional alienation in the society and provides the ethical value system of executive decision making must be transformed by values of social justice."

### Responsiveness to Minorities

To the question as to the responsiveness of the city manager to the needs of minority groups, most respondents, except Sherwood, felt that city managers in general would be capable of responsiveness in this situation, but that it was an individual matter with the answer depending on a blend of education, experience, and personal philosophy. Sherwood says, "In its classical form, at least, the plan is not responsive. You have just one full-time person brokering the relationship with the environment. People who want to change the sytem can't mobilize the resources. The manager has access to more information and all the levers."

However, Norton Long of the University of Missouri at St. Louis says, "I think there is no doubt that the manager can communicate with and be truly responsive to minority groups. As an alert, well-trained professional, he is better prepared intellectually to deal with the problems than most. His constraints are those of his power base. His membership in a national profession with great career mobility both emancipate him, if he is able, from parochial inhibitions and job security anxieties and give him a wide, enlightened professional reference group to provide him standards of action and critical appreciation. In many ways, the manager, like the professional school superintendent, is both freer and more sensitive than most politicians with respect to minorities."

Adrian, too, seems to feel "... that an intelligent, well-trained manager can probably communicate with and be responsive to minority groups better than can the typical councilman in cities that elect at large. According to Cape, however, "From the minority group point of view, most managers are probably unacceptable since these officials are unable or unwilling to acquiesce for one reason or another in many reasonable requests and demands that are extremely important factors for the minorities."

Cape's analysis of the minority view of the manager seems to harken back to the Bollens and Ries analysis of how lower classes viewed the manager plan in the early decades of the 20th century. These authors said, "Council-manager government may have meant good government to the middle class, but it meant perpetuation of a Brahman dominance to the lower classes."[13] Acknowledging that the antecedents and history of the manager plan have clearly suggested that the role of the manager is that of a "business executive" for the middle-class civic polity and that some might argue that this is an integral part of the plan itself, Miller says, "I tend to feel that this need not be so and that it has more to do with the attitudes of those who have promoted the plan, those who have developed and directed educational training programs for managers, and the ideological preferences of the manager recruits."

A number of managers and professors felt that one of the factors which enhanced the ability of a manager to communicate with minorities was his ability to appoint staff resources. This was a two-way affair. Several people cited the minority staff member's ability to communicate minority viewpoints to the manager. At the same time, the human relations director or other minority staff member may be much more capable of relating to the minorities than can the manager. He needn't appear as an establishment figure, has the time to devote to cultivating his acquaintances and building trust among the minorities, and can even abandon establishment dress patterns if that seems to be important. Sherwood claims, "These are good ideas, but are more like band-aids than the fundamental changes called for by the situation."

Banovetz offers some suggestions to managers facing the future. He advises council-manager communities to move more rapidly: (1) "To follow John Pfiffner's advice and build a staff of social scientists within city hall so that the necessary communication channels can be established which will provide the manager with the kinds of informational and attitudinal inputs and feedbacks needed to make sound policy judgments and recommendations"; and (2) "It means that greater efforts must be made to broaden the base of persons employed by city hall, and particularly, the persons employed as assistants to the manager, to include representatives from low-income groups and persons from those groups who will be deemed by those groups to be viable spokesmen for their point of view." Contrast that with Bollens and Ries: ". . . the more a manager gets involved in matters of representation, responsibility, political participation, and civic education, the less he is able to perform his professional roles."[14]

Adrian goes on to state that, ". . . it is wrong to blame the council-manager approach for the hiatus that exists today in so many places between city hall and the ghettos and barrios. The major cause of this communications gap, I am personally convinced, stems from other mistakes of the Efficiency and Economy movement: in particular, the movement advocated a city council that is much too small in size to provide adequate representation. Its emphasis is upon efficiency and decision making and a desire to have councilmen concentrate on community rather than neighborhood concerns. Similarly, the reform movement, seeking to reclaim city government for the business community from the working class, advocated at-large elections of councilmen. I can think of no other device that could make minority group communication with city hall more a hostage of the whims of the dominant middle class and upper working class."

I also asked my correspondents, "Does the rush toward councils of governments and regional governments indicate that the city manager has failed and will take his place on the shelf with elected chiefs of police?" The answer to this question was a unanimous "no." Long, for instance, says, "It doesn't seem to me that the current interest in councils of governments and regional governments in any way reflects on the city manager but rather on the adequacies of existing governmental territorial competences and the needs to transcend present territorial limitations." Adrian states, "These developments in no way reflect upon the success of the council-manager plan. They are simply efforts to cope with regional problems without destroying local self-government, which the council-manager plan symbolizes in many states...."

Edward Hearle, vice president of Booz • Allen Public Administration Services of Washington, D.C., observes that, "... managers are perhaps inclined to support regional councils of governments because they are management professionals and in tune with the kinds of rationality which regional councils are intended to encourage."

### Needed: New Pioneers

From my admittedly limited sampling, it seems to me that the council-manager plan should be adaptable to dealing with major social problems and that the manager, for the most part, should be able to communicate with and respond to the needs of minority groups. If we are not doing the job today, it may not be the system but the need to take the first step, the need to jump in and get our hands dirty ... to commit major resources."

So far, with a relatively few notable exceptions, we are just talking a good game and patting ourselves on the back that we have recognized the importance of social issues. Now that the people problems have come to the fore and are crying out for our attention, they still have to struggle with the established programs for a piece of the budgetary action and, so far, they are coming out distinctly second best. Go to most any city in the country and try to see what percentage of the budget is spent on working with alienated youth versus the percent spent for fire protection, or contrast the amount spent on problems of racism with the amount spent on collecting garbage. Compare the fiscal effort expended on job training for the hardcore unemployed with that devoted to paving of streets. You'll soon see that the people problems are still the "have-nots" of municipal budgeting. This is not to say that fire protection, garbage collection, and street paving are not provided in response to basic urban problems. They are. But alienated youth, racism, and the hard-core unemployed are basic urban problems, too, and the commitment to solve them is not yet reflected in most municipal budgets. Query: If an item is not included in the budget, is there really a commitment to solve the problem? Of course, a blanket statement is unfair; some cities and some managers have made progress here and there in each of these areas.

There are exceptions, but we need more such exceptions. In fact, what we need right now are some new pioneers. We need pioneers who will make major breakthroughs on the questions of low-income housing in their cities, pioneers who will score lasting victories in manpower training programs for the hard-core unemployed, pioneers who will learn to deal effectively with alienated youth, and pioneers who can reach out to the impoverished barrio or ghetto and make the Chicano and the Black feel that somebody in the establishment really cares. These pioneers will take some big steps forward, experiment, experience failure, but do the new things that will one day become routine for those who follow. They will learn to link the necessary resources with new organizational mechanisms in order to achieve social objectives. Perhaps some of the voluble New Public Administration Group will find their role here.

The International City Management Association has been going through a process of organizational self-renewal the past three years . . . and with considerable success at that. The membership base has been broadened to include significant groups heretofore excluded and to recognize overall management performance of an agency, not just organizational form. Through the vehicles of a new position-taking process and the review of drafts of federal urban action proposals, city managers are gaining a voice in national urban policy formulation and review. The policy paper on managing for social and economic opportunity, the ICMA-sponsored workshop in Kansas City on race relations in 1970, and a proposed policy paper on the governance of neighborhoods are at least good beginnings on the social action front and in improving responsiveness. Now more individual managers must start the process in their own cities and in themselves.

## The City Manager in the 1970 s

Beginning, therefore, with the feeling that change was upon us, that although the plan seemed healthy and growing, there were serious questions and challenges as well as problems and opportunities, that there is a fairly good feeling that managers and the plan should be capable of responding to the major social problems of the future, given the strong desire and the necessary training to do so, I turned to six people (two of them as a team) to ask their view of the city-manager scene at the start of the '70's. Tom Fletcher, city manager of San Jose, California, and formerly deputy mayor of Washington, D.C., starts off by cataloguing the problems, proposing solutions, discussing educational needs for urban management, and affirming the need for change in the profession. Charles Henry, city manager of University City, Missouri, then looks at the roles of the city manager in the 1970's. Professors Robert Boynton and Deil Wright follow with a new analysis of mayor-manager relationships in larger cities and contrast their findings with traditional views of the council-manager plan. Next, Picot Floyd, city manager of Savannah, Georgia, gives his views on how we will staff and organize to solve some of the problems of the decade. Finally, Walt Scheiber of the Washington, D.C., Council of Governments deals with the implications for managers of the growing trend toward COGs and regional governments.

### Plan Has Come a Long Way

Since its earliest beginnings in 1908, the council-manager plan has indeed come a long way.[15] The articles in this symposium indicate that the changes are continuing. Hopefully, an even more effective council-manager plan will emerge as we learn more about managing change and dealing with complexity, for cities will need all the creative leadership they can obtain to solve unsolvable problems and improve the quality of life for all of their residents.

K.F.M.

Claremont, California
September 4, 1970

P.S. The protesters didn't enter the bank or burn it down either.

### Footnotes

1. For a recent review of the changing world of another public executive, see Sidney P. Marland, Jr., "The Changing Nature of the School Superintendency," *Public Administration Review,* Vol. XXX, No. 4 (July/August 1970), pp. 365-367. Marland says, on p. 367, "It is likely that a similar sequence of high expectations and corresponding executive change will modify the counterpart role in all public administration."
2. John M. Pfiffner, "Policy Leadership for What?" *Public Administration Review*, Vol. XIX, No. 2 (Spring 1959), p. 124.
3. Edgar L. Sherbenou, "Class, Participation, and the Council-Manager Plan," *Public Administration Review,* Vol. XXI, (No. 3 (Summer 1961), p. 135.
4. *Managing for Social and Economic Opportunity* (Washington, D.C.: The International City Management Association, October 15, 1969), p. 2.
5. John C. Bollens and John C. Ries, *The City Manager Profession Myths and Realities* (Chicago: Public Administration Service, 1969), p. 33.
6. John W. Gardner, *No Easy Victories* (New York: Harper and Row, Publishers, 1968), p. 23.
7. Thomas O. Paine, "Space Age Management and City Administration," *Public Administration Review,* Vol. XXIX, No. 6 (November/December 1969), p. 657.
8. *Report of the National Adivsory Commission on Civil Disorders* (New York: Bantam Books, 1968), p. 287.
9. This statistic and those which follow in this paragraph were taken or constructed from data appearing in *The Municipal Management Directory 1970* (Washington, D.C.: The International City Management Association, 1970), p. 7; Orin F. Nolting, *Progress and Impact of the Council-Manager Plan* (Chicago: Public Administration Service, 1969), pp. 15-16; Orin F. Nolting, "The City Manager of Tomorrow," *Public Management,* Vol. 50, No. 10 (October 1958) p. 234; and a telephone conversation with the ICMA staff, September 2, 1970.

10. Commission on Civil Disorders, *op. cit.*, pp. 287–288.
11. Bollens and Ries, *op. cit.*, pp. 25 and 28.
12. "The American City and Civil Disorders," *Urban Data Service* (Washington, D.C.: The International City Managers Association, 1969), p. 12.
13. Bollens and Ries, *op. cit.*, p. 9.
14. *Ibid.*, p. 47.
15. For a general review of the historical development of the plan, see Nolting, *Progress and Impact, op. cit.*

LLOYD D. MUSOLF

## Separate Career Executive Systems: Egalitarianism and Neutrality

THE CALIFORNIA Career Executive Assignment (CEA) system was analyzed in this article, with a critique in terms of values of civil service egalitarianism and political neutrality. As originally published, the article also analyzed a then-current Nixon administration proposal for a Federal Executive Service (FES) and compared both the CEA and FES to the Senior Civil Service proposal of 1955.

Professor Musolf, then director of the Institute of Governmental Affairs at the University of California, Davis, served in 1970 on an ASPA blue ribbon task force on the FES. Considerable exchange of ideas occurred there, drawing on California CEA experience, with some continuing impacts on efforts in the federal government to create an executive service corps.

SEPARATE PERSONNEL systems for the higher civil service rest upon a persuasive rationale. Today the vast array of government responsibilities requires an unprecedented level of managerial competence. The diversity of modern government demands managers who are able to move across organizational and functional lines, as well as a variety of professional specialists. This need for increased responsiveness, flexibility, and specialization requires singling out the top rungs of employees for special treatment. This familiar argument is bulwarked with envious comparisons. "Separate systems for executive personnel," a brochure of the California State Personnel Board states, "are the hallmark of many other [i.e., non-American] career public services, and private industry typically applies very different personnel practices to management personnel."[1]

---

The assistance of numerous California state government officials, representatives of the California State Employees' Association, and Seymour S. Berlin, director, Bureau of Executive Manpower, U.S. Civil Service Commission, is hereby gratefully acknowledged. The usual absolution to all save the author for errors and inadequacies applies.

## Career Executive Assignment in California

The California legislature established a separate system for top-ranking executives as a result of the State Personnel Board's initiative. Featuring the effects upon the higher civil service of an increasing number of "exempt" appointments by the Brown Administration, the Board sought to build a backfire with a special personnel system for merit system executives. The decision to use this instrument recognized several facts of life.[2] In the first place, the confining rules of the merit system—veterans' preference, the rule-of-three, tenure—became onerous mainly at executive levels, where loyalty and responsiveness to program changes are essential to democratic government. In addition, by concentrating on the higher civil service and its need for special treatment, the expected storm of opposition from the powerful California State Employees' Association (CSEA) might be weathered. This strategy was successful; an enabling bill was passed and survived determined CSEA challenges to its constitutionality in the courts.

The bill provided for:

1. Creation of a category of the civil service called Career Executive Assignment into which the Board could place high administrative and policy influencing positions as they became vacant.

2. Authorization for the Board to develop a merit system which would best staff and utilize these positions, and which was not bound by the selection, classification, and pay portions of the general civil service law.

3. Nonpunitive removal from a Career Executive Assignment, appealable only if allegedly made for reasons of racial, religious, or political discrimination.

4. Restriction of competition for Career Executive Assignments to permanent civil service employees and authorization for their absolute right of return to their general civil service post if removed.[3]

The rules which the Board hatched on the basis of this legislation had the following features:

1. The classification and pay structure was retained.

2. Selection was to be based on the rule-of-three-categories-of-excellence in which the top category of ten is certified; if there are less than ten names, then all names in the second (and, if necessary, the third) category are certified. (This method was more politically defensible than the rule-of-the-list method, which the Board staff and agency management preferred.)

3. All positions to be included in the system were to be identified immediately, even though general civil service incumbents might occupy them for many years to come.

4. A parallel career executive class was created for every regular civil service class identified as appropriate.[4]

Together the statute and the conservatively drawn regulations constituted a solid craft that appeared capable of steering a cautious course in dangerous waters. Placing merit system individuals in temporary positions answered the cry of political heads for more responsiveness and flexibility from the civil service. At the same time, the puissant state employees' organization could not successfully claim that merit had been ignored or even that the new system created a differentiated rank and pay system.[5] Senior civil servants were reassured by the provision against competition from outsiders for the Career Executive Assignment (CEA) positions and by iron-clad guarantees of return to their merit slots should they be removed. One could easily conclude that it is highly probable that only a plan which simultaneously acknowledged or at least recognized the claims of all these elements stood a chance of being adopted.

There remained the critical question of how well the plan would work in practice. Though experience to date is hardly conclusive, it can be reported around three questions. First, how were Career Executive Assignment appointees to be identified and adequately distinguished from political appointees and the regular civil service? Next, how was the transition to Career Executive Assignments to be accomplished? Finally, did the plan establish a basis for a broader-gauged higher civil service in the State of California?

## Identification

Achieving a definable image for the CEA system has been a challenge which has been only partially met. As noted, the State Personnel Board had proposed Career Executive Assignments in reaction to the threat of increased "exempt" appointments, but, in the view of the California State Employees' Association, the new law would easily lend itself to partisan political purposes. Some of its spokesmen conjured up a vision of competition among candidates on a CEA roster for a reputation as the most active member of the ruling party. The willingness of the legislature to act was taken as confirmation that it saw such a possibility in the statute. The Board, however, believed these fears to be overdrawn, especially in view of California's "good government" tradition and the Board's monitoring capabilities. In the view of one observer at the time, the statute could be read as implicitly distinguishing "between social bias and partisan bias, between enthusiasm for a governmental program and enthusiasm for a political party."[6]

Rather than an excess of partisan turnover, even the most modest projections of removals from Career Executive Assignments have not been met, to the point where one can ask whether the system is achieving the flexibility that was sought. Between 1963, when the statute was enacted, and October 1970, there were nine removals, and the majority of these were unconnected with the transition from the Brown to the Reagan administrations.[7] (It is true that, in anticipation of being removed, some state executives fled to the friendly and more lucrative climes of Washington rather than return to their merit system posts.)

What accounts for this result, which not only confounds the predictions of overly partisan CEA use, but does not appear to match the theory under which the law was sponsored? One factor is the humanitarian reluctance of agency heads to force salary reductions on veteran officials by demoting them to their regular civil service position. In addition, newly appointed agency leaders inevitably must rely upon available expertise to avoid lost motion. Conceivably, the governmental inexperience of some of the appointees of a governor who had never held political office before accentuated the latter factor. In any event, the unusually low number of removals has somewhat reassured the CSEA about the partisanship that the law might engender.

More basically, the low removal rate may relate to the problem of defining what CEA is all about. Thus, one interviewee suggested that appointing authorities have difficulty verbalizing what they are looking for in executive qualities and a similar difficulty in verbalizing why a CEA appointee should be removed. More than one interviewee felt, however, that if Jess Unruh had been able to defeat Governor Ronald Reagan in 1970, CEA removals might have risen sharply. The Reagan administration has used the CEA category for various nonline positions and new positions with a somewhat political tinge. For the present, the stability of CEA positions resembles that for the regular civil service.

Differentiating CEA positions from others was also made more difficult by the lack of a distinction in salaries. Although the State Personnel Board could have established a separate scale, it chose not to in order to increase CEA's political acceptability. The Board has also resisted pressure from the CSEA to identify the cut-off points in salary for CEA positions, reasoning that this was not a valid distinction. Though both of these moves were grounded in realism, they had the effect of muting the Board's own assertions about the distinctiveness and prestige of Career Executive appointments. The effect upon CEA appointees and prospective appointees can be imagined. The State Personnel Board staff continue to toy with the notion of a separate CEA salary scale, but has encountered difficulty in reflecting performance evaluation in salary terms (the identity problem again). Reflecting merit distinctions in salaries would also face CSEA opposition. In any event, a separate scale is probably unlikely unless and until the state government's financial crisis evaporates.

**Transition**

By employing a parallel career executive class for every regular civil service class, a conservative transition to the new system was assured. The decision to proceed slowly was one taken by the Board's executive officer after he had convened an advisory committee to discuss implementation.[8] Though the committee agreed that the new system would hopefully lead to the broadest servicewide development and promotional selection of career executives, the group split on the matter of achieving this aim. One group wished to proceed gradually, incorporating as many established practices as possible; the other group was willing to delay the implementation if necessary in order to achieve an innovative system. The use of parallel classes is one sign that the gradualistic approach won out at the executive officer and Board level.

## Implications

The device of employing parallel classes has some implications that deserve brief discussion. Basically it meant that Career Executive Assignments were shaped in the same mold as existing classes and positions in the higher civil service. A characteristic of the regular civil service classes at the CEA level is that the number is about two-thirds of the number of positions. There are many one-position classes. The duplication of this structure in CEA was something of a paradox, given the emphasis on flexibility and broadened recruitment. The parallel class arrangement, however, had some practical advantages. Some observers think that it helped reduce the chances that CSEA will win a law suit on the charge that Career Executive Assignment constitutes a second merit system in violation of the state constitution. CSEA in turn can appreciate narrow classes because they permit easier surveillance of attempts to bring positions under CEA.

The State Personnel Board has diplomatically touted other advantages. First, parallel classes, it is argued, permit orderly transition. The incumbent of a regular higher civil service position could rest easy in the fact that, though his position had been identified as suitable for Career Executive Assignment, it would only be after his retirement that the position might be filled on that basis. The snail-like progression in CEA appointments as a result of this system can be observed by studying the following presentation of the statistics over time:

### CAREER EXECUTIVE ASSIGNMENT

| Date | Classes | Positions | Appointees |
|---|---|---|---|
| Jan. 1964 | 153 | 218 | — |
| 1965 | 170 | 239 | 29 |
| 1966 | 177 | 248 | 46 |
| 1967 | 190 | 287 | 62 |
| 1968 | 196 | 327 | 107 |
| 1969 | 210 | 353 | 142 |
| June 30, 1970 | 235 | 420 | 225 |

By 1975, it is estimated that 90 percent of the *present* eligible positions will be filled by CEA appointees, but it is highly likely that positions will continue to be added in the intervening years. About 70 percent of the original 218 positions now have CEA incumbents.

The second advantage of parallel classes cited by the State Personnel Board is that they preserve flexibility for recruitment. There is no need to go back to the Board to get authorization for a regular civil service class if recruitment through CEA proves impossible. Furthermore, there is no need to identify a CEA class each time openings occur in the regular civil service.

Recruitment flexibility is not perceived as an unalloyed advantage by CEA types and the employees' organization. If a dual-listed position should be filled under the regular civil service, open recruitment would be employed and an outsider might win a permanent berth. If the CEA system is employed, only an insider is eligible to compete, but he would receive no more salary than the putative outsider and he would receive it for no longer than he held the position. His regular merit slot might have a considerably lower salary. A natural by-product of this arrangement is that CEA appointees strive to move laterally rather than fall back and accept lower pay. In practical terms, the State Personnel Board is unlikely to push the alternative of recruiting from the outside very strongly, and removals from CEA positions are likely to be few (as experience to date already confirms). Both of these consequences appear to limit the innovative effect of the new system. The parallel class arrangement has also been something of a frustration for CSEA. Though it has fought Career Executive Assignment as a threat to the regular civil service, the organization also favors promotion from within, a feature of CEA and not of the merit system. Those within CSEA who are eligible for managerial positions view CEA more favorably than do the rank and file. The former emphasize the small number of removals while the latter stress the ideological threat to the merit system.

### Broadening

As suggested in an article soon after CEA was established, the new scheme posed a triple challenge: "To the political leaders, a challenge to look beyond partisanship; to the agencies, to relax narrow career lines; and to top civil servants, to accept broader-based competition and uncertain tenure."[9] How have these challenges been met? The answer to the first is fairly clear. The fear that CEA would be subject to partisan abuse has not materialized to date. A change of party might well see a substantial increase in removals and even the elimination of certain CEA positions that reflect the program emphases of the Reagan administration, but these developments would be within the expectations of the system.

Answers to the second and third challenges are more complicated. Certainly State Personnel Board statistics indicate that competition within the civil service for positions has been substantially broadened. By the end of 1970, 219 CEA promotional examinations, consisting of oral interviews by an ad hoc examining board set up for each vacancy, had been held. Of these, 150 were servicewide, 25 were multidepartmental, 30 were departmental, and three were "subdivisional." The other 11 were on an open basis, meaning that the alternate regular civil service class was utilized and outsiders were permitted to compete. Servicewide examinations are increasing; 95 percent of the examinations are now on this basis.

The executive roster acts as an instrument for acquainting agencies with extra-departmental candidates. Established in 1967 as a servicewide listing of merit system members interested in the possibility of Career Executive Assignment, the roster enrolled more than 1,500 members by October 1969. As of January 1, 1968, when there were already 1,100 members, enrollment essentially reflected the distribution of occupational backgrounds found in the total management population, except that the medical and legal professions were under-represented. The roster includes more information than is available in its federal equivalent, which stresses the record of job experience and is limited to personal information supplied by the applicant.[10] California has less elaborate coding of job experience and qualifications, but requires completion of the Basic Administrative Aptitudes Test and a variety of performance data from superiors, peers, and subordinates (rating is restricted to superiors). In 1968 terms, California roster members average about 48 years of age, most have had both line and staff experience, about 80 percent have obtained at least one college degree, and seven percent already hold (or have held) a CEA appointment.

The executive roster has other advantages in addition to acquainting hiring authorities with a much wider range of potential candidates than was possible before. The publicity given to a vacancy is thought to deter agencies from non-competitive practices in filling slots. Furthermore, an educational function is claimed for the roster: a department will learn about manpower resources for the future, even if its present slot is "locked up." Screening committees, which eliminate candidates considered unsuitable, are employed in about one-sixth of the examinations and serve as another vehicle for acquainting the hiring authorities with the range of manpower.

The roster has also drawn some criticism. It is said that there are too many who apply and need processing but are not of the caliber to be seriously considered for vacancies. Conversely, the eternal bridesmaids become discouraged and cynical. Some who have sat on examining boards feel that the information in the roster may be too tentative to permit discriminating selection.

Dissatisfaction with the present situation has attracted various suggestions for change. The most drastic is put forth by those who deemphasize specialization most: reduce the roster to 200-odd members through careful culling by an examining board with stable membership and give these selected individuals intensive training, career counseling, and rotating assignments. Agreement on *which* 200 would be difficult at this stage of CEA history. Hiring authorities, who lack time to do the selecting themselves, would be highly skeptical of culling done by others. Some observers defend the present arrangement on the ground that "also-ran" is better than "never-was" and that without CEA and the roster, selection would retrogress to the rigidity of the rule-of-three.

In between are those who recognize the limitations of CEA and the roster, but feel that modifications can improve what is basically an advance in dealing with top civil servants. They recognize that, although examinations are now almost always servicewide, in eight or nine out of ten cases the successful candidate is still from the department with the vacancy, and it is unlikely that departments will (or perhaps should) give up their preeminent role in selection. Improvement, these observers argue, could come through wider use of screening committees followed by interviews for those who survive. This modest change, it is claimed, would be inexpensive in comparison with evaluating 1,500 individuals in order to arrive at a roster of 200 and would also be easier for present roster members to accept than permanent elimination ("I was screened out for *that* job"). Screening committees are being used increasingly as the number of competitors for positions increases, but they are far from perfect. The process can easily degenerate into counting years of experience.

There are other suggestions which, for one reason or another, have not been put into practice but are mild enough to continue to draw support: (1) have the State Personnel Board send a department with a vacancy a list of likely candidates (not too different from the Board's present practice of sending special invitations to take an examination to those best qualified; (2) give yearly examinations for broader groupings (e.g., Resources Administrator I, II, III), followed by specific examinations if needed for specific vacancies; (3) evaluate performance of roster members continually through agency reports on decision-making performance on a management-by-objectives approach (discovered to be too controversial, time-consuming, and costly); (4) convert the roster into a mandatory pool of competitors as in the present Executive Assignment System at the federal level (at present, the Personnel Board can invite non-roster members of the merit system to compete for a specific post).

## Trends and Portents

What can be said about the Career Executive Assignment experiment to date? The very act of survival is a mild triumph, given the entrenched opposition to separatism from the California State Employees' Association and a reluctance to broaden recruitment on the part of departments in which narrow professionalism is strong. Beyond survival the accomplishments become rather sketchy. Certainly there has been progress in broadening the approach to executive recruitment even if appointment habits have changed far less. As CEA appointees gradually replace individuals holding regular civil service appointments in the top managerial positions, some of the familiar walls and barriers of the traditional civil service are eroding—through some of this would occur anyway quite independently of CEA.

Yet the prudent caution exercised in the adoption of Career Executive Assignment has dulled its image, unspectacular as it may have been. CEA has never caught the public eye nor, for that matter the enthusiasm of those most involved. Public indifference may be inevitable but hardly a sense within the civil service that the system has been drifting. There are, nevertheless, signs that the momentum of change may increase. Governor Ronald Reagan's directive to departments on "the selection and development of state managers" in April 1970 included the stipulation that "Appointing powers when filling C.E.A. and middle management positions will make every effort to consider all qualified candidates—not just those immediately visible." The challenge to the new State Personnel Board exectuive officer who takes office in 1971 is to revitalize Career Executive Assignment and relate it more closely to manager development.

Separatism in the California civil service has brought a certain amount of flexibility, with the possibility of more. The attained flexibility in the selection process, for example, consists of such elements as the following: better information on a wider number of manpower possibilities; slow recognition that selection is conducted in a fishbowl and with the need to justify choice in terms understandable outside a department; and increased willingness to accept broader minimum qualifications because applicants need not be screened out to the same degree with a rule-of-three categories than with the rule-of-three.

Much greater flexibility could be realized throughout the civil service with a bolder Career Executive Assignment. If CEA were opened to outside competition, one thoughtful CEA incumbent has suggested, the act would create a different philosophy in junior positions. The notion that seniors would move in and out of government might encourage juniors to do likewise in the knowledge that positions at the top were open to outside competition. The prediction may be awry (even the one making it said he would feel threatened by this course of action), but at the very least it indicates the kind of rethinking that can occur with even a mild movement toward flexibility.

### Footnotes

1. California State Personnel Board, *Management Manpower Bulletin*, No. 1 (March 1, 1967), p. 3.
2. See John F. Fisher and Robert J. Erickson, "California's Career Executive Assignment: I Meeting the Challenge for Better Managers," *Public Personnel Review*, Vol. XXV (April 1964), p. 83.
3. *Ibid.*
4. *Ibid.*, p. 84.
5. The constitutionality issue, long quiescent, has been reopened by CSEA recently in two suits challenging the extension of CEA to new positions.
6. Lloyd D. Musolf, "California's Career Executive Assignment: II A Perilous But Necessary Voyage," *Public Personnel Review*, Vol. XXV (April 1964), p. 88.
7. Based upon interviews with California State Personnel Board staff. Many of the subsequent statements in this article are based on extensive interviews with the same staff and with line officials holding Career Executive Assignment appointments.
8. Fisher and Erickson, *op. cit.*, p. 84.

9. Musolf, *op. cit.*, p. 89.
10. John W. Macy, Jr., "Assurance of Leadership," *Civil Service Journal*, Vol. VII (October–December 1966), p. 5.

## HARLAN CLEVELAND

# The Future Executive*

THIS SELECTION consists of two *PAR* excerpts from Harlan Cleveland's subsequently published book, *The Future Executive.* The first part below is from the book's Preface, and the second is from Chapter 7, "The Exhilaration of Choice," in which the "feel" of executive work is described.

This book was particularly important in its analysis of executive brokerage and interorganizational roles. It described the growing webs of horizontal linkages of organizations and the resulting complexities faced by present and future executives.

Cleveland was president of the University of Hawaii when this book was published. Earlier he had been dean of Syracuse University's Maxwell Graduate School of Citizenship and Public Affairs, and, after that, assistant secretary of state (U.S.) and U.S. ambassador to NATO. He was also ASPA national president shortly before publication of this book.

### Preface

FOR HALF a lifetime as a public executive, I have wrestled with complexity in public and private employ, in Europe and Asia as well as in the United States. That this experience must have produced some useful ideas about executive leadership is this book's presumption, in both senses of the word.

A career as an executive is not something you plan for yourself. It's the series of accidental changes of job and shifts of scenery on which you look back later, weaving through the story retroactively some thread of logic that was not visible at the time. If you try too carefully to plan your life, the danger is that you will succeed—succeed in narrowing your options, closing off avenues of adventure that cannot now be imagined, perhaps because they are not yet technologically

---

*From "Preface" and Chapter 7 "The Exhilaration of Choice" (as it appeared in *PAR*) from THE FUTURE EXECUTIVE by Harlan Cleveland Copyright © 1972 by Harlan Cleveland. Reprinted by permission of Harper & Row, Publishers, Inc.

possible. When a student asks me for career advice, I can only suggest that he or she opt for the most exciting "next step" without worrying where it will lead, and then work hard on the job in hand, not pine for the one in the bush. When your job no longer demands of you more than you have, go and do something else. Always take by preference the job you *don't* know how to do. If you build into your life enough variety of experience, you will be training for leadership, in the role I have called the Public Executive.

This book is addressed to those who are, or wish to become, executive leaders in the realm of public responsibility—which includes not only those who work in "the government" but also a great many executives in private business, non-profit organizations, and the professions. Others can listen in if they will, but it is the self-conscious executives who most need to think about their role, because they seem to be inheriting the earth—though not because they are meek. It is not a comfortable moment to inherit the earth, just when the earth is revealed as polluted, overpopulated, and in mortal peril from Man's civilizing intervention in Nature. But it is just these cosmic dangers which are causing people to turn to those men and women who see their task in life as bringing people together in organizations to make something different happen.

In this book I suggest that the Public Executives will soon number one million in the United States alone. Do we have a profession, those of us who lead by trying to get things done? What makes us think that taking thought, describing reality, and spinning theories will improve our performance on the job? How important is it, anyway, for the executive to know—rather than just to feel—what he is doing and why?

The classical professions were endowed with a special status because they dealt with that which determined life and death. Law and medicine, the military, and the ministry have this in common. When people realize that they are dependent on a few for some function, they want those upon whom they depend to be obviously and certifiedly special. But the Public Executive usually graduates through some speciality; he carries no license to administer the destiny of others. He need have no knowledge of a mystery like the men of the cloth, and he cannot impress the public with the special words and hieroglyphs that lawyers and doctors get to use. Nor is the professionalism of administration a specialized and repeatable technique like musketry or cannonmaking. Half a century ago, in the high fashion of scientific management, it may have seemed so. But we know now that efficiency has a built-in tendency to take us rapidly to where we will not want to be when we get there. We know this instinctively as we sniff the thickening air, stall in the urban congestion, and count the dead that were killed by systems analysis.

The profession of administration took its rise from concepts in engineering and mechanistic psychology. In this century much of its power came from reform movements that sought to limit bossism and corruption by taking part of government out of politics, as it was said, in the interest of efficiency. But now the Public Executives don't just implement, they initiate. They don't just carry out the laws, they write most of them. They don't just advise, they act. Just when industrial society's sense of direction is cast loose from "growth" as its mooring, just when "policy" seems elusive and fogbound, just when the other sciences have run amuck, we find the policy sciences in the ill-prepared and hesitant hands of the Public Executives.

A person who has never managed on his own some form of organized cooperation probably cannot be taught what public responsibility is like, in a classroom or elsewhere. The best of the university graduate programs in business management and public administration insist on an internship experience at the tenderest possible age. Formal education for executive responsibility is mostly, and properly, offered for men and women in mid-career who are graduating up one of the ladders to leadership from specialist to general executive. The best arrangement is to catch them just when they are beginning to feel like a lover of realistic art who wanders by mistake into a gallery of abstract paintings.

Even the formal mid-career training course can be but a small part of an executive's education. Most of it takes place in action. Every executive is a teacher: a good part of his time and effort is devoted to sharing with his more specialized colleagues his own perception of the process in which they are engaged together. For cooperation is the conscious interaction among specialists, and those who understand most deeply what the others are doing, and why, are likely to do their own jobs best.

I have tried in this book to capture and record the essence of what I have learned in action, so that it can be used by those who choose self-fulfillment by bringing people together in organizations to make something different happen. What emboldens me to write it down is the observation that much of what has proved most valuable in education for leadership is the work of reflective practitioners. One of the earliest books about how to interview, hire, and supervise people was written by a Public Executive who served local princes in China 1,700 years ago. Of the codified insights which serve Americans today as general theory in public administration, some of the most durable seem to be the legacy of men of action with a taste for teaching, from Confucius and Kautilya and Julius Caesar and Thomas Aquinas through Machiavelli and Clausewitz and Madison to Woodrow Wilson and Churchill and Barnard and Brownlow and Appleby.

● ● ●

*Chapter 7*

**The Exhilaration of Choice**

The future executive will be brainy, low-key, collegial, optimistic, and one thing more—he will positively enjoy complexity and constant change.

People who shy away from executive work often say they feel imprisoned by the multiplicity of options and the ambiguities of jurisdiction which are the stuff of large-scale organization systems. The effective executive, on the other hand, is likely to be a person who delights in the chance to choose the best path according to his own lights. For the public executive, the "feel" of administration is the exhilaration of choice.

* * * * *

At EXPO 67 in Montreal, the tasteful exhibit from Czechoslovakia attracted the most attention, and its outstanding feature was a remarkable film about the selection of options in motion. The screenplay starts conventionally enough: The day is warm; a beautiful girl, scantily clad, is ironing in her apartment. By some series of accidents I cannot remember, she goes out into the hall wearing nothing but a towel, and the door slams behind her. Of course, she doesn't have her key, and she is distraught as she imagines her iron, still on, burning the fabric and setting the apartment house afire. She knocks on the door of the apartment next door; a man emerges. He too has a problem; knowing that his wife will be back in a moment, should he invite the nearly naked girl into his apartment while he tries to help her?

Suddenly the movie stops, the houselights go on, and a real-life man appears through a trapdoor on the stage in front of the darkened screen. The man is the actor we have just been watching on the screen. "Stop the movie!" he cries, and turns to the audience. "What shall I do now?" He explains that each member of the audience has a console at his side, and can vote whether he should invite the toweled blonde into his apartment or slam the door in her face. The audience votes, chivalry wins by a narrow margin, the houselights go off and the movie reappears, pursuing the action that follows from the option we have selected. The wife returns, draws the obvious conclusion, and leaves her man; there is still an iron presumably setting the whole building on fire; it is not long before another excruciating choice presents itself. Again the movie stops, the trapdoor opens, the girl actress this time appears in the flesh (though properly clothed according to Eastern European standards) and asks the audience for a decision. Evidently the movie maker had a whole scenario worked out for each option, no matter which fork in the road each audience elected each time the movie was shown. After a hilarious hour, with more audience participation than I have ever seen in a movie house, the ambiguities are resolved in an ironic O. Henry finish.

The enormous popularity of this film at EXPO 67 is easily explained: the ethical dilemmas it presented were transmuted from a celluloid image to the reasoning conscience of each member of the audience. Instead of observing other people's dilemmas, the dilemmas suddenly became ours.

The central function of the executive is to choose among alternative action options as he goes along—not just for himself but for others too. The more responsibility he carries, the harder the dilemmas he faces: if they were not hard, they would not reach him for resolution. In Washington one observes that issues reaching the President or even the Secretary of State are no longer rational choices. My rule of thumb in the State Department was that if an answer could rationally be given a 51 to 49 chance of being "right," the problem could be settled by brokerage among the bureaus without bothering the Cabinet level. By the time an issue gets to the ultimate political executives, it has been proved insoluble by logic and reason; the chief ingredients in high policy are gut feelings and ethical hunch.

Even Robert McNamara, who as Secretary of Defense tried so hard to apply reason to policy, concluded that "Management is, in the end, the most creative of all the arts, for its medium is human talent itself." Like painting or sculpture or dance, the management of social complexity cannot be taught by rote, but it can be learned by example and inspiration and unremitting practice. What Michel de Montaigne said of the arts and sciences is doubly true of the qualities of executive leadership: they are not cast in a mould, but are formed and perfected by degrees, by often handling and polishing, as bears leisurely lick their cubs into form.

\* \* \* \* \*

What makes the executive's life exciting is that the choices he makes, or helps make, are *in motion*. It used to be said of the good executive that he was "driving"; a more accurate word would now be "steering." The momentum is already built in—the executive's task is to give it direction, to cause the momentum to serve a subjective human purpose by channeling it in a system managed by human beings and not by blind fate.

Because I used to race sailboats in my youth, I have often thought the feel of executive responsibility analogous to the feel of a small boat in competition. The skipper must know well what his craft will and won't do, and what his crew can handle especially in emergencies. He has to have done his homework—looked up the timing and force and direction of the tides and currents that afternoon, listened to the weather forecast, studied windshift tactics and the racing rules. He must know as much as possible about the psychology of the other skippers and the performance of their boats—some faster in light airs, some able to point higher on a windward beat, some especially swift on a spinnaker run. With all these data stored for instant retrieval, he must analyze a constantly moving situation, in which the air, the water, the other boats, and his own boat are continuously changing their relations to one another. And then he makes decisions—several major "policy" decisions per minute if the class is large and the competition keen. Win or lose, he is unlikely to be bored.

A year after the British electorate had retired him as Chancellor of the Exchequer in a Labour Government, Roy Jenkins proposed skiing as the best way to describe the exhilaration of choice in motion. He contrasted private writing and public responsibility: "A hard period of writing is like a walk up a steep mountainside. There is no natural momentum behind one. It all has to be self-generated." But the writer "can mostly control his own pace, and his intermediate failures are private rather than public. There are no onlookers to mock his periods of ineffective immobility.

"Ministerial work, on the other hand, is much more like skiing down a slalom course. The momentum is all on one's side, provided it can be controlled. There is little difficulty about generating the will to proceed. There is a rapid and relentless movement from one event to another ... each event comes up with such rapidity that there is relatively little danger of falling through hesitation or overanxiety. They have to be taken as they come, on the run; and a lot of things are better done this way...."

Neither analogy is very close. The object of executive work is usually not to win a race but to make cooperation work. And the slalom image would be better if at each gate the skier were presented with two or three alternative ways to proceed. But both images convey the essential sense of motion. Because the whole environment of administration is constantly in motion, nobody can quite know just how the situation looks to an individual executive except the executive himself. Within the limits of relevance, therefore, he must choose his own path, and live with the consequences.

To some, the obligation to choose too fast and too often will seem a burden, a cause for complaint and a reason for frustration. But to those who have the stuff to be our future executives, the momentum will carry its own excitement, and the opportunity to participate in destiny decisions will more than repay the days of committee-sitting and the nights of homework.

\* \* \* \* \*

For many public executives, perhaps most, the exhilaration of choice is the primary reward for service and the chief ingredient in "morale." But that feeling of joy in getting things done by getting decisions made has to be generated from within—for the nature of modern leadership is that the leadership doesn't show. To maximize his own morale, the public executive has to learn to *internalize credit* for what he does.

For a few executives, especially those in top positions, public notice and even approbation are available as inducements to develop the skills and carry the ethical burdens that go with his function in society. (There is of course the offsetting risk of public opprobrium. For a time a new recruit to the ranks of public executives may feel that the choices he makes are so complicated, and the criteria of his success so obscure, that it is almost impossible for outsiders to judge his performance on the job. The probability is indeed diminishing of any interested public being able to understand what the decision was about or what his part in it was. Yet this does not necessarily make life safer for the public executive. For when a judgment *is* rendered, the public's ignorance, combined with its ultimate power, may render the verdict more unfair than it might have been in simpler times or more static societies.) For most public executives, however, their very function precludes their taking credit for the most important things they do. The staff man who writes a policy speech for the President; the analyst whose staffwork enables his boss to keep the firm in the black; the personnel manager who keeps a crack designer from quitting in disgust, and thus ensures better design work on next year's car; the general counsel who drafts a major piece of legislation (of which a senator is said to the the "author" because he introduces it); the American ambassador who thinks up a useful initiative, and then persuades a foreign colleague to float it publicly—none of these can take credit for their work without interfering with the desired results. The mark of a good colleague is that he not hog the credit for collective accomplishment, and the mark of a good staff man is that the person functionally responsible for a decision not be deprived of the credit for making it.

On several occasions while I worked in the State Department, I contributed major chunks of thinking and writing to President Kennedy's statements and foreign policy speeches. In the nature of things, the Kennedy biographer who served as the President's chief writer later attributed to his own initiative ideas that thus originated in other parts of the federal bureaucracy. The President did not live to say what he himself remembered, but it is altogether probable that he would have considered that the ideas in his policy speeches were his own; wherever originated, he had made them his own by understanding them and taking public responsibility for making them presidential policy.

President Kennedy was acutely conscious of where credit and blame might fall. On one occasion, after we had worked out in his office a complicated scheme for handling some foreign policy issue, he sent us back to our offices with a cheerful parting shot: "I hope this plan works," said the President of the United States. "If it does, it will be another White House success. If it doesn't, it will be another State Department failure." But I was in the Cabinet Room the day it became clear that the Bay of Pigs invasion was a fiasco; President Kennedy promptly took full responsibility for the mistake.

Of course there are many kinds of social rewards for executive work short of applause from the general public. Usually a few people know the situation well, and their private congratulations count for much. The Central Intelligence Agency operative and the FBI undercover man, who may not even be able to tell their wives what they are doing, know that people in their own organization whose opinion they value are aware of their assignments and recording their triumphs.

Nevertheless, most of the credit for accomplishment—and most of the blame for failure, too—is internalized. I learned in the diplomatic service to derive active pleasure from reflecting on my part in defusing several peace-and-security crises and averting several near-wars, without having to boast to anyone outside my immediate family. The capacity to internalize the credit for what you do is certainly an acquired skill, unnatural to the human psyche. An executive needs to acquire it early, for the nature of modern leadership is that it doesn't show—and especially that it doesn't show off.

*PAR,* Volume 32 (May/June, 1972)

FRANK P. SHERWOOD

# The American
# Public Executive
# In the Third Century

THIS ARTICLE was first published as part of *PAR*'s U.S. Bicentennial issue. In it, Frank Sherwood took a cautiously optimistic view of future prospects for American public executives and the governments which they serve. He set forth agendas for public administration based on realities present in 1976. He particularly raised questions about the exchange relationships between growing executive burdens and diminishing returns for their efforts, noting that he had "some question about the qualifications of anyone who can be so easily seduced into leadership responsibility." His final paragraph poses an especially clear challenge.

Frank Sherwood wrote in 1976 from the perspectives of a past dean of the University of Southern California's School of Public Administration, the initial director of the Federal Executive Institute, the founding director of USC's Washington Public Affairs Center, and a past president of the American Society for Public Administration.

THE NOTION of the public executive is a relatively recent one, having emerged only in the last quarter of the 200 years of American independence.

To be sure, the idea of the political leader having executive responsibilities for governmental performance is not altogether revolutionary. Presidents have in particular gained notoriety for their ability to make things happen in the nation. But involvement in a foreign policy dispute, a war, a landmark piece of domestic legislation, or a political drama tends more frequently to shape the way in which we remember a President. With the exception of a few cabinet officers and a handful of mayors, who operated during the first 150 years, executive performance in government excited little attention.

Since the passage of the U.S. Budget and Accounting Act in 1921, Presidents have experienced a continuing expansion of executive power, largely in recognition of their general management responsibilities. In many states and cities in the nation there has been a companion move toward the "strengthening of the executive." But the idea of the public executive extends beyond the political leader, who must be regarded as a relatively transitory figure. Increasing numbers of public executives are career people, who, by design or by accident, have given a lifetime to providing our governments with leadership. In this context the city managers are perhaps most illustrative. There were enough of them by 1914 to hold their first professional meeting, slightly more than 60 years ago. Today there are about 3,000 recognized council-manager cities and a good many people who regard themselves in that career system.

In most of the larger governments in the United States the concept of the public executive has tended to evolve more slowly. Typically we have been more aware of the political leader who has been presumed to have executive credentials and also of the growing army of civil service technicians, charged with performing the day-to-day work of the organization. Nevertheless, there are indicators that the career public executive is emerging, perhaps most clearly in the State of California. There, more than a decade ago, a cadre of "career executives" was formed. Now involving approximately 500 jobs in the state apparatus, the career executive program is designed to create a role separate from that of political leader and specialist civil servant. Things have moved somewhat more slowly in the federal government; but the establishment of the supergrades (GS-16, 17, 18) about a quarter-century ago was an important step toward recognizing leadership responsibility in the career system. Since that time, proposals for a Senior Civil Service, for a Federal Executive Service, and for an Executive Personnel System all provide evidence that the leadership function in the governments of the United States is becoming an increasing concern.

While the past half-century has witnessed an emergence of the executive in government (here assumed to imply general management responsibilities for the performance of the enterprise), there remains much ambivalence about the desirability and need for such a role. The city managers are still unique in the degree to which they can rather openly assert their special quality and status in the exercise of leadership at the local government level. Otherwise, there have been only sporadic efforts to address the dimensions of the public executive role specifically and systematically. Even including council-manager governments, our systems of recruiting, developing, utilizing, motivating, and providing rewards and sanctions to public executives remain primitive and ill-defined. Certainly one of the tasks ahead is to give more attention to the management problems of big government, to confront our political beliefs, and to come to some conclusions on how we propose to construct leadership systems to deal with the complex of demands of the third century.

This insistence on greater attention to the nature of the public executive role should not be taken as mere rhetoric. Five years of observing more than 1,500 federal executives in residence at the Federal Executive Institute, as well as the highest government officials in various interactive situations, convinces me that we are paying a big price for our inattention. If it is important that some people feel themselves especially responsible for what happens in the society, then the message expressing those expectations must be clear and unequivocal. It is not there today.

## Changes in Organizations: Their Influence on Leadership

The concept of hierarchy puts great emphasis on an organizationally defined leader. Legitimacy, always important in the power game, is endowed through the pyramid of authority and responsibility. Such a system has many functional advantages. It provides substantial incentives to certain types of people, particularly those with power motivation and status needs. The organization chart is a rather graphic picture of social stratification. Hierarchy is also quite effective in draining the last ounce of energy and commitment from the person in the catbird seat. That person is in effect whipsawed. On the one hand, there is the dominant message of responsibility for whatever happens in the domain, enough in itself to generate many guilt feelings. On the other, there is the quixotic assurance that leadership is equivalent to power. Hence, one bears a double guilt: that which comes from leadership responsibility and the more personal concern of whether one has used one's full potential in the discharge of those responsibilities.

As a result, the hierarchical organization tends to be very effective in getting the most from its leaders, and, for some of the reasons noted above, the leader in the U.S. culture is strongly moved to internalize the values and goals of the organization. As the organization goes, so goes the leader. Indeed, there is still a number of people who believe it is the leader who sets the goals, which makes even more understandable the extreme dedication with which the hierarchical leader often pursued organizational interest.

Another collaborator in this symposium, Neely Gardner, is very careful not to predict a move away from hierarchy. Indeed, an early draft of his article comments, "Big bureaucracy shows little sign of changing or of permitting the emergence of non-hierarchical structures." He observes that we became "hooked" in the Second Century and that "... boundary maintenance is our mother's milk and goal displacement our rest and recreation." This is not to say Gardner supports goal displacement. In fact, he believes we face an organizational crisis; but he cannot bring himself to offer his non-hierarchical organization as any more "than a scenario or discussion piece. . . ." It is not, he says, "a concrete plan of action."

Such caution it seems, is well placed. In over 30 years of observing the governmental scene, I see profound changes in individual attitudes, but very few in operational ways of thinking about organizing. Despite a decided weakening in the power that may be attributed to formal authority, the principle of hierarchical organization seems as firmly implanted and vital as it did in the early '40s.

What may undergo some change in the third century is an alteration in boundary conditions and turf arrangements. Gardner may have erred, for example, in linking big bureaucracy with non-hierarchical structures. Theoretically, small, as well as large, organizations can be structured hierarchically; and one may look at virtually any cabinet department to realize that the operative hierarchy is not at the departmental but at the bureau level. In short, it is possible to conceive of some changes in early third century organization life, with attendant public executive implications, that do not necessarily suggest a drastic move away from the hierarchical principle.

Bigness itself is under considerable attack today. Perhaps we have come fully to realize that the further a decision maker is from a problem, the harder it is to appreciate the priorities and needs of that situation. There is a tendency to abstract reality and to rely far too much on symmetrical orientations. The emerging literature of "Public Choice" makes a persuasive argument for much greater variety in our government institutions. This line of thought, coupled with empirical data that now make us suspicious that scale is likely to lead to effectiveness and efficiency, could very well gain greater influence in the future. This may not lead to the breakup of any of our titans, but it may limit the creation of new ones. Again, it should be noted that hierarchy will likely prevail in these organizations regardless of size. Indeed, the Public Choice people seem to limit their nonhierarchical argument to the interorganizational dimension. Hierarchy continues to be triumphant within.

At the same time that we question the viability of the big organization, we must face the reality of greater independence among organizations and in the society as a whole. An increasing number of our problems are planetary, not even national. Alberto Guerreiro Ramos points out, in a manuscript not yet published, we may have been trapped by our tendency to think of "all-purpose" organizations.[1] If we were to "delimit" organizations, as Ramos suggests, the effect would be to expand greatly the complexity and scale of the society of organizations.

A very fundamental point in the Ramos thesis is that our view of reason has been displaced over the centuries. Particularly since the 16th century, reason has been increasingly associated with instrumental rationality, i.e., a "reckoning of consequences." So dominant has been this emphasis on instrumental rationality that we have lost our capacity to see that the goal of one human association may be different from another. All organizations have been cast in the same mold of purpose, that is, to maximize their resources and to optimize goal achievement. Every interest in the organization, collective or personal, is assumed to be subject to the same intellectual discipline. By this type of reductionism we have come to believe that organizations can serve all purposes. At one and the same time they are assumed able to pursue a utilitarian end, such as the provision of a refuse collection service, and also provide an arena within which an individual may actualize himself or herself.

Ramos argues that we trap ourselves with such assumptions. In his view, the economizing imperatives of utilitarian organizations necessitate that there be demands on the individual, in effect leading to the subordination of personal to organizational interest. Where there is an absence of delimitation—a specifying of purpose—the risk of organization breakdown is high. Nothing gets done very well. What we should seek, then, is a world in which organizations are delimited both in scope and purpose. We should use our intellective powers, in the Platonic sense, to conceive our basic purposes and then to create human associations consistent with those goals. The consequences, in Ramos' vision, would be enclaves of organizations pursuing very discreet and different tasks, with an explicitness of purpose, and very likely following widely varying organizing strategies. The self-actualizing organization, for example, might be nonhierarchical; the utilitarian association would very likely be quite hierarchical.

Whether we will consciously move toward delimitation is, of course, problematical. But there is plenty of evidence that our highly pluralistic society already embraces many of Ramos' models. In certain respects it would appear that Ramos may be making the most laudable of scholarly contributions, helping us to understand and hasten a process which may already be under way.

There is another dimension of the "society of organizations" emerging in the third century which deserves attention. As we come to realize the scale at which some social requirements must be comprehended, it is clear that smallness and isolation have their limitations. Put simply, there is an inevitable tension between the interests of an area or community and of programs whose requirements extend far beyond any boundary. While we need people who see a community in its totality and who can help to shape a delivery system that is congruent with that community's special needs, our extreme interdependence requires that there be people concerned with global health, national education, and public safety, among many other social needs. Characteristically, we think of the area representative as the generalist, the program representative as the specialist. But such distinctions are becoming less and less useful, particularly when the generalist uses such status to claim a special right to represent the public interest. In effect, both are specialists; and the need is to recognize the legitimacy of both roles.

A recent consulting experience emphasized for me the extreme difficulty in conceiving of leadership systems that are essentially horizontal and parallel, in which responsibility continues to be present and in which authority is even further reduced. In this sense the canard of authority commensurate with responsibility dies very hard, unrealistic though the concept has always been. There are some real challenges ahead in helping executives become comfortable with interorganizational conditions of interdependence and reciprocity of influence. However, there is no intention to suggest that a leader can be derived wholly of influence and power. The balancing of influence becomes essential in this interorganizational world.

The prediction of heightened interorganizational activity will have great effect on the role imperatives of the public executive. Already, there is an increasing interest in the concept of networking—a word which is likely to be greatly over-used in the first decade of the third century. But the concept has important, and very likely lasting, significance. It assumes increasing numbers of situations in which organizations will be in system relationships but not in a "center-periphery" sense. The network is characterized by absence of a center and by the expectation that all the elements have equal obligations to influence and be influenced. Again, it seems quite evident that the effectiveness of a "society of organizations" will depend on the skill and wisdom with which the various organization representatives collaborate.

## Porosity of Organizational Boundaries and Its Implications

Consideration of interorganizational factors raises another problem which is apt to have increasing importance for the third century public executive: the extreme porosity of organization boundaries, which have sometimes been called "Swiss Cheese." Interventions in the internal business of organizations, in the name of a huge variety of public purposes and needs, have increased manifold in the last quarter century. In this sense there is no way to "delimit" organizations. Public or private, the way they do business is going to be determined in very substantial part by outsiders. The labor unions, growing rapidly in the public sector, are a part of this intervention system.

Much of the literature would seem to suggest this is a healthy development. Organizations, it is argued, must be congruent with their environment. Indeed, their structure and processes are "contingent" on the structure and processes of the environment. Put another way, a lack of stability in the environment ought to be replicated inside the organization. Thus the executive might look upon these interventions as an insurance that incompatibility between organization and environment will be minimized.

But things do not fall into place so easily and seductively for the executive. First there is the need to contend with the growing dilemma of the level of influence potential appropriate to the executive role. Certainly the leader ought to have at least a little capability to influence circumstances for which people in the society assume he has responsibility. While there is no possibility of equalizing authority and responsibility, it does seem a little too much to believe figureheads can make a difference.

Of at least equal importance is the way in which an executive thinks about the organization and its need for stability. Indeed, it is not alone an executive question. It is an issue for all organization members. Like many others, I have been a devotee of contingency theory, largely because the alternative has always conjured a "head in the sand" posture. We certainly don't need many ice plants in a day of electric refrigerators. The problem, however, is not that categorical. Because a society is turbulent, it does not necessarily follow that everything in it should be. As this is written, Italy is undergoing one of its most extreme crises. Certainly it was a world situation that evoked the internal turbulence; but it has been the failure of belief in the internal leadership to promote stability that has accentuated difficulties. An executive stance a little less congruent with the environment might have been helpful and more promising of stability and purpose to Italy.

These notions suggest a somewhat different executive role inside the organization. First, it means we may have to call a halt to the erosion of leadership influence, specifically authority. Second, it changes somewhat the way in which an executive thinks about his transaction with the environment. The boundary role signifies more than representation and communications linkages. It suggests credibility for the executive in his interpretation of environmental imperatives; and that in turn implies some willingness on the part of the membership to accept the judgment—the influence—of the leader. Further, as the organized interventions from outside increase, much of this acceptance may come as a result of the need to "hang together."

When presented to professional colleagues, this line of reasoning has excited an interesting response. Clearly the argument supports a greater influence capability for the executive in seeking stability in a condition of turbulence. Such influence is typically translated as authoritarianism. So strong is the democratic bias in the academic community that any proposal for greater leadership influence excites a profoundly negative response. Further, there is a deep, expressed belief that executives have a very limited repertoire of behaviors. Give them an ounce of authority and they will think it applies in the family, in interorganizational negotiations, and in the metaphysical world. Thus there is the rather profound question of whether we can look to a time in the third century when public executives will have substantial imperatives to operate in a horizontal fashion in their interorganizational relationships (and some intra-organizational ones), at the same time reverting to rather classical vertical behaviors in their own shops. Personally, I am rather optimistic that such a range of repertoires has existed in the past and can be further developed in the future. What is disturbing is the flatness with which the disagreement is expressed, with consequently great constraints on the ways in which we can think about problems of organizations and their environments.

## On Nourishing the Public Executive

Certainly we have asked a lot and will ask even more in the future of those sturdy souls willing to accept formal leadership responsibility in public organizations. Hopefully, that is apparent from what has been written above. Yet the rewards of leadership, particularly in the public sector, are perhaps at an all-time low. Money and other forms of extrinsic reward are fairly obvious problems. It is on the intrinsic side, however, that we may be facing real problems in the third century in attracting people into public leadership roles. While the public sector has its special disabilities, it is likely that the absence of intrinsic rewards is fairly general.

Consider the nature of the motivation to become an executive, to lead. As a fair amount of reserach has indicated, leadership motivation primarily results from a desire to make things happen, to influence. It may be purely a power motivation, or some combination of power and achievement drives. Contrast that need with an organization reality of a world of negotiation, of horizontal relationships, of changing value systems that emphasize individual potency, of increasing interventions from a number of societal directions, and a general deprecation of the need for, and value of, leadership influence. Further, to the extent that the leader continues to be an allocator of values, he or she faces a world of extreme conflict. Indeed, it is probably fair to say that a large number of leadership positions (and even more in the future) are "failure prone."

With good salary floors and attractive retirement systems at the middle management level, it becomes increasingly difficult to understand how the need for status or the power motivation (such as it can be fulfilled) remains *that* important. Indeed, I have some question about the qualifications of anyone who can be so easily seduced into leadership responsibility.

At the beginning of the third century, it appears that there is a real need to take a look at the exchange relationships struck between organizations and their leaders. A careful review, I believe, will reveal a very serious shortfall in the leader's "profits" and an urgent requirement to redress that balance in order to populate some of our toughest jobs with our best people.

### Summary

A century is a long time. If we did not understand that already, its length takes on further point when it is realized that real interest in the role of the public executive is a product of only about half that period of time. If I were to be asked what I would most like to see happen in the years ahead, it would be continued and growing interest in the processes of executive leadership in the governments of the nation. Greater attention at both the political and career levels should have its consequence for the quality of governmental performance.

We have to contend with cultural norms that are heavily rooted in hierarchy and which limit our interest and our capacity to think creatively about processes of human collaboration. However we might wish otherwise to change ourselves, that seems to be a reality with which we must contend.

Hierarchy, however, is no longer a guarantee either of stability or of leadership dominance. Increasingly, hierarchical leadership carries with it a heavy dose of responsibility and a rapidly lessening capacity to influence events central to the discharge of that responsibility.

Further, it is a world in which we may see a much greater number of organizations, perhaps with more highly articulated and sharpened interests. In such a society of organizations, the public executive will have a major responsibility as an ambassador and as an interpreter of that environment to his own organization. The leader will have to know and understand a great deal more as he seeks to interpret what is happening around his or her organization.

Within the organization there are contradictory possibilities. On the one hand many of the forces of fragmentation will also be found. Organizations are not, and never have been, as monolithic/monocratic as frequently alleged. Thus the leader's ability to deal horizontally will again be tested. At the same time, as many forces play upon the organization's equanimity, the leader may have to assume more of a vertical role, as a stabilizer and supporter of the whole enterprise. In playing these multiple roles, public executives will be called upon to exhibit a repertoire of competences which I believe wholly possible, but about which others have expressed deep doubts.

In the last analysis, the quality of organizations in the third century is largely going to depend on whether it's fun to be a boss. Above all, let's hope we do not lose sight of that imperative.

## Footnote

1. The above is the author's interpretation of the Ramos manuscript and bears all the frailties of such attempts to summarize.

RICHARD J. STILLMAN, II

## The City Manager: Professional Helping Hand, Or Political Hired Hand?

THIS ARTICLE was one of several in a two-part *PAR* symposium edited by Frederick C. Mosher and Richard Stillman, II on "Professionals in Government." A comprehensive review of issues and literature on city managers was presented by Stillman. His assessment of forces favoring and impeding professionalism among city managers was a central thrust toward which much of the analysis was directed.

Richard Stillman was a professor at California State College, Bakersfield, when this article was published. He had served eralier as an assistant to two city managers. He had written extensively already on city management, including a 1974 book, *The Rise of the City Manager*.

NEARLY 100 million Americans reside in cities served by city managers or chief administrative officers (CAOs). Today, 2,655 city managers and CAOs are appointed by city councils as full-time administrators of their community governments. In a typical council-manager plan city, a small council made up of five, seven, or nine representatives, generally elected on a nonpartisan, at-large basis, serves as the chief policy-making body of the city principally through its legal powers of approving city ordinances, personnel policies and budgetary appropriations.[1] The council appoints a chief executive officer, a city manager, or CAO who generally serves without tenure "at the council's pleasure."

A complex working relationship evolves between the elected legislative policy makers on council and the appointed chief administrator. Under the manager

---

The author wishes to thank the following individuals who kindly took the time to review and comment on this article: Professor Ronald O. Loveridge, University of California, Riverside; David Arnold, director of publications, International City Management Association; David Bauer, chief administrative officer, New Haven, Connecticut; James Buell, assistant city manager, Bakersfield, California; and Marjorie Sauer, assistant to the academic vice president, California State College. Vice President Phillip Wilder and Dean Richard Wallace at Cal State Bakersfield generously provided research and travel funding for the author's work.

plan, the mayor generally performs part-time ceremonial functions, with the manager assuming full-time, day-to-day responsibilities over all or most line functions of local government. CAOs normally have fewer direct line departments of the city to supervise by comparison to managers, though both managers and CAOs exercise vital and powerful roles through budget preparation and personnel recruitment, as well as through formal and informal adivsory activities with council.[2]

The "professional" nature of managers' work in terms of their on-the-job activities, skills, experience, training, and career is legally prescribed by most council-manager city charters, as well as promulgated as official doctrine by the International City Management Association (ICMA), the professional association of city managers and CAOs. For instance, the typical council-manager charter that outlines the manager's job reads: "As chief administrative officer, the city manager provides professional counsel to the city council. . . . His work is performed with professional independence. . . ." The Introduction to the ICMA's Code of Ethics for managers also emphasizes that one of their primary pusposes is: ". . . to strengthen the quality of urban government through professional management."[3]

However, political scientists over the last two decades, drawing on sophisticated community power studies and decision-making analyses, have evolved another view of managers and CAOs strikingly different from that of traditionally autonomous professionals subject to an independent code of ethics, peer group review, and their own standards of expertise. Rather, a manager is viewed from this perspective as one of the chief actors in community politics, responsive to local interests and decision makers and, in turn, influencing the general course of city affairs.

In the words of Norton Long, managers are in reality "politicians for hire," or as Karl Bosworth put it more concisely, simply "politicians" who derive their considerable influence within city hall and the community at large from their control over budget preparation, personnel appointments, and formal as well as informal council advisory functions.[4] For this "realist" school of political scientists, the very term "professional" simply disguises one of the best politicians in town, and, as they view it, "professional" is both a meaningless and deceptive term that fails to describe a manager's "real" activities and functions.

This article will attempt to sort out the two prominent but seemingly contradictory views of managers/CAOs—that of "professional helping hands" versus "political hired hands"—by beginning with a brief look at their unique triad of historic values which did much to create their contemporary occupational identity confusion.

### The Business Corporation, Neutral Expertise, and Pragmatic Reform

Unlike other public officials, city managers were originally conceived as the centerpiece of a normative reform theory or "model" for restructuring and redirecting the very purposes of local government. Thus, the manager's occupation was at its very inception deeply enmeshed within a peculiar frame of political values that was the handiwork, not of a seasoned public official nor profound political thinker, but of a relatively obscure New York City businessman, 28-year-old Richard S. Childs, who pursued a part-time hobby of municipal reform. Shortly after graduating from Yale College, Childs in 1904 with another prominent Progressive of that day, Woodrow Wilson, set out to rid cities of boss rule by promoting the "short ballot" idea, which sought to improve and rationalize voting processes through shortened ballots. He later was attracted for similar reasons to "the commission plan," first popularized in Galveston, Texas, but in 1909 his eye fell accidentally on an experiment in Staunton, Virginia, that had recently hired "a manager" as chief full-time administrator.[5] From his one-room New York City short ballot office, Childs soon produced a steady stream of anonymous articles and stories praising the virtues of city manager government as superior to the commission plan (giving the mistaken impression that the manager plan was already in widespread operation). Childs wielded a powerful pen that made him a virtuoso at publicizing manager government. News editorials and after-dinner speakers soon were repeating his catch-phrases that became stock-in-trade programs of the Progressive municipal reformers. By 1918, 100 cities, one as large as Dayton, Ohio, had adopted "the manager plan." Ironically, while all this occurred, the man who claimed to be "the plan's inventor" remained so inconspicuous that no one had ever heard of him at the first meeting of city managers (I doubt few managers today have ever heard of Richard Childs).

To Childs' credit, however, he recognized early that to mobilize support for the idea it "must be condensed to a catch-phrase first, even if such a reduction means lopping off many of its vital ramifications and making it false in many of its natural applications." Childs had an undeniable knack at simplification and promotion, yet as a Progressive reformer, Childs also had a genuine and vital concern about the need for better local government by means of widening popular participation in community affairs through structural change. The manager plan was his prime vehicle of structural reform that, as Don Price rightly observed,[6] rested on the manipulation symbols then dominant (and still I would venture to argue popular today) in American culture—the business corporation, neutral expertise, and pragmatic reform.

These three fundamental values behind the plan I would argue operate simultaneously on three levels: at the first level in engendering popular support and public acceptance for the plan and hence creating the very occupational role a manager performs in a community; at a second level in influencing the particular and unique formal structure within which a manager's job is performed; and on a third level in giving rise to the persistent and fundamental value problems associated with this line of work. Table 1 illustrates the "interrelatedness" among the three fundamental values of the plan and the three levels of "impact" upon the city management occupation.

While much of Table 1 is self-explanatory, I would argue that the enduring and critical value problems of city managers depicted under Level Three stem

Table 1

| Triad of Values Implicit in "Plan" | Means for Impact | Level One: Symbolic and Popular Appeal of "Plan's" Values to Voters | Level Two: Structural "Impact" of "Plan's" Values on City Management Practitioners Today | Level Three: Critical Operational Issues Posed for Managers by Values of the "Plan" |
|---|---|---|---|---|
| Corporate Value | Formal model for city government enacted by law in council-manager charters. | Pattern of local government modelled on business corporation denoting central values of economy/efficiency. | Provides a formal bureaucratic hierarchy for local government with a sharp differentiation between policy-making role of council and administrative authority of manager. | Clear-cut idealized dichotomy between politics and administrative poses perpetual and complex practical problems of relations between manager and council in matters of governance, policy formulation, and cooperative direction. |
| Neutral Expertise | City charter that establishes a professional city manager's post. | Word "manager" denotes energetic, nonpolitical leadership. | Centralizes decisional authority and responsibility in *one* individual who takes a "communitywide approach" to solving city problems. | Complex problems associated with finding the "public interest" or "community good" in order to apply neutral expertise in achieving a pluralistic community's desired goals. |
| Pragmatic Reform | Immediate demands for improvements and changes in local government by city council and community when "plan" is adopted. | The council-manager plan denotes a reform measure designed to generate specific changes in government as well as general civic progress. | Council-manager government serves to respond to specific community needs by reforming community government structure and providing improved and "effective" municipal services. | Reformers have frequently oversold the plan by promising the manager can do the impossible, like lower taxes, etc. |

frequently from the difference between the popular expectations of the plan (Level One) and the practicalities of governance that managers encounter in making the plan work (Level Two). The business model, for instance, which sells well to voters by establishing a council-manager government on the basis of a business corporation and which sharply separates policy from administration, is in practice a terribly difficult, if not an impossible dichotomy to achieve on a daily working basis, because, as numerous political scientists have noted,[7] so much policy "slips and slops" into administration that the distinction between the two becomes both fuzzy and blurred.

Similarly, the second value of neutral expertise implicit in a manager's official title may warm the hearts of voters because of its apolitical symbolic appeal, but neutrality on the practical level of running cities is extraordinarily hard to achieve in pluralistic communities where a five-man council may indeed have five different opinions about any issue it faces. Also, the value of pragmatic reform may sell the plan well, but sometimes at a price, in that managers are expected to achieve the humanly impossible under the plan, such as reducing taxes in an inflationary economy.

In short, the persistent disparity between the ideals implicit in the plan—ideals that, of course, make the very existence of a city management occupation possible—and the human practicalities of day-to-day operational problems of urban governance force managers to assume perpetually a sort of schizophrenic double identity—"a professional identity," one defined by law in city charters and given popular credence from the general public's support of "the plan"—and a "political identity" that requires them to exercise a great deal of savvy of an astute politician in terms of "fitting" the ideals of the plan into a real world. No other public official is forced to operate within a legacy of this sort of a triad of values that causes persistent tensions and identity crises in terms of his/her own self-image.

## The Shape of City Management Today: Its Contemporary Values and Social Trends

What is the shape of the city management field today? In what directions is it evolving? While I do not pretend to offer up a list of all changes that are occurring within city management (the diversity of the field makes a comprehensive listing impossible), among the eight most noteworthy major trends over the last two decades that influence the direction of this line of work as well as the individual roles of managers are the following:

*1. A continued popularity and growth of managers/CAOs and a rise in the multiplicity of their responsibilities but with a concomitant "dispersion" of their authority.*

Since World War II, an average of 65 cities annually have adopted council-manager government. War and depression have slowed the growth of the plan, but the relative prosperity of the 1960s and 1970s with demands of growing city/suburban populations for better municipal services and new federal money from revenue sharing has helped to spur the growth rate of city management. Furthermore, with the broader ICMA criteria for general management recognition established in 1969, a record 159 communities were recognized as approved council-manager cities in 1973, and 110 were approved in 1975. The statistical growth of the plan of course leads to increased occupational opportunities for city management practitioners. As indeed recent surveys have shown, managers themselves remain relatively optimistic about the future expansion of their field.[8]

As the plan itself has grown, so too have managerial responsibilities widened. New demands for their expertise applied to new areas like environmental protection, affirmative action, pollution control, and energy conservation have contributed to significantly expanding their roles, activities, and interests. Managers, like front line soldiers on the battlefield, are frequently the first public officials to face the assault of new issues and innovations affecting government, and thus are frequently the first to learn how "to cope" with the new problems.

Along with rising responsibilities, managers have faced in recent years a concomitant "dispersal of authority," due on one side from the rapidly increased "intrusion" over the last decade by federal/state authorities into what once was the manager's pretty much exclusive "turf." The intergovernmental layer cake that turned into a marble cake has meant the dispersal of the once clear lines of authority of managers over their own internal administrative functions. Federal and state oversight and interest in city government has risen, thanks largely to its generous fiscal support which usually has strings attached.

The challenge to managerial authority comes equally from below as well. Public employee unions' growing demands at the bargaining table for better pay and working conditions make unions now equal or almost equal partners with managers in setting administrative priorities and policies for communities. Similarly, new minority participation in local government further has served to widen the circle of citizenry in the community decision-making processes, and further serves in "fuzzing" the manager's traditional authority. As one manager who recently resigned his post in one small community told the newspapers on his departure:

> I have a philosophy that local government doesn't have as much effect on city government as regional and state policies. Most of the policies the city implements don't originate locally ... and 95 percent of the revenue the city receives, including where it is obtained and how it can be spent, is controlled by the state and federal government. Local government is an ebbing entity ... that is becoming increasingly diverse and complicated.[9]

*2. In response to the growing cross-pressures on managers from "above" and "below," the traditional core values of their occupation have also been significantly broadened from an emphasis on technique-oriented engineering efficiency to more general public management based upon recent social science knowledge.*

One of the best barometers of the widening concerns and values of city management is found by an examination of the most widely used educational publication of the ICMA's Municipal Management Series (commonly referred to as the Green Book Series, which first appeared in 1934). These green books for 40 years have attempted to outline "the best" practices of the field of local government administration, covering such subjects as police administration, planning, fire protection, community health, and public works. The "flagship" of the green books has traditionally been *The Technique of Municipal Management.* In its last edition in 1958 its expressed purpose was "to define the job of management in municipal administration and to suggest techniques and practices which will help municipal officials." This book, as its title suggested, was something of a how-to-do-it manual for city managers, and its chapters enumerated many of the best techniques for efficient internal management of local administration, including sections on: "Techniques of Directions," "Programming Municipal Services," "Administrative Planning and Research," and "Administrative Measurement."

The 1974 edition of this book, edited by James M. Banovetz of Northern Illinois University, was retitled *Managing the Modern City,* and adopts a much broader perspective of the subject for training practitioners. Drawing on the last two decades of organization theory, decision making, and human relations research, the new edition attempts to relate modern social science research to the practical world of municipal affairs. In contrast to the 1958 edition, representative chapters cover such topics as: "The City: Forces of Change," "Environment and Role of the Administrator," "Decision Making," "Leadership Styles and Strategies," "Administrative Communication," and "Administrative Analysis." New emphasis is placed on computer technologies and intergovernmental relations, as well as PPBS. Clearly in the years that transpired between this book's 1958 and 1974 revisions, the vertical and horizontal dimensions of city management values and interests were considerably broadened and extended.

*3. Despite the growth of the city management field and its ever-widening concerns, city managers remain a fairly small, homogeneous occupational group with a strong small town-suburban orientation.*

City managers as a social group from their very beginnings have shown consistent homogeneous social patterns: white, male, in their early 40s, middle-class, protestant. Their incomes have grown over the years (currently averaging $19,962 per year) and their remuneration compares favorably with other professionals today—the average lawyer now earns $22,000 and a school superintendent $20,000.[10] But blacks, women, young, or religious minorities are found only in token numbers in the city management field. The heavily suburban, small-town setting in which most manager plans function is one of the chief causes for the small numbers of minorities by comparison to other professional groups.[11]

*4. Managers increasingly are better trained with less engineering-oriented education, combining both an "administrative generalist" and "specialist" background.*

Managers have always been a well-educated group of men. Even in 1934, Ridley and Nolting reported 64 percent of them held baccalaureate degrees; in 1975 an ICMA survey showed 76 percent having bachelors degrees, and 48 percent of these had masters degrees.[12] An even higher percentage of their assistants (86 percent) today have baccalaureate degrees. In recent years there has been a noticeable shift, however, away from engineering as the preferred preparation for city management. In 1934, 77 percent of managers held bachelor degrees in engineering, but today that figure is only 18 percent, with 34 percent of modern managers majoring in political science or government and 78 percent of those who hold masters degrees obtaining them in the field of public administration. Today only 3 percent of managers' advanced degrees are in engineering.

A generalist management background in public administration seems now to be the preferred training for the field and also may be an indication for the reduced demands on the part of city councils for technicians as opposed to administrative generalists. Most managers now cite the more administrative generalist educational areas as being the most useful job preparation for city management, particularly the fields of budgeting and finance, administration and organization theory, public relations, and personnel. Also, informal specialization in narrow skill categories of solid waste removal, collective bargaining, or grantsmanship is found among many managers. Increasingly, a generalist administrative education coupled with "skill specialties learned on-the-job" seems to be the most common training background for city management. No doubt, the advanced degree gives the practitioner a professional image while the on-the-job training gives the pragmatic skills for coping with daily hazards of occupational survival.

5. *While there is still no prescribed professional career pattern in city management, informal common career patterns have developed that seem to prefer the "in-and-outer" administrative generalist.*

Statistics show career patterns informally have developed in the city management field. Most managers take their first jobs in the field in their late 20s or early 30s, frequently after working as an assistant city manager or with a consulting firm in city management. Their average local government service is 13 years, while their average tenure in a single city is five years. More than a third of the managers today were alerted to the field by college or graduate training, and another third by a job after school.

Generally, most seem to "drift" into the field from many jobs, but primarily most have been experienced administrators prior to becoming city managers: 29 percent had some previous experience in government service, 47 percent had prior business administration experience, and 16 percent had some engineering background before taking their first job in the field. Unlike most careers, breadth of experience in different types of challenging administrative jobs in public and private agencies is encouraged, even preferred, and so city management remains one of the few "open fields" that a person can enter comparatively late in life without having been specifically trained. Indeed, many do take up city management as a second career after service in the military or private industry.

6. *Managers see themselves as "career professionals," though not all are "careerists."*

Surveys of managers emphasize that the chief perception they hold of themselves and their community roles places them squarely in the "professional category." While only 23 percent of managers view themselves as in an established profession like law or medicine, 75 percent see themselves in a new professional field, akin to diplomacy or school superintendency. Less than two percent claim that their line of work is not professional at all. Moreover, they reflect an optimism about the future of their careers, with more than half believing that there will be increasing numbers of cities adopting city management form of government.[13]

However, recent surveys of managers also find that not all managers can be classed as "careerists" in their field. Only one-quarter of the managers spend most of their working careers as city managers. Better than one-half of the managers are more accurately classed as administrative generalists or "in-and-outers" moving into and out of city management from and to a wide variety of jobs in both business and government. A quarter of the managers must be categorized as "local appointees" or "hometown boys" who took the job because it was easily available to them. Local appointees by definition have no aspirations beyond the local horizons. The high percentage of in-and-outers and local appointees within city management is perhaps ultimately due to the political hazards, as Paul Ylvisaker aptly described: "A manager's job tenure is only secure until the next council meeting."

7. *The professional association of city managers, the International City Management Association (ICMA), has significantly broadened its outlook and scope of activities in recent years, but nonetheless, remains a weak voluntary association with little or no influence over the entrance, promotion, training standards, and ethical performance of individual city managers.*

In the late 1960s, the ICMA undertook several important reforms which were healthy as a whole for the urban management field: it moved its national headquarters to Washington, D.C., staffed its ranks with new leaders, enlarged its research and training programs, adopted a new code of ethics, and changed its name from "manager" to "management" association in order to include administrative professionals in the many related management fields of local government.[14] Yet, in spite of its intense new look of the last decade, the ICMA, unlike the American Bar Association or American Medical Association, exercises no control over the entrance or promotion into the field of city management. And while the ICMA has a code of ethics and publishes the popular Green Book Series, and *Public Management*, it enforces neither ethical nor educational standards for city managers.

The ICMA can recommend and indeed does actively encourage such standards, but the hiring and firing of managers remains squarely with independent local city councils across the nation. The limited extent to which managers are aware of any peer group influence in their field was demonstrated by a recent survey that asked managers to rank the top three city manager practitioners—few could even name one person.[15]

8. *Increasingly city managers seem to take an activist view of their community policy roles, but three variables—city size, politics, self-definition of leadership roles—largely seem to determine the extent and nature of a manager's policy activity.*

While Richard Childs and other early founders of the manager plan stressed "a neutral expert role" for the city manager, a number of community power studies written by political scientists over the last two decades seem to agree that the city managers today are not merely inconspicuous public administrators, but rather their empirical analyses conclude that managers play very influential roles in determining public politics within their respective communities.[16]

After a careful analysis of several council-manager cities in Florida, Gladys Kammerer and her associates found "no managers ... who were not involved in making, shaping, or vetoing policy proposals." A similar study, conducted in North Carolina by B. James Kweder, pointed out that "... in many cities the city manager clearly emerges as a person who has the greatest influence on what is happening at every stage of the policy-making process." Aaron Wildavsky's *Leadership in a Small Town,* which examined decision making in Oberlin, Ohio, revealed that the city manager was frequently the central figure in determining the important outcome of community policy issues. Oliver P. Williams and Charles R. Adrian made similar observations in two out of the four Michigan cities they studied: "the city manager was the key leadership figure and policy innovator." Even surveys of managers themselves show a remarkable shift away from a view of themselves as neutral experts and toward a proactive policy involvement.[17]

While contemporary political scientists and surveys of managers' own views on their policy roles have concluded that managers are no longer merely neutral administrators, the extent and scope of a manager's policy-making role seems to be also very much influenced by three key variables. The first, as would be expected, city size, is an important factor determining a manager's policy involvement. Large city managers, because of the urban diversity and sizes of their city resources, are more inclined to be involved with broader, more abstract policy matters such as shaping the city budget, advising city councils, negotiating with unions, dealing with inter- and intra-governmental matters—policy issues akin to those of large corporation executives.

On the other hand, small town managers whose role involves more technical matters like parking, snow removal, sewer repair, and the like are involved more frequently with the mundane technical side of administration. Limited staff assistance and fewer resources force small town managers to solve on their own many diverse technical as well as non-technical problems of communities. Like small businessmen, small city managers must not only make up their financial accounts, but also stock the store themselves.

The political environment of the community also decisively shapes the policy role that managers play in their communities. Edward C. Banfield and James Q. Wilson classed manager cities in five categories ranging from small homogeneous, "faction-free" cities to large, highly factionalized communities.[18] Those cities they found with a high degree of political conflict force managers frequently into roles of "negotiators" and "conflict resolvers," while the more homogeneous communities or those with the large stable majorities provide managers with greater consensus on policy matters and, therefore, give managers a freer hand in finding effective and efficient techniques for implementing agreed-upon goals.

As John Bollens and John Ries have pointed out,[19] managers tend to fare better in those homogeneous, growing communities as opposed to stable or declining cities with considerable political conflict. The former group of cities demand technical competence to cope with their growth, which is the premium stock-in-trade skill of managers, while the latter type of city, one enmeshed in continuous political combat, requires an able politician more versed in the arts of negotiation and compromise rather than efficient administration.

Ronald Loveridge, in his excellent role analysis of San Francisco Bay area city managers, emphasized a third important determinant influencing policy involvement among city managers: i.e., self-definition of their own leadership role. Professor Loveridge's analysis found four classes of managers in terms of how they perceived themselves as "activists" in their policy roles in communities:[20]

A. *Political Leaders* who take the broadest view of their policy role and see themselves as idea men and change agents in communities. These managers espouse a political readiness to act as plaintiffs for good government and the public interest.
B. *Political Executives*. This group of managers believes they should be policy innovators and leaders yet they are less willing to stick their necks out in pushing councilmen toward major policy decisions. They take a more pragmatic and less moralistic view of their political roles as managers.
C. *Administrative Directors* are convinced that managers should actively participate in the policy process but, nevertheless, they articulate a reluctance to be a novel administrator or open community leader. They tend to be preoccupied with the art of the possible, stressing the constraints and the problems, the council's authority as opposed to the manager's expertise.
D. *Administrative Technicians* define their policy roles within the narrowest context with a focus on administrative or housekeeping functions. They see themselves as staff advisors who are clearly subordinate to city councils and rather than proposing or instituting changes, they view themselves as curators of the established goals.

Professor Loveridge's fourfold classification of the self-perceptions of management leadership roles influences very directly the breadth or narrowness of the managers' goals, strategies, and results which they expect to achieve in community government. Loveridge argues the "political leader-type" frequently has the best contemporary education in public administration and exhibits great willingness to introduce new ideas for making broad city improvement projects by openly soliciting or "playing politics" with council members for their votes on various issues. At the other extreme, Professor Loveridge points up that "administrative technicians" have very often limited formal managerial training and are more inclined to view their own roles in communities as strictly subserviant to the city council's wishes. While city size is not found to be correlated with "type of managerial style," Professor Loveridge believes there may be a certain self-selection process that occurs, with cities seeking out managers and managers seeking out cities most compatible to their own particular favored style of public management.

## Taking Stock of the Occupation

What can be said about city manager professionalism from the standpoint of the foregoing summary of current statistical and social trends in city management? Can managers be classed as "professionals" or not? What are attributes that favor as well as prevent ranking city management as a professional career? Table 2 shows them to have a foot on both sides of the fence.

Table 2 should emphasize clearly that city managers are different from other public professionals. They have developed into a clear-cut occupational field as administrative generalists in city management—but they are a Janus-faced occupation that looks simultaneously in the directions of "professionalism" with its peer group-defined norms of expertise and behavior as well as being very much in politics with primary orientation toward and demands for community responsiveness and accountability.

Managers cannot totally embrace either role of professional or politician. If managers became neutral experts without reference to the political facts of life, they would jeopardize their own survival, but if they became politicians without responsible knowledge or expertise in urban affairs, they jeopardize their credibility and worth to the public they serve. In short, managers cautiously and continuously tread a middle ground between the two poles of politics and expertise.

## The Future of the City Manager: As An Envoy of the Potomac?

What does the future hold for the city management field? If the past 70 years of unabated growth of the "manager phenomenon" is any guide to the future, the prominence and influence of city managers, individually and collectively, in the context of American community life will no doubt continue, even expand. The technological and social complexities of modern urban life increasingly require their specialized administrative talents in coping with the myriad of

## Table 2

| Attributes Favoring Professional Status | Attributes Favoring Non-Professional or Political Status |
|---|---|
| *General influence on American Life*<br>Significant and growing in terms of numbers of managers/CAO's with increasing job responsibilities | "Dispersing authority" due to increased participation of federal/state action in local government and new minority/union participation |
| *Ethos and outlook*<br>Outlook characteristically of an administrative generalist | Exercise of administrative/leadership skills highly dependent upon and subject to shifting political nature of community life, causing the bulk of managers to be "in-and-outers" |
| *Informal social background of managers*<br>Homogeneous/middle class occupation with professional level salary | Social make-up of city management, especially influenced by parochial small town, suburban political pressures |
| *General educational preparation*<br>Survey shows increasing college/graduate educational preparation | No required degree or certification to obtain employment |
| *Core skills necessary on the job*<br>Informally favors administrative generalist background with preference for skills of budgeting, personnel, and management, as well as newer specialties like energy conservation or federal grantsmanship (which depends on needs of individual communities) | No skills specified by law for employment |
| *Career patterns*<br>An informal route of career advancement developing for many managers through assistant managerships, consulting work, business or related government careers | None legally or formally specified |
| *Lifetime occupation*<br>Possibility for all managers | The bulk of managers are "in-and-outers"—moving across a broad range of comparable administrative type jobs |
| *Self-perception of occupation*<br>Most managers see themselves akin to public professional groups like diplomats or school superintendents | Less than one quarter of managers believe that they are "an established profession" like law or medicine |

**Table 2** (*Continued*)

| Attributes Favoring Professional Status | Attributes Favoring Non-Professional or Political Status |
|---|---|
| *Peer-group influence of professional association—the ICMA* | |
| The ICMA informally promotes professional and ethical codes of conduct through training programs, meetings, and publications | No formal control by the professional elite or professional association relative to entrance, work standards, promotions in profession, nor does ICMA attempt to enforce ethical code of behavior on the practitioner. Employment of manager remains subject to local council's decision |
| *Degree of professional autonomy in relation to politics and community affairs* | |
| Classic theory of the manager plan as well as most manager charters view managers as neutral experts in municipal affairs | Reality of management role deeply affected by nature and distribution of community politics. Extent and scope of manager involvement in policy leadership is influenced by (1) community size, (2) degree of political conflict, and (3) self-definition of leadership styles |
| *Conflict or Possible Competition with Other Professional Groups* | |
| In theory managers are viewed as the chief professional administrator *in charge of* various professional services | In reality possibilities exist for wide array of conflict with community professional as well as minority and union groups |

insistent problems like energy, pollution, crime, minority recruitment, urban planning, and mass transit. Moreover, as the local public sector is pressed urgently by citizen and federal government alike to deal with these kinds of problems, city managers and their counterparts—CAOs, county managers, town managers, city administrators—with their central and full-time responsibilities on the local scene for planning, budgeting, personnel selection, and advice to council will remain the indispensable link between the conceptualization and achievement of community goals.

At the same time, strong countervailing pressures in the opposite directions, away from the extended application of professional expertise, are at work in the city management field. Growing demands for widespread citizen participation, minority employment, and union involvement—in short, widening political representation—are constant pressures on city managers and urban government as a whole. Managers are now and will remain at the delicate fulcrum point where these fierce twin cross-pressures for both narrow expertise and wider citizen representation meet and are balanced.

Yet, on the horizon is the ominous and rapidly growing intergovernmental intrusion "from above" with which most managers (like most local public officials) must contend. Greater federal and state presence on the local scene unquestionably will mean an ever-increasing dispersal of the manager's real authority over internal community functions. Many managers already spend a third or more of their time on intergovernmental matters, and this percentage seems to be growing every year.

Our cultural mythology of "home rule" to the contrary, American city managers may indeed play at the present time a role more akin to the French Prefect in responsiveness to the national capitol's dictates and demands than we or even they care to imagine. Today Washington's "unseen hand" is as invisible and omnipresent as ever was Adam Smith's.

The hard fact is, so long as local government continues to ebb as an entity in the national structure of governance, for better or worse, we may expect managers in service more as envoys of the Potomac than of Peoria. And no doubt in response to this shifting locus of authority, the traditional twin images of the manager as "a professional helping hand" and "political hired hand" will have to be recast to fit the new political realities of this line of work. Certainly these future changes will demand a reappraisal of traditional managerial functions, educational preparation, career orientation, professional associations, and the like, though the old political mythology and verities of managers' roles changes slowly, if at all.

## Footnotes

1. It is important to emphasize at the outset the distinction between the "manager plan," which is essentially a theory of local government, and the "city manager," which is a recognized and established public service occupation. This article focuses principally on the latter subject though, of course, the "plan" and "occupation" are closely related.
2. In recent years the distinction between CAOs and managers in terms of their functions and authority has grown increasingly "fuzzy," and since the ICMA includes CAOs (along with "kindred spirits" like town managers, city business managers, etc.) now in their membership, this article also will lump them together within the city management field. For a separate discussion of CAOs, read Edwin O. Stene, "Historical Commentary," in *Public Management* (June 1973), p. 6; Charles R. Adrian, "Recent Concepts in Large City Management," in Edward C. Banfield (ed.), *Urban Government* (New York: Free Press, 1969); and James B. Hogan, *The Chief Administrative Officer* (Tucson: University of Arizona Press, 1976).
3. My unproven observation is that four very real pressures are constantly upon managers moving them in the direction of increased professionalism in terms of their work substance and attitudes: (1) greater numbers of higher

educational institutions throughout the nation, specifically schools of public administration and public affairs, are turning out increasing numbers of students with professional administrative skills and outlook; (2) an increasing competition for a limited number of openings in the city management field helps to insure a high quality "crop" of managers (particularly true in the tight white collar labor market today); (3) well-trained and upwardly mobile managerial staffs found in most middle-sized and large cities constantly press both expertise and professionalism upon managers; and (4) city managers' regional associations, perhaps even more than the national ICMA, serve informally as "professional informational exchanges" and a very important avenue for many managers in terms of keeping their professional expertise current.

Readers will note throughout my essay that I back off from trying to define the actual substance of city management professionalism for in my view it leads into a hopeless semantic bog that is represented by the essay of Robert Kline and Paul Blanchard, "Professionalism and the City Manager: Examination of Unanswered Questions," *Midwest Review of Public Administration* (July 1973), pp. 163-175.

4. Norton Long, "Politicians for Hire?" *Public Administration Review*, Vol. 25 (June 1965), p. 119; Karl A. Bosworth, "The City Manager is a Politician," *Public Administration Review*, Vol. 18 (Summer 1958), pp. 216-222; and for both a lively and more contemporary essay following this line of reasoning written by a city manager, read: William V. Donaldson, "Continuing Education for City Managers," *Public Administration Review*, Vol. 33 (November/ December 1973), pp. 504-508. For an excellent insight into the role of city managers in the budgetary process, refer to Arnold J. Meltsner, *The Politics of City Revenue* (Berkeley: University of California Press, 1971), pp. 51-60.

5. For the unusual story of the development of the council-manager plan, read John Porter East, *Council-Manager Government: The Political Thought of Its Founder, Richard Childs* (Chapel Hill: University of North Carolina Press, 1965); and Richard J. Stillman 2nd, *The Rise of the City Manager, A Public Professional in Local Government* (Albuquerque: University of New Mexico Press, 1974).

6. Don Price, "The Promotion of the City Manager Plan," *Public Opinion Quarterly* (Winter 1941), pp. 570-571. There is considerable controversy in the historic literature over Childs' actual role in the development of the manager plan. Price terms Childs' role as "a manipulator of symbols"; Herbert Emmerich saw it as "an inventor of the plan"; but Childs liked to describe himself as the "minister" who performed the marriage between the commission and manager plans. My own view is that Richard Childs is best understood from the historic perspective as a child of the American Progressive Era and its reformist spirit.

7. There is an immense literature on this subject. Perhaps one of the best and most thoughtful analyses of this issue is found in Clarence E. Ridley, *The*

*Role of the City Manager in Policy Formulation* (Chicago: International City Manager's Association, 1958). For more current views of this subject, read Arnold J. Meltsner; Timothy A. Almy, "City Managers, Public Avoidance, and Revenue Sharing," *Public Administration Review,* Vol. 33, No. 1 (January/February 1977), pp. 19-27; and Robert P. Boynton and Deil S. Wright, "Mayor-Manager Relationships in Large Council-Manager Cities: A Reinterpretation," *Public Administration Review,* Vol. 31, No. 1 (January/February 1971), pp. 28-35.

8. See Stillman, p. 73. For the high degree of general satisfaction with this field by its practitioners even among those who leave city management altogether, read Fremont J. Lyden and Ernest G. Miller, "Why City Managers Leave the Profession: A Longitudinal Study in the Pacific Northwest," *Public Administration Review,* Vol. 36, No. 2 (March/April 1976), pp. 175-181.

9. Sali and Walt Damon-Ruty, "Former Taft City Manager Tells Viewpoints," *The Bakersfield Californian* (March 10, 1977), p. 33. I realize that this issue of the dispersal of authority of city managers and of all public professionals in general is an important subject that desreves considerably more attention than I have given it. Certainly the subject deserves book-length treatment rather than a few paragraphs. In my view one of the best books to date to treat this subject in relationship to cities as a whole is Norton Long, *The Unwalled City: Reconstituting the Urban Community* (New York: Basic Books, 1971).

10. Survey data drawn from the following sources: Laurie S. Frankel and Carol A. Pigeon, *Municipal Managers and Chief Administrative Officers, A Statistical Profile, Urban Data Service Reports,* Vol. 7, No. 2 (Washington, D.C.: International City Management Association, February 1975); Richard J. Stillman, chap. 4; *Directory of Recognized Local Governments, 1977* (Washington, D.C.: ICMA, 1977); *The Directory of Assistants* (Washington, D.C.: ICMA, 1977); and Robert Huntley and Robert MacDonald, "Urban Managers: Organizational Preferences, Managerial Styles and Social Policy Roles," *Municipal Yearbook* (Washington, D.C.: ICMA, 1975), pp. 149-159.

11. No large city over 500,000 (except Cleveland) has ever adopted the manager plan, and Cleveland threw it out after two years. Several manager plan communities, though, adopted it prior to growing over 500,000. Most large cities like New York, San Francisco, and New Orleans have opted instead for vesting administrative authority in a CAO or deputy mayor. Perhaps large-city municipal problems are less administrative and more political, so voters prefer to have a strong mayor "on top" and an administrator "on tap" rather than the reverse under manager government. The classic debate over the application of the manager plan to large cities appeared in the pages of the *Public Administration Review* between Wallace S. Sayer, "The General Manager Idea for Large Cities," Vol. 14 (Autumn 1954), pp. 253-258 and John E. Bebout, "Management for Large Cities," Vol. 15 (Summer 1955), pp. 188-195.

12. Clarence Ridley and Orin Nolting, *The City Manager Profession* (Chicago:

Univeristy of Chicago Press, 1934). Also for good early statistics on city managers, see Joseph Cohen, "The City Manager as a Profession," *The National Municipal Review* (July 1924), pp. 391–411. Certainly the most significant determinant of managerial selection are the attitudes and preferences of city councilmen. For one of the best discussions of this subject, read Efraim Torogovnik, *Determinants in Managerial Selection* (Washington, D.C.: ICMA, 1969). In the Torogovnik study public administration ranked first as the preferred background of managers by councilmen, with business administration and engineering second and third respectively.

13. Here I can be criticized for sidestepping the whole issue of what constitutes city manager professionalism, but as I pointed out in footnote 3, in my view one enters a hopeless semantic bog when one attempts to define this term. The important point I feel is that most managers believe themselves to be professionals, even though the substance of their professionalism has never been adequately defined.
14. For an extended account of the significant changes that have occurred within the ICMA during the last decade, read Stillman, chap. 3. I must also emphasize that I do not want to leave the impression from this essay that the ICMA is totally impotent with regard to enforcement of professional standards; indeed, from time to time it does expel members for the most flagrant violations of its professional code of conduct. For a recent case of expulsion, see *ICMA Newsletter* (Feb. 28, 1977), p. 1. Nevertheless, I feel my point still stands that ultimate authority for enforcement of professional standards rests not with the ICMA but local city councils.
15. Stillman, p. 74.
16. For the rather complex evolution of thinking on this subject over the last 70 years, refer to Stillman, *ibid.*, chaps. 1-3. I should qualify this point somewhat by pointing out that while "the early founders" like Childs did stress a neutral role for managers, the early managers hardly approached their work in a neutral manner. Indeed, not handicapped by federal or state guidelines and mandates as are modern city managers, early managers probably exercised considerably more control over internal city matters and were not hesitant to exercise very broad policy initiatives over many areas of city activities, see particularly the early chapters of Leonard White, *The City Manager* (Chicago: University of Chicago Press, 1926). Today perhaps the real change is that the managers' own view of their policy roles (as reflected by the ICMA's Code of Conduct) better reflects their actual community policy involvement. The paradox today may be that this pro active ideology may vastly overestimate their real power and authority over community affairs, given their general "dispersal of authority."
17. The results of the Stillman survey of city managers, pp. 73-74, contrasts sharply on this subject by comparison with the 1934 Ridley and Nolting survey.
18. Edward C. Banfield and James Q. Wilson, *City Politics* (New York: Vintage, 1963), pp. 168-186.

19. John C. Bollens and John C. Ries, *The City Manager Profession: Myths and Realities* (Chicago: Public Administration Service, 1969). More recently, the Bollens-Ries thinking has been refined further by Cortus T. Koehler in "Policy and Legislative Oversight in Council-Manager Cities," *Public Administration Review*, Vol. 33, No. 5 (September/October 1973), pp. 433–441. Koehler divides councilmanic policy oversight into three types: "average," "blind faith," and "politician," and depending on the composition of these type councilmen in the makeup of any council, the degree of manaagerial autonomy over policy issues is thus determined.
20. Ronald O. Loveridge, *City Managers in Legislative Politics* (Indianapolis: The Bobbs-Merril Co., 1971). Unquestionably the Loveridge book is one of the best on city managers to appear in recent years. Timothy A. Almy, "Local-Cosmopolitanism and U.S. City Managers," *Urban Affairs Quarterly* (March 1975), pp. 243–272, is an interesting and useful essay that builds further upon Loveridge's typology by utilizing Gouldner and Merton's localism-cosmopolitanism concepts. Professor Almy demonstrates empirically how the local vs. cosmopolitan backgrounds of managers significantly shape their policy roles.

## Further Reading

The two outstanding classics on the city manager and the city manager plan, which are still useful in terms of providing historical perspectives on the development of the city management field, are Leonard White's *The City Manager* (1926) and Harold Stone, Don Price, and Catherine Stone, *City Manager Government in the United States* (1940). Two interesting early statistical surveys of managers are found in Joseph Cohen's "The City Manager as a Profession," *The National Municipal Review* (July 1924); and Clarence Ridley and Orin Nolting, *The City Manager Profession* (1934). For the best current surveys on contemporary city managers, read Ronald O. Loveridge, *City Managers and Legislative Politics* (1971); John Bollens and John Ries, *The City Manager Profession: Myths and Realities* (1969); and Richard Stillman, *The Rise of the City Manager: A Public Professional in Local Government* (1974). John Porter East's *Council Manager Government: The Political Thought of Its Founder, Richard Childs* (1965) is the most authoritative and thorough analysis to date of Child's thought, ideas, and involvement with the development of the manager plan.